CULTURE IN THE AGE OF THREE WORLDS

CULTURE IN THE AGE OF THREE WORLDS

MICHAEL DENNING

VERSO
London • New York

First published by Verso 2004

1 3 5 7 9 10 8 6 4 2

Verso
UK: 6 Meard Street, London W1F 0EG
USA: 180 Varick Street, New York, NY 10014–4606
www.versobooks.com

Verso is the imprint of New Left Books

ISBN 1–85984–577–0
ISBN 1–85984–449–9 (pbk)

British Library Cataloguing in Publication Data
Denning, Michael, 1954–
Culture in the age of three worlds : reflecting on genocide
1. Culture
I. Title
306

ISBN 1859844499 PB
ISBN 1859845770 HB

Library of Congress Cataloging-in-Publication Data
Denning, Michael.
Culture in the age of three worlds / Michael Denning.
p.cm.
Includes bibliographical references and index.
ISBN 1-85984-449-9 (pbk. : alk. paper)—ISBN 1-85984-577-0 (hardcover : alk. paper)
1. Culture. 2. Culture—Study and teaching. 3. Social movements. 4. Social history—20th century. I. Title.
HM621.D46 2004
306'.071—dc22

2003025291

Typeset in 10.5/13 Bembo by SetSystems Ltd, Saffron Walden, Essex
Printed in the USA by R. R. Donnelley

CONTENTS

1 Introduction 1

PART ONE
Rethinking the Age of Three Worlds

2 Globalization and Culture: Process and Epoch 17

3 A Global Left? Social Movements in the Age of Three Worlds 35

4 The Novelists' International 51

PART TWO
Working on Culture

5 The Socioanalysis of Culture: Rethinking the Cultural Turn 75

6 The End of Mass Culture 97

7 The Academic Left and the Rise of Cultural Studies 121

8 What's Wrong with Cultural Studies? 147

PART THREE
The American Ideology: The Age of Three Worlds as the American Century

9 "The Special American Conditions": Marxism and American Studies 169

10 The Peculiarities of the Americans: Reconsidering *Democracy in America* 192

11 Neither Capitalist Nor American: The Democracy as Social Movement 209

12 A Cultural Front in the Age of Three Worlds? 227

Notes 235

Acknowledgments 269

Index 272

For the organizers of
GESO

I

INTRODUCTION

As we look back on the last half of the twentieth century, it seems clear that culture moved to the foreground. It is not, to be sure, that there had been no culture before 1950, but it was always in a period's background. Historians dutifully included it in a supplementary chapter on arts and culture as they surveyed the age of Jackson or Victoria. But suddenly, in the age of three worlds, everyone discovered that culture had been mass produced like Ford's cars; the masses had culture and culture had a mass. Culture was everywhere, no longer the property of the cultured or the cultivated. Just as an earlier bourgeois gentleman had been pleasantly surprised to discover that he had been speaking prose all along, so now even Americans found that their barbaric yawp was culture. And what's more, culture mattered – this was not your grandparents' culture, the quaint customs and artifacts collected by folklorists. Rather, under its various guises – the omnipresent commercial signscape, the unending stream of mass entertainments, the regular consumption patterns of a world of shoppers, the millions of adolescents migrating to high schools and universities, and, eventually, as a common denominator, the uncounted gigabytes of digitized information – this mass culture was part of the wealth of nations, an engine of what those intoxicated by the new discovery called a "postindustrial" society.

With the discovery that culture was everywhere, the study of culture and the critique of culture became an increasingly central part of political and intellectual life. In recent years, this has come to be called "the cultural turn" in the humanities and social sciences, and is often associated with the rise of "cultural studies." This book is a product of, and reflection on, that cultural turn, which, I will argue, was a fundamental aspect of the age of three worlds, that short half-century (1945–1989) when we imagined that the world was divided into three – the capitalist First World, the Communist Second World, and the decolonizing Third World – as if each were a separate planet involved in an elaborate and dangerous orbit around the others.

In a sense, this book is about the emergence of "cultural studies." But it takes its distance from most contemporary celebrants and critics of cultural studies in two ways, seeing it at once more widely and more narrowly. I view cultural studies more widely, because I take the cultural turn in political and intellectual life in the age of three worlds to be a much broader phenomenon than the specific "cultural studies movement" which spread unevenly across the universities of North America, Northern Europe, Australia, and Taiwan from its quasi-academic roots in Labourist Britain (where it had developed out of the intertwining of adult education initiatives in the Workers' Educational Association and the Open University with the redbrick and polytechnic tradition of "Birmingham cultural studies"). In contrast to this "diffusionist" understanding of cultural studies, I will suggest that the cultural turn erupted around the world, though its idioms were not always mutually comprehensible. This global cultural turn was a consequence of the uneven development of a global culture out of the cultural and ideological struggles between the three worlds. Thus, even some of those who ignore or refuse the word "culture" – either for ideological reasons or because of its different connotations in different languages – are nonetheless part of this cultural turn: the choice of "sign," "ideology," "discourse," "communication," "consumption," "everyday life," or "habitus" as one's name for the region others called "culture" is itself part of the debate that constitutes the cultural turn. Moreover, despite my own use of the term "culture" and my biographical affiliation with the Birmingham-derived "cultural studies," I am not interested in asserting any particular privilege for the term "culture" or "cultural studies" over these competing accounts; rather, I seek to translate and mediate between them. It will then not be surprising that I see many of the critics of the methods and ideologies of the Birmingham-derived "cultural studies" as themselves part of the larger turn to the cultural.

On the other hand, I view cultural studies more narrowly, because I will argue for the historical specificity of the cultural turn in the age of three worlds. Unlike the recent lively accounts by Francis Mulhern and Terry Eagleton, which highlight the concept of culture to assert substantial continuities between earlier forms of *Kulturkritik* and postmodern cultural studies, I will argue – most explicitly in chapter four – that the concept of culture undergoes a sea-change at mid-century: this is one reason why many of the cultural studies of the age drop the word "culture" for a variety of alternatives and neologisms.[1] The great modernist notions of culture – the literary sense of culture as arts and letters and the anthropological sense of culture as habits and customs – were entirely inadequate to understand the culture industries and ideological state apparatuses that dominated the age of three worlds. So new concepts, new frameworks were forged. Thus this is not a book on the idea of culture generally, but on culture and its synonyms in a specific moment, the age of three worlds. This historical specificity also suggests that the moment of cultural studies is a moment which has in some sense passed. Indeed I would suggest that the academic triumph of cultural studies in the 1990s came as the age that generated it was disappearing. So this book is an attempt to reckon with that break, that line between our own moment – the moment of "globalization" – and the period that now appears to have ended, the age of three worlds.

The cultural turn, the rise of cultural studies in this wider sense, was a fundamental aspect of the age of three worlds for two linked but distinct reasons: first, the study of culture, under several names (perhaps most commonly "communications"), developed into a new social science precisely because of the emergence of a new and relatively autonomous region of social life; and second, the turn to culture marked the distinctive politics of the social movements of a New Left that formed in all three worlds. This double genealogy of cultural studies – at once a reformation of the disciplinary landscape of the modern state and university, and a renovation and renewal of radical thought – continues to cause confusion and conflation. Just as an earlier social science, sociology, was seen variously as an ally or antidote to socialism, so cultural studies was both an ally and antidote to the cultural radicalisms of the New Left.

In an era when the cinder blocks of the mass university became a characteristic landscape, cultural studies (and its kin: semiotics, American studies, media studies, communications) has tended to see itself as an interdisciplinary or transdisciplinary reformer of academic boundaries, often promising to restore the wholeness of knowledge which reigned before the division of the faculties. Thus it was also seen as a secessionist, poacher, or imperialist by the established disciplines – literature and history on the one hand, sociology and anthropology on the other – each with its own notion of culture. However, it is better to see the differentiation of cultural studies in a way not dissimilar to the earlier division of the social sciences, mapped elegantly by Immanuel Wallerstein. The four modern social sciences derived, he suggests,

> from the dominant liberal ideology of the nineteenth century which argued that state and market, politics and economics, were analytically separate. . . . Society was adjured to keep them separate, and scholars studied them separately. Since there seemed to be many realities that apparently were neither in the domain of the market [economics] nor in that of the state [political science], these realities were placed in a residual grab-bag which took as compensation the grand name of sociology. . . . Finally, since there were people beyond the realm of the civilized world, . . . the study of such peoples encompasses special rules and special training, which took on the somewhat polemical name of anthropology.[2]

The differentiation of cultural studies in the age of three worlds was, I will suggest, the result of the emergence of yet another aspect of social reality – the culture industries, the mass media, mass communications – which seemed to have its own autonomy, its own logic, and its own power. Though intertwined with state, market, and civil society, the "media," as it is called in daily life, seemed to occupy an imaginative space equal to the state and the market. Thus the study of the logic of this new world, the logic of mass communication, the logic of culture in a new sense, became the fifth social science, a postmodern social science, linked, as we shall see, to that other reorganization of the social sciences in the age of three worlds: area studies.[3]

But the cultural turn was never simply this academic tropism toward the light and heat of the mass media. From the start, it was also a moment of renewal and renovation in radical and socialist thought, generated from the crisis of Stalinism, from the contradictions of what was seen as a new form of capitalist society, and from the victories of decolonization. In 1959, a somewhat hostile observer, Daniel Bell, looked at the recently launched journals of the New Left and noted that their

> pages . . . are full of attacks against advertising, the debaucheries of mass culture, and the like. And often, phrasing these criticisms in the language of the early Marx, particularly in terms of alienation, gives these attacks a seeming political content. But the point is that these problems are essentially cultural and not political, and the problem of radical thought today is to reconsider the relationship of culture to society.[4]

A central ideologue of the era he dubbed the "end of ideology," Bell was skeptical of this new "cultural radicalism" (and we shall later consider the long line of variations on his complaint that its political content is seeming); but regardless of the justice of his judgment, his observation was accurate. In the decades that followed, one of the basic problems of radical thought *was* to reconsider the relationship of culture to society (hence the great influence and totemic status of Raymond Williams's *Culture and Society*), to grapple with the foregrounding of culture in the age of three worlds.

Though the New Left cultural turn eyed the mass media (Bell was not wrong about those "attacks against advertising [and] the debaucheries of mass culture"), its forms of thought rarely limited themselves to the technologies or to a media studies. For a generation of New Left thinkers around the globe, the issue of culture was not simply the fact of the existence of the new technologies of mass information and communication, but the reshaping of the everyday lives and struggles of subaltern classes and peoples by those new forms. If the modernist notions of culture named those social sites where the commodity form and its law of value did not yet rule – the high arts, on the one hand, and the lifeways of "primitive" peoples, on the other – the new postmodern concept of culture was premised on the generalization of the commodity form, not only in symbolic production (the industries of culture, entertainment, and advertising), but throughout daily life. This new notion of culture encompassed the means of consumption and subsistence of workers, what Marx had obliquely called "the pleasures of the laborer." But if Marx had famously bracketed the analysis of workers' consumption – noting of "the maintenance and reproduction of the working class" that "the capitalist may safely leave this to the worker's drives for self-preservation and propagation" – the New Left thinkers made culture and its cognates the vehicle for a reconsideration of the very processes of social maintenance and reproduction under capitalism.

As a result, the cultural turn raised the specter of a cultural politics, a cultural radicalism, a cultural revolution, a specter that haunts the age of three worlds. The idea was contested from the beginning: in the very first issue of the British *New Left Review* in 1960, E.P. Thompson was already responding to the skeptics: "'The danger is,' writes our colleague Alasdair MacIntyre, in a reproof to the New Left in the current *Labour Review*, 'that one will fight a series of guerilla engagements on cultural questions which will dissipate socialist energy and lead nowhere.'" In reply, Thompson insisted that "*any* serious engagement in cultural or political life should not dissipate, but generate, socialist energy."[5] If culture had come to the foreground throughout society, how could politics not be cultural? The debate over the status and efficacy of culture as a site and form of political resistance, of the relation between culture and social movements, echoed across the age of three worlds and beyond; it will run throughout this book.

Finally, the cultural turn marked New Lefts in all three worlds. This was rarely noticed at the time, because the dramatic differences in form and strategy between the social movements of the First, Second, and Third Worlds overshadowed common concerns. And most contemporary accounts of cultural studies still miss the global aspects, and see its spread at the end of the century as an example of the globalization of North Atlantic academic trends. For example, the cultural critic Beatriz Sarlo notes that "in Argentina we do not call it 'cultural studies' . . . which is a term that has been put into mass circulation by the US academy."[6] I don't dispute this; in many cases the slogan of cultural studies has simply meant the marketing of US academic discourses, and the erasure of distinctive regional intellectual traditions of cultural analysis and criticism. But a closer look at the various New Left intellectual formations in each of the three worlds suggests that they underwent parallel or analogous cultural turns. In part, this was due to the common, if uneven, experience of mass commodity culture (film, radio and television broadcasting, recorded music, mass spectator sports) which took hold across the world's exploding plebeian metropolises: from Sarlo's own Buenos Aires where a mestizo migration from the countryside created the populist city of tango, football, and Peronism (Sarlo notes that Argentina's first televised image was that of Eva Peron) to the Calcutta in which Dipesh Chakrabarty grew up, a postcolonial city where a new culture industry of Bengali comedians, singers, and soccer teams on film and radio was created by the "culture war" between *bangals*, the post-Partition refugees from the villages of East Bengal, and *ghotis*, the established residents of Calcutta.[7] But the cultural turn was also due to the globalizing effect of the Communist experience: the post-1917 generation steeped in the cauldron of Leninist militancy, Popular Front anti-fascism, and a revolutionary anticolonialism. If the genuinely internationalist ideology of the Communist movement nurtured the remarkable spread of anti-imperialist solidarities, its equally vigorous Soviet loyalism reproduced the rigidities of Comintern Marxism on every continent. One of the central rigidities was the economism of Communist Marxism, its discounting of culture – merely a superstructure – and of national and regional particularities.

Thus a common aspect of the New Lefts of the age of three worlds was the turn to the superstructures, the reconsideration of culture: it is as evident in the founding of the Brazilian Centro Popular de Cultura (CPC) as in the founding of the British *New Left Review*; in Frantz Fanon's address on "Racism and Culture" at the 1956 *Présence Africaine* congress as in Roland Barthes's celebrated analysis of the photograph of the Negro soldier in his 1957 *Mythologies*; in Antonio Candido's 1959 *Formation of Brazilian Literature* as in Raymond Williams's 1958 *Culture and Society*.[8] It is not that these figures influenced each other; in fact, precisely because the cultural turn was usually a turn to what Gramsci had called the "national–popular" – the regional and national particularities often ignored by the abstract internationalism of Comintern Marxism – explicit cross-national theories and debates about culture did not develop (witness the "exceptionalism" of even the radical American studies movement, which I discuss in part two). But parallel developments can be seen throughout the era.

In retrospect, the New Left flowering after 1955–56 – from the Khrushchev revelations to the uprising in Budapest, from the battle of Dien Bien Phu to that of Algiers, from the Suez crisis to the Bandung conference, from the Montgomery bus boycott to the Sharpeville massacre, from the CND marches to the Anpo protests, from the independence of Ghana to the charismatic guerilla revolution in Cuba – stands out as the first of three moments. If this first moment saw the resurrection of the "humanist" young Marx and a variety of existential and phenomenological radicalisms, the second moment, that of the global wave of uprisings and insurgencies in 1968, saw the popularization of the cultural turn in the form both of denunciations of the dominant culture, as ideological state apparatus, cultural imperialism, consciousness industry, or society of the spectacle, and of theorizations of cultural revolution. Triggered by the utopian demands unleashed in the vast and violent upheavals against forms of Soviet-style modernization in Maoist China as well as in the guerilla ideologies of Che Guevara and Amilcar Cabral, notions of a cultural revolution became the vulgate of Naxalites in Bengal and Situationists in Paris, of Black Panthers in Oakland and liberation theologians in Bogotá, and energized the emerging movement for women's liberation.

The third moment – the defeat and repression of the New Left social movements marked by the end of the "thaw" and the invasion of Czechoslovakia, by the coups and military dictatorships in Indonesia, Africa, and Latin America's Southern Cone, and by the authoritarian populism and free-market fundamentalism of the Reagan and Thatcher regimes – continued the cultural turn of New Left thought, though its visionary and utopian modality, imagining a cultural revolution, gave way to reflections on the failures of popular nationalisms and the contradictions of popular culture. This is the moment of several relatively independent Gramsci revivals: at the same time that the radical intellectuals of the

Birmingham Centre were reappropriating Gramsci's work on popular culture to make sense of the new Thatcher regime's "great moving right show" and the changes in British working-class subcultures (evident in Stuart Hall's influential essays on Thatcherism and in Paul Willis's *Learning to Labour*, as well as in the early work of Hazel Carby and Paul Gilroy in *The Empire Strikes Back*), a young Argentinean intellectual exiled in Mexico, Néstor García Canclini, was wrestling with the Latin American revival of Gramscian notions of popular culture to understand the effects of urban markets on the crafts of Mexican artisans (*Culturas populares en el capitalismo*), and a group of young South Asian intellectuals took up Gramsci's notion of the "subaltern" to criticize nationalist histories and initiate a "subaltern studies."

At the time, hardly anyone connected these projects. The New Left intellectual tradition that most vigorously tried to think the world as one – the dependency and world-systems theorists – were rarely concerned with culture (as one Brazilian intellectual told me, for dependency theorists, culture was merely perfume). The sense of the discontinuities between the three worlds – and thus between the philosophically oriented "critical theory" of the First World, the dissident formations of the Second World, and the peasant and guerilla Marxisms of the Third World – meant that the project of a transnational cultural critique never surfaced. It was not until the three worlds dissolved into one, and radical critics of globalization called for a cultural studies that would cross borders and attend not only to the popular and the subaltern but to the hybrid and the creole, that one can not only see the beginnings of a transnational cross-fertilization but also re-imagine the elective affinities between the earlier projects.

It is perhaps not surprising that many of the central figures of this contemporary transnational cultural controversy over alternative modernities – a name in part for the age of three worlds, now seen as the era of nation-focused modernization and development from whose success or failure one is now escaping – and their hybrid subjects were formed intellectually in the earlier moment's reckoning with the crisis of the popular in particular national situations. Paul Gilroy's account of the antinomies of modernity's racial practices in *Between Camps* has its roots in *The Empire Strikes Back*, the pioneering Birmingham study of the place of race and migration in the crisis of popular Labourism; García Canclini's mapping of the hybrid cultures of Mexico City's modernity is explicitly a rethinking of the "crisis of the popular" outlined in his early study of Mexican artisans; Aihwa Ong's powerful outline of the alternative modernities of East Asia's "repressive developmentalist states" and the emergence of a "flexible" pan-Asian culture and subjectivity in the Chinese diaspora grows out of her insistence on the importance of cultural struggle in her pioneering study (conducted in the late 1970s) of the contradictory meanings of cases of spirit possession among young Malaysian women assembling semiconductors in the then-new "export-processing" factories; and Dipesh Chakrabarty's critique of historicism and his insistence on the specificity of Bengali modernity in his project of "provincializing Europe" is explicitly a self-critique, a return to the unresolved questions in his early culturalist – "culture," he wrote, was "the 'unthought' of Indian Marxism" – recasting of Bengali working-class culture through a subaltern reading of jute industry archives. It would be absurd to trace these works back to a single source, an ur-cultural studies, and it would be a mistake to ignore the theoretical and political differences among these, and other, figures. But it would be equally misleading not to register the elements of a common situation, a common crisis that they address, both in the work of the late 1970s and in more recent work.

The break between the theme of the national–popular and those of hybridity, flexibility, and the diasporan stands less as a theoretical or political advance or declension (both positions have been argued) than a symptom of a wider historical change. If culture was the unthought of Indian (and other) Marxism in the age of three worlds, it may be that it no longer is. "If the 1930s left had undersold culture," Terry Eagleton quips, "the postmodern left overvalued it." This suggests that a happy medium might exist: a fair price for culture good for any decade. I doubt it. Rather I would argue that the very sense of a radical alteration in the valuing of culture – and of cultural politics – marks a new era, a new political situation. If cultural studies is now in crisis or in question, it is less because it was overvalued than because its moment, the age of three worlds, is over.[9]

This is where this book begins. If this is a work of history – culture in the age of three worlds – it is also a reflection on the present, on, to borrow a classic title from Perry Anderson, the "origins of the present crisis." For this book tries to understand the emergence of a global culture in a time when few would have imagined that that phrase could be used in the singular. What is the meaning of this shift from the plural (three worlds) to the singular (a global culture)? The first part, "Rethinking the Age of Three Worlds", tries to illuminate the break between our own moment, the moment of "globalization," and the period that now appears to have ended, the age of three worlds, by charting the sources and lineaments of a global culture. Is global culture simply the international marketing of cultural commodities by transnational culture industries which have enclosed and privatized the cultural commons, the public domain? Is it simply those deterritorialized spaces and experiences – shopping malls, airports, tourist hotels, and the hardware and software of the ubiquitous electronic entertainment machines – that are mass produced to be as identical as possible? Or is the culture of the global city a proletarian culture in some yet unimagined and unfigured sense of that word, the symbolic product of masses of migrants forming social movements and plebeian public spheres of yet untheorized forms? In chapter two, "Globalization and Culture: Process and Epoch," I suggest that behind the powerful accounts of globalization as a process lies a recognition of a historical transition, of globalization as the name of the end, not of history, but of the historical moment of the age of three worlds. The debate over globalization is largely a debate over the meaning and legacy of that short half-century, a period when the question of a global culture takes shape. Chapter three, "A Global Left? Social Movements in the Age of Three Worlds," juxtaposes the anti-globalization movements of our time to the social movements of the age of three worlds, the movements of 1968, both to interrogate our ways of understanding social movements and to argue that the Seattle WTO protest stands in a tradition of IMF riots that mark a break from the politics of 1968. Chapter four, "The Novelists' International," is the book's major experiment in writing a transnational cultural history. Arguing that the effort to create a proletarian culture in the early decades of the century was a fundamental part of the globalization of the novel, it suggests that what we inherit as a global culture is not simply an emporium of commodities marketed around the world, but a powerful body of narratives that emerged out of the clash of the three worlds.

The book's second part, "Working on Culture," explores the debates about culture and politics that have accompanied the cultural turn in the intellectual life of the last quarter of the twentieth century. There was a dramatic shift in the meaning of the concept of culture at mid-century, as a new generation of radical intellectuals developed a new cultural politics and elaborated a variety of socioanalytic theories of culture. What were the consequences of this cultural turn? Did the new cultural studies neglect class? What kind of politics is cultural politics? Chapter five, "The Socioanalysis of Culture," explores the change in the meaning of culture in the age of three worlds, and outlines the major cultural theories to emerge from the New Left – market-based theories, state-based theories, and recognition-based theories. It then argues that these need to be supplemented with a labor theory of culture.

Chapters six and seven deal with the moment when cultural studies, under that name, was first imported into the United States, and became part of the Reagan–Bush "culture wars." Chapter six, "The End of Mass Culture," argues that the Reagan years – which marked the definitive end of the political hopes of the New Left – witnessed a dramatic shift in the New Left's theories of popular or mass culture, in part to understand both the defeat of the New Left's countercultures and the continued cultural turn in politics, figured not least by Reagan himself, Hollywood star become president. Chapter seven, "The Academic Left and the Rise of Cultural Studies," attempts to situate the so-called culture wars of the 1980s and the journalistic moral panic over "political correctness" in 1990–91 in the context of the rise of cultural studies. Chapter eight, "What's Wrong with Cultural Studies?," addresses several common objections to contemporary cultural studies, including its apparent retreat from class, and its exaggeration of cultural politics and cultural resistance. In response, chapter eight becomes an opportunity to defend, define, and develop the slogan of cultural studies for our new times of globalization, after the end of the age of three worlds.

Because of the post-World War II emergence of the United States as a dominant world power, the age of three worlds often seemed to be the "American Century," a phrase coined by Henry Luce, the publisher of *Time* and *Life*, in his 1941 manifesto. Throughout the world, global culture came to be seen as American culture, and New Left cultural criticism was often inaugurated by lessons in how to read Donald Duck. A distinctive American ideology emerged in the age of three worlds: "democracy" came to be seen as a peculiarly "American" product, and was wrenched apart from socialism and Marxism, both now counterposed to Americanism. Inside the United States, notions of Americanism, the "American way of life," and American exceptionalism flourished, and "un-American activities" were the subject of Congressional investigations. The final part of this book, "The American Ideology: The Age of Three Worlds as the American Century," explores the Americanisms of the age of three worlds. The intensified intellectual interest in US culture in the decades after World War II found expression in a new academic field, "American studies," whose origins lay in a curious fusion of two Americanisms with contrary political inflections, namely Popular Front Communism and Cold War anti-Communism. Chapter nine, "'The Special American Conditions': Marxism and American Studies," examines the relation between Marxism and notions of American exceptionalism in the formation of the "discipline" of American studies, and in its subsequent transformation by a generation of New Left scholars.

This genealogy of American studies is followed by a reading of the figure who so often stood as the canonic authority for notions of American exceptionalism and American democracy: Alexis de Tocqueville, whose *Democracy in America*, written in the 1830s, had an extraordinary revival in the United States during the age of three worlds. Chapter ten, "The Peculiarities of the Americans: Reconsidering *Democracy in America*," argues not only that Tocqueville was ill-served by his revivalists, but that the key antinomies in his work – the unresolved tension in his notion of "civil association" and the rhetorical and theoretical disruption that African enslavement and Indian dispossession work on his account of democracy in America – offer avenues toward a historical materialist understanding of the "exceptionalism" of settler capitalism.

If chapter ten focuses mainly on Tocqueville's text, chapter eleven,

"Neither Capitalist Nor American: The Democracy as Social Movement," returns to Tocqueville's historical moment in an attempt to separate democracy from both American exceptionalism and capitalist triumphalism. In the age of three worlds, anti-democratic interpreters of democracy – from Schumpeter to Huntington – narrowed the definition of democracy and obscured its roots as a social movement: "the democracy." Reconsidering the history of "the democracy," I argue that the battle to establish and defend universal suffrage parliamentary states and to extend democracy into civil society – a social democracy – has been the work of neither bourgeois revolution nor middle-class modernization, but of working-class social movements. The final chapter, "A Cultural Front in the Age of Three Worlds?" grew out of my involvement in the effort, sparked by the "labor teach-ins" of the late 1990s, to create an alliance between the labor movement and writers and artists in the academy. It reconsiders the history of the relations between labor and culture in the decades after World War II, suggesting that the well-rehearsed story of the hostility between labor and the New Left has obscured some remarkable elements of a cultural front in the age of three worlds.

PART ONE

RETHINKING THE AGE OF THREE WORLDS

2

GLOBALIZATION AND CULTURE: PROCESS AND EPOCH

One of the key words of the last decade of the twentieth century was "globalization." Though the *Oxford English Dictionary* places the first use of the word in 1961, there are hundreds of books with the word in their titles in the 1990s; it appears that the first book to use it in its title was published in 1988. With its various kin – transnational, postmodern, and postcolonial – "globalization" displaced "international," the key word of an earlier moment, which had modified not only such grand capitalist forces as International Business Machines (IBM) and International Telephone and Telegraph (ITT), but the First, Second, and Third Internationals of the world working class. What historical change is figured by this new word, by this shift from the "international" to the "global"? If the idea of globalization almost always points to a sense that, to travesty Virginia Woolf, human nature changed on or about November 9 1989 (the opening of the Berlin Wall), what implicit narratives of the past enable this assertion of the end of history, this freedom from any past? And does this new word have a place in the critical understanding of the culture of the present?

In many ways, as the skeptics remind us, globalization is not new, but is a long-term tendency of capitalism; by some measures the world economy is not more global than it was in 1914, at the beginning of what Eric Hobsbawm has called the "short twentieth century." And one of the earliest accounts of globalization was that classic German pamphlet of 1848 with its fable about the pitiless, icy, and brutal hero with the French name but uncertain nationality who is chased across the globe "like the sorcerer who is no longer able to control the powers of the nether world whom he has called up by his spells." "The need of a constantly expanding market for its products chases the bourgeoisie over the whole surface of the globe," our narrator tells us.

> The bourgeoisie has through its exploitation of the world market given a cosmopolitan character to production and consumption in every country. . . . In place of the old wants, satisfied by the productions of the country, we find new wants, requiring for their satisfaction the products of distant lands and climes. . . . The intellectual creations of individual nations become common property . . . from the numerous national and local literatures, there arises a world literature. . . . The cheap prices of its commodities are the heavy artillery with which it batters down all Chinese walls. . . . It compels all nations, on pain of extinction, to adopt the bourgeois mode of production; it compels them to introduce what it calls civilisation into their midst, i.e., to become bourgeois themselves. In a word, it creates a world after its own image.[1]

It is a great story, and most of the key antinomies of contemporary writing about globalization can be found in Marx's succinct paragraphs in the *Communist Manifesto*: the corrosive force of the market against the protectionism of the state and its nation; the promise or threat of cheap commodities; the promise or threat of a world literature, a world culture, a world civilization in the image of, to use our hero's later name, capital.

Marx's words have led a number of contemporary thinkers to dismiss the globalization discussion as simply hype, "globaloney," the latest fashionable rhetoric of capitalist triumphalism. I have much sympathy with these skeptics, but my disciplinary background in the rhetorical sciences makes me curious about the emergence of new words. A new word may not signify a new world, but it points to some change. And if globalization claims to name a new world process, a new world order, it also gestures to a new kind of "inter-discipline," to use the old vocabulary, a new way of looking at the world. "Globalization falls outside the established academic disciplines," Fredric Jameson has recently suggested,

> as a sign of the emergence of a new kind of social phenomenon, fully as much as an index of the origins of those disciplines in nineteenth-century realities that are no longer ours. There is thus something daring and speculative, unprotected, in the approach of scholars and theorists to this unclassifiable topic, which is the intellectual property of no specific field, yet which seems to concern politics and economics in immediate ways, but just as immediately culture and sociology, not to speak of information and the media, or ecology, or consumerism and daily life.[2]

So I am less interested in the celebrations of globalization in the corporate literature than in the ways the notion is reorienting work in critical theory. One can see this "speculative, unprotected" approach of scholars and theorists in three major US anthologies that map the encounter with this "unclassifiable topic" of globalization in powerful yet various forms. There are over fifty contributors to these anthologies, so my characterizations will be necessarily, but, I hope, usefully reductive.

The first anthology, *Culture, Globalization and the World-System*, edited by Anthony King, grew out of one of earliest globalization conferences. The conference was held in Binghamton, New York, in 1989, a symbolic year for our purposes. With major contributions by Immanuel Wallerstein and Stuart Hall, one could characterize this anthology as "world-systems theory meets cultural studies." In other words, it marks the encounter of two of the central forms of New Left critical theory with the idea of globalization. World-systems theory had grown out of one of the richest intellectual debates of the Third World liberation movements: the controversy among Latin American, Caribbean and African intellectuals over dependency theory and the development of underdevelopment. Cultural studies was the product of the New Left's critical reflection on the cultural industries and the state's ideological apparatuses. Both traditions had tried to get beyond what Anthony King calls the "nationally constituted society as the appropriate object of discourse, or unit of social and cultural analysis," and were thus committed to "conceptualizing 'the world as a whole.'"[3] Like many of the early globalization discussions, the conference was dominated by the worrying parallel between a world economy structured around an international division of labor and a global mass culture that seemed to follow in its wake. Was globalization a force of cultural homogenization, or was there a countermovement of resistance, translation, hybridization, indigenization, and creolization? No consensus is reached, and the conference papers and responses stay at a relatively abstract level. There are only about a dozen references to specific cultural texts, figures or genres in the entire volume and the ones cited are common indices of global culture: Fanon's *Black Skins, White Masks*, the music of Bob Marley, Stephen Frears and Hanif Kureishi's *My Beautiful Laundrette*, Nigerian highlife and juju music, Salman Rushdie's *The Satanic Verses*, Nagisa Oshima's *Merry Christmas, Mr. Lawrence*, and Wim Wenders' *Paris, Texas*.

The second anthology, *The Cultures of Globalization*, edited by Fredric Jameson and Masao Miyoshi, grew out of a 1994 conference at Duke University in North Carolina. We might call this collection "comparative literature meets area studies," under the sign of globalization. Again it is worth noting that both comparative literature and area studies were developed in the post-World War II research university to provide a framework for the study of the "international;" if both often had close ties to the postwar modernization and development projects of the US national state, both also became a space for critical research. Taking the concept of globalization as a reflection, in Jameson's words, of the "immense enlargement of world communication" and the "world market," the Duke anthology pays close attention to the export and import of culture, and particularly to the assault on the state subsidies and quotas that tried to protect national cultures – national cinemas and musics. The emergence of Third World national cinemas and vernacular musics like reggae mark a moment of "import-substitution," now giving way to the export-processing zones of transnational postcolonial culture, an international "culture fever," to borrow the phrase used to name China's version of the 1980s culture wars. The volume's contributors are divided over this shift, and over the role of markets in culture: are they merely carriers of what Leslie Sklair calls "the culture-ideology of consumerism," or can they be, as Manthia Diawara argues about the West African markets, a source of resistance to the unholy alliance of neocolonial states and multinational corporations, a place that upholds the "right to consume" and a place that can be, "as C.L.R. James discovered in his analysis of the Accra market in 1946, a basis for revolutionary action?" The heated debate over the promise or threat of globalization is summed up by Indian art critic Geeta Kapur, who notes of the postcolonial migrant intellectual that "hybridity is the survivor's credo in the age of globalization": "Let us concede that it is the privilege of those who live their lives within the format of a national culture to resist globalization, as against the privilege of those who lead more global lives to seek its emancipatory features."[4]

The third major anthology, *The Politics of Culture in the Shadow of Capital*, edited by Lisa Lowe and David Lloyd, developed out of another 1994 colloquium, this one at the University of California. It can be seen as a meeting of US ethnic studies, particularly women of color discourse, and postcolonial or subaltern studies. US black, women's and ethnic studies emerged out of the liberation movements of 1968 as well as their critique of the class and gender orthodoxies of social democracy and Communism; postcolonial and subaltern studies were founded on the critique of the orthodoxies of anticolonial nationalism. All shared a politics of recognition, using a history or ethnography from below to reverse the silences and invisibility to which the subaltern, the underothers, had been condemned. So the Lowe and Lloyd anthology is less concerned with charting the onslaught of cheap commodities, global mass culture, or the state-led defenses of a national culture. Its editors refuse the model of cultural homogenization, and the reduction of culture to commodification; but they also refuse the modernization and development ethos of the postcolonial state. Rather their mapping of culture in the "shadow of capital" points to the connections between culture and social movements, and the ways social movements create "new forms of political subjectivity," for which the term "subaltern" stands as an empty signifier. The contributors rely less on the interpretation of cultural texts and more on the global articulation of local struggles, what they call the transnationalization of social movements. The anthology's rich collection of particular studies ranges from the turn of the century Filipino "bandits" to end of the century Zapatistas, from Indian political theater to Basque pirate radio, from the transnationalization of feminism in China to the transnationalization of gay liberation in the Philippines. If a "global narrative" emerges from the anthology, it is that of transnational factory women, the "global racialized feminization of . . . labor," which anchors the key essays by Aihwa Ong and Lisa Lowe, as well as Lowe's interview with Angela Davis.[5]

What might one conclude about globalization from these three landmark anthologies? First, they all illustrate the ways the discourse on globalization has created a new transdisciplinary debate, promising a transnational or global cultural studies which would cross national borders, and reorient our research agendas and curricula. When I taught a seminar on globalization, my students enthusiastically followed the lead of the contributors to the anthologies, writing essays on subjects that ranged from the globalized graphic design of Tibor Kalman's *Colors* magazine to the role of Thomas Mapfumo's chimurenga music in the Zimbabwean anticolonial struggle, from sex tourism in Thailand to the cinematic links between Kurosawa's *Seven Samurai* and Sturges's *Magnificent Seven*. Even though neither they nor I was sure what exactly counted as the culture of globalization – whether by period, geography, genre, or media – they had no difficulty in identifying particular texts and practices which seemed to be traversed by processes of globalization, by global flows.

So my second conclusion is that globalization is understood largely as a process, a circuit of the global flow of commodities and communications (not unlike the classic American tale of consumerism), rather than as a historical narrative or a common culture, a "world culture." Thus, it is not difficult to understand particular texts or events – the film *Titanic* or a disease like AIDS – as participating in the process, but it is much more difficult to figure out how they are connected to each other or to a historical narrative. My students and I were repeatedly faced with this problem in reading the globalization anthologies, particularly the Lowe and Lloyd anthology: how was one supposed to connect the particular case studies? Throughout the seminar, we tried to draw up chronologies and canons: what were the key dates by which we could mark the era of globalization? What were the most representative or most valuable cultural texts of the age of globalization? Though we brainstormed a variety of blackboard canons, the exercise seemed a strange one. Understanding the culture of globalization did not seem to depend on making a list of texts, in the way that understanding the American novel might. One might say that this is exactly the point: if the name of globalization in the world of thought is postmodernism, then perhaps we should endorse this lack of a master narrative or established canon.

However, master narratives, or tall tales, are not easily dispensed with; the refusal of one kind of tall tale usually means that another sort is sneaking in the back. And if there is no apparent overall historical narrative, nor any clear generic one, the abstract logic of the process proves to be such a master narrative. The fundamental arguments focus on the nature of the circuit, the flow: is it a logic of homogenization or one of hybridization? At what point in the circuit is power generated, and at what points does it encounter resistance? Arjun Appadurai's well-known "general theory of global cultural flows" – made up of five dimensions: ethnoscapes, technoscapes, financescapes, mediascapes, and ideoscapes – is built on the image of movement through a medium, "this mobile and unforseeable relationship between mass-mediated events and migratory audiences."[6] For my students, this model of global cultural flow as the master narrative of globalization was an ingrained common sense, making certain topics seem like ideal globalization papers. In general, they fell into three genres: first, the worldwide distribution and reception of some culture industry practice, like the advertising of Marlboros in Southeast Asia or the place of hip hop in French youth culture; second, the emergence of hybrid, creolized popular forms – Jamaican reggae, for example – and the question of whether they had been co-opted, commodified, and westernized, or whether they remained part of a resistant subaltern social movement; and third, the promise of a form that would create a new global community, based on the virtues of migration and media, this latter figured by the Internet, the World Wide Web, and the idea of a global net.

Cynics who regularly dismiss new forms of intellectual work because of the appearance of new formulas – recall the dismissal of the flurry of writing about sexuality, performance, and popular culture as Madonna studies a few years ago – would have no difficulty in lampooning this already emerging set of standard topics and stances as simply the latest fashion. But any teacher who sees the passion with which students take up these issues and stances, indeed anyone who sees their frustration at being able to argue both sides without arguing their way out, knows that we are not seeing a lack of originality and independent thinking but a genuine antinomy, the failure of even the most sophisticated and self-critical social thinking to solve a conceptual contradiction because its underlying social contradiction has not been solved in reality.

Globalization, like postmodernism, is thus not something one can be for or against; it stands as an attempt to name the present, and its antinomies (homogenization *versus* hybridization, universal market or global net) are the sign of the unfinished nature of the present. However, despite the tendency of globalization discourse to displace large-scale historical narrative with the ahistorical timescales of market and communication theory – the moment of globalization began intellectually, one might say, with Fukuyama's widely-read announcement of "the end of history" – I would like to suggest that there are several implicit histories and, indeed, implicit canons within the contemporary work on the culture of globalization.

Globalization is a periodizing concept, even when it announces the end of history. We were in the "era of globalization," as one of the early globalization ideologues, the Indonesian information minister Harmoko, put it. In most cases, this present begins in 1989 with the end of the Cold War, the end of the World War II settlement, which had been figured by the Berlin Wall. In 1999, the *New York Times* globalization ideologue Thomas Friedman went so far as to borrow a Merrill Lynch advertising slogan for a chapter title: "The World is Ten Years Old."[7] If history is a nightmare from which we are trying to awake, 1989 did mark the end of a particular history, a freedom from history, the ability to say that something we were stuck in was over. For the right, it was the end of Communism; but for the left, which had long since divested itself of its utopian and even solidaristic investments in the Soviet Union and the people's democracies, it was also a new freedom. The old manifesto could be read with new eyes, and it seemed an uncanny foreshadowing of the new posthistorical world.

But does globalization really refer to the world since 1989, as is so regularly insisted, or is it really a retrospective account of the period which now seems to have ended, of the world before 1989? This kind of displacement would not be that unusual; many of the announcements of the modern in the early twentieth century were disguised ways of naming, understanding, and exorcizing what they could now call the Victorian, the genteel tradition, and most of the protestations of the postmodern were veils for new narratives of modernity and modernism – the postmodern Foucault, after all, spent his time in the Bibliothèque Nationale tracking the history of nineteenth-century prisons. Curiously, all three of the anthologies with which I began draw us back to the world before 1989. A reader looking for an account of the contemporary would be disappointed with them, as some of my students were. Three dates stand out in the implicit history of globalization: 1492, 1791, and 1945.

The first two dates derive from the sense that globalization means the reconceptualization of modernity from a planetary perspective, overthrowing the entire narrative of the Western humanities and social sciences which saw the formation of modernity as a European story: the formation of the European languages in the Renaissance and Reformation classics of Dante, Rabelais, Cervantes, Shakespeare, and the vernacular Bibles of Martin Luther and the King James edition; the emergence of the modern European novel, of modern thought from Bacon and Descartes to Kant and Hegel; even Marx's extraordinary account of the transition from feudalism to capitalism through the example of England. Between 1850 and 1945, Walter Mignolo argues, the rest of the world appeared in scholarship under the guise of civilization studies, the classic Orientalisms, or anthropology, the study of the "peoples without history."[8] The reassertion of 1492 as the beginning of the modern world-system in the contemporary discourse of critical globalization places the conquest of the Americas and the slave trade as founding moments. In Enrique Dussel's powerful reconceptualization of the history of philosophy, modern thought begins in the sixteenth century with the debate over slavery, and the counterdiscourse of modernity, the philosophy of liberation, begins not with Kant, as Habermas would have it, but with Bartolomé de las Casas and his critique of slavery and Indian conquest.[9] If globalization marks the end of European history, it also marks an entry into history for the peoples without history.

Similarly, the reassertion of 1791, the year of the San Domingo revolt, the other half of the French Revolution, places modern social revolution under the sign not of the Parisian sansculottes, but of the Haitian slaves, a symbolic beginning not of two centuries of European urban insurrection but of two centuries of global anticolonial revolt. As a result, C.L.R. James's famous history of the Haitian revolution, *The Black Jacobins*, has rightly achieved canonic status in the critical globalization studies (or transnational cultural studies) – it is the only text that gets an essay-long treatment in the Lowe and Lloyd anthology. For *The Black Jacobins* is not only a forebear of the notion of a "black Atlantic," but James is the source of the powerful argument that modernity began in the so-called periphery of the world-system when he argues that the New World plantation slaves were the most modern people in existence at the time.

The third date, 1945, is perhaps the most common reference point in this work. After the twentieth century's Thirty Years War, the old empires were staggering and colonialism was dying. But the newly christened Third World only escaped anthropology and entered scholarly discourse under the sign of modernization and development; it was to mimic the stages of European development. If modernity in its grand form had been taken to begin with the ideals of the Enlightenment, the more plebeian modernization (the litany of schools, newspapers, legislatures and civil services) stepped forward after World War II. Consequently, the discourse of globalization is largely a reflection on the legacies of the period which now seems to have lasted from 1945 to 1989, a period dominated by a particular imagination of the globe, the image of three worlds. The rhetoric of the three worlds – the capitalist First, the Communist Second, and the decolonizing Third – emerged in the early 1950s, and, though it was challenged on all sides, it dominated the period. Both US and Soviet ideologists tried to resolve the three into two, asserting that the world was really divided between the West and the East, the Free World and the Socialist Camp, as they called themselves (though the Sino-Soviet split in the early 1960s was an imaginative as well as a political crisis); and modernizers of several stripes also tried to resolve three into two, asserting that the key divide was between the North and the South, the developed and the underdeveloped, the modern and the traditional. Nonetheless, the asymmetrical three – West, East, and South – never lost their imaginative hold until the East gave way, and the South divided into rich and poor with the emergence first of the oil states and then of the NICs (the Newly Industrialized Countries of East Asia). As a result, as William Greider's title *One World, Ready or Not* tells us, whatever else globalization means, it means that there are no longer three worlds. The eclipse of the very term Third World by terms like postcolonial and subaltern is a marker of that reality.

Paradoxically, it is precisely the end of the age of three worlds, as one might call the half-century after World War II, that makes its history haunt every account of globalization. Underneath the apparently abstract explorations of the circuits of global flow, one sees arguments about what took place in the age of three worlds: Robert Brenner's controversial account of *The Economics of Global Turbulence* – one of the most ambitious attempts to outline the economics of globalization – is built on a narrative of the postwar boom and downturn; Fernando Coronil's magnificent contribution to Latin American subaltern studies, *The Magical State*, unravels the fetishes of oil money and rent in a political narrative, echoing Marx's *Eighteenth Brumaire*, of postwar Venezuelan state modernization and development. The established tale of the age of three worlds is that there were three stories: the long boom of US, Japanese, and German Keynesian capital that created a global Fordist mass culture characterized by sex, drugs, and rock and roll; the long and uneven struggle between the Stalinist bureaucracy and the forces of "thaw" and *glasnost* in the apparently separate world of centrally-planned people's democracies; and the rapid decolonization of the Third World followed by various forms of state-led development and modernization, whether through capitalist import-substitution or Soviet-style central planning. What the three worlds, and these three stories, shared, Eric Hobsbawm has argued, was a commitment to secularism, planning, equal rights, education, and modernization.

To speak the word "globalization" is to say that these worlds and their ideals have not only failed, but are gone, over. The task of the various forms of critical globalization studies is to understand why, to find the fault lines that generated the earthquake, to read the history of the age of three worlds against the grain. The heart of this project is, I would suggest, the elaboration of a transnational history of the age of three worlds, that is to say a history that does not take the nation-state as the central actor. The difficulty of the project can be glimpsed by reading Eric Hobsbawm's remarkable history of the "short twentieth century," *The Age of Extremes*, the fourth in his tetralogy of modern history begun with *The Age of Revolution*, *The Age of Capital*, and *The Age of Empire*. On the one hand, Hobsbawm's social and cultural history admirably abandons the national focus, arguing that the Cold War was not that important, that it will take its place in history alongside earlier forgotten great power alliances, that the division and reunification of Germany was finally no more consequential than earlier such divisions. The real story of what he calls the golden years lies not in such Cold War events as the Korean War or the Berlin crisis but in the profound social changes that reshaped the planet: the death of the peasantry (for 80 percent of the world, he argues, the middle ages ended in the 1950s and was felt to end in the 1960s); the massive urbanization of the world as displaced peasants created the vast informal economies of the global shantytown, the global barrio, the global ghetto; the rise of occupations requiring formal education and the consequent emergence of students, universities, and cultural industries as a powerful social force throughout the world – not least in what Wallerstein has called the "indigenization" of the state apparatus in the Third World; the transformation in household structures that revolutionized the work, sexuality, residency, and consciousness of women and young people; and the massive relocation of manufacturing that led to the "deindustrialization" of the North and the industrialization of the South.[10]

Curiously, the actors in Hobsbawm's history remain nation-states and national leaders. Not only are the social movements of the age of three worlds relatively absent, movements which live in a chronology of uprisings and massacres: Birmingham, Sharpeville, Watts, Prague, Soweto, Kwangju. So too are the transnational corporations which seem to loom large in popular imagination: IBM, ITT, United Fruit, the Seven Sisters of oil, Ford, Sony, and Nike. A central task of a transnational cultural studies is to narrate an account of globalization that speaks not just of an abstract market with buyers and sellers, or even of an abstract commodification with producers and consumers, but of actors: transnational corporations, social movements of students, market women, tenants, racialized and ethnicized migrants, labor unions, and so on. In chapter three, I will look more closely at the social movements of the age of three worlds.

But if there is an implied history to globalization – the yet to be written planetary history of the age of three worlds to which the three anthologies all contribute – there is also an implied canon, a common body of texts, in our understanding of the culture of globalization. In teaching my seminar on globalization, I began with a blackboard game: what are the most representative or valuable cultural texts since 1945? It produced strange and wonderful lists, predominantly but not entirely US-based, juxtaposing films, novels, musical recordings, photographs, and built environments (see Table 1).

Though students enthusiastically joined in creating this list, they resisted my suggestion that this list of texts be the syllabus for a course on the culture of the age of three worlds. Moreover, they resisted my restricting the list to particular authored texts. They wanted to include products like the Apple Mac, Coke, and Nike (though there was an argument over whether Nike referred to the shoe or the broadcast advertisements), and even networks like the Internet (which is like saying that one of the key cultural texts of the American Renaissance was the telegraph network – surely true, but it rarely appears on the same list as Emerson, Melville, Douglass, and Stowe).

Is it ridiculous to make such a global list? Without a doubt, but perhaps no more ridiculous than to make a list and define, however roughly, the English novel, American jazz, French painting. Over the last decade one finds more and more rough guides to world music, world cinema, and the world novel. The rational kernel of such rough guides is the "globalization of markets," to use the title of Theodore Levitt's 1983 *Harvard Business Review* essay, the mass distribution of commodities beyond the boundaries of the nation-state.[11]

The development of a global market in cultural commodities creates, as Marx argued, a world literature, and, one might add, a world music and a world cinema. However, for much of the last century, this was more imagined than real. In retrospect, the rise of mass culture in the late nineteenth and early twentieth centuries looks like the development of *national* cultural markets. National culture industries producing mass-

Table 1
The Blackboard Postwar Canon

Pablo Neruda, *Canto General*, 1950
Ralph Ellison, *Invisible Man*, 1952
Inoshiro Honda, *Godzilla*, 1954
Disneyland, 1955
Chinua Achebe, *Things Fall Apart*, 1958
Miles Davis, *Kind of Blue*, 1959
Alfred Hitchcock, *Psycho*, 1960
Betty Friedan, *The Feminine Mystique*, 1963
The Beatles, "I Wanna Hold Your Hand," 1964
——, *Rubber Soul*, 1965
Gabriel García Márquez, *One Hundred Years of Solitude*, 1967
Miles Davis, *Bitches Brew*, 1969
Jimmy Cliff, *The Harder They Come*, 1972
Francis Coppola, *The Godfather*, 1972
Thomas Pynchon, *Gravity's Rainbow*, 1973
George Lucas, *Star Wars*, 1977
Francis Coppola, *Apocalypse Now*, 1979
Afrika Bambaataa, "Planet Rock," 1982
Michael Jackson, *Thriller*, 1982
Stephen Spielberg, *E.T.*, 1982
Toni Morrison, *Beloved*, 1987
AIDS Quilt, 1987
Public Enemy, *It Takes a Nation of Millions*, 1988
Salman Rushdie, *The Satanic Verses*, 1988
Nike's Michael Jordan campaign

reproducible forms – films, vinyl records, radio broadcasts, and illustrated magazines with half-tone images – displaced the city as the site not only of live performance and exhibition, but even of book and newspaper publishing. They also enclosed the cultural commons as all sorts of vernacular art forms that had circulated as common property, or part of the public domain, were recorded, copyrighted, and sold as commodities.

Before the 1980s and 1990s, these "national media systems were," as Robert McChesney has noted, "typified by domestically owned radio, television and newspaper industries." Despite "major import markets for films, TV shows, music and books . . . dominated by US based firms, . . . local commercial interests, sometimes combined with a state-affiliated broadcasting service predominated."[12] Nevertheless, the years after World War II saw the beginnings of a global cultural market, often experienced as a tide of "Americanization," because of the prestige of US films, products, and musics. Against this stood the powerful, if unsuccessful, alternatives posed by the Second and Third Worlds: the attempt to delink the culture of the Communist world from the world cultural market, and the struggle by postcolonial states to orchestrate a new world information order.

In the wake of the age of three worlds, a radical privatization and deregulation of mass communications established a global market in cultural commodities, dominated by a handful of world-spanning corporations, among them Sony, News Corp, Disney, AOL-Time Warner, Viacom, and Bertelsmann. Not surprisingly, national cultural canons of art, film, music, and literature have been eroded, and the idea of a world cultural canon comes to make more sense. When it came to researching and writing papers and presentations, my students each wrestled with the question of identifying representative texts that seemed to transcend national boundaries.

Their choices were not random, but had some regularity, figured in the strange pairing of Nike and Bob Marley. Perhaps there is not one global culture in this period but two overlapping ones, both to a large degree self-conscious about their global ambitions. The first – figured by Nike – is commodity aesthetics, the culture of the transnational corporations, the culture figured by the grand four-letter words of globalization: Coke, Nike, Sony. It is a culture which is less about grand symbolic narratives than about supplying (for a profit) the means of everyday subsistence: the means of cheap transportation from Ford to Volkswagen to Toyota; the means of cheap communication from telephones and radios to TVs and PCs; the fundamental "proletarian hunger-killers," to borrow Sidney Mintz's phrase, the sugared, caffeinated, carbonated waters that began with Coke and the basic meat and potatoes that make up the McDonald's happy meal; the demotic fashion of blue jeans and athletic shoes that still bothers leftists of an earlier generation like Hobsbawm and Sherif Hetata; and the miniature electronic entertainers from the Walkman to the Game Boy. Perhaps there are some grand narratives embodied here – Shigeru Miyamoto's tale of a Italian-American plumber in Brooklyn, *Super Mario Brothers*, might be a candidate – but for the most part, this global culture is in many ways indifferent to content, open to hybridization.[13]

The other global culture – figured by Bob Marley – has its social roots in the huge migration from the rural Third World to the trench towns of the planet; but its aesthetic roots lie, curiously enough, in one of the first explicitly international cultural movements, the worldwide movement of plebeian artists and writers to create a proletarian culture, a socialist realism. Though the checkered literary politics of the Soviet Union and the various national Communist parties have often obscured it, much of what emerges as the vital elements of a global culture comes out of this internationalism, as it intersected with the national-popular hopes of the anticolonial movements: not just with poets like Brecht, Neruda, Hikmet, Césaire, Hughes and Faiz, but also with novelists like Richard Wright, Jorge Amado (generally regarded as the most widely-read Latin American novelist), Ngugi wa Thiong'o, Naguib Mahfouz, Gabriel García Márquez and Pramoedya Ananta Toer, those making up the emerging canon of the world novel. If the first generation of these artists are figures inspired by the Bolshevik Revolution of 1917 and the Baku conference of 1920, which turned the eyes of the Communist movement to the anticolonial struggles, later generations find inspiration in the African independence struggles, the Bandung conference of 1955, and the Cuban Revolution of 1959. It is they who transmute the earlier proletarian modes of socialist realism into forms of what will be called magical realism. There is a direct line as well between the pioneering cinematic alternative to Hollywood (the left-inspired Italian neo-realism) and the various Third World cinemas (*cinema nuovos*) of the age of three worlds. Nor is it surprising that some novelists become filmmakers, most famously the Senegalese Sembene Ousmane, or that there should be collaborations between radical filmmakers and radical novelists, between Orson Welles and Richard Wright in the US, between Youssef Chahine and Mahfouz in Egypt, between Bruno Barreto and Amado in Brazil.

Moreover, the soundtracks of these new national cinemas are often vehicles for the vernacular musics that begin to cross national borders: one thinks of the famous boss nova soundtrack for *Black Orpheus* in the late 1950s. The postwar years are the time when the New World musics that took shape in the first half of the century – jazz, tango, samba, son – become the basis and inspiration for an extraordinary profusion of local musical renaissances, ranging from Motown to bossa nova to juju to reggae. A variety of liberationist philosophies run through these musics as they often stay close to social movements. It is no accident that Bob Marley stands as a canonic figure in this sense of global culture, for his union of politics and vernacular music is echoed in Thomas Mapfumo's chimurenga, the tropicalismo of Gilberto Gil and Caetano Veloso, the blues rock of Bob Dylan, the Afropop of Fela. One can see why the controversy over Paul Simon's *Graceland* has not died down. Some of my students saw it as an act of cultural imperialism, commodifying South African music and politics to exoticize the postmodern angst of a US star; others saw it as a quintessential example of a hybrid world music which fused US pop and the migrant music of Ladysmith Black Mambazo under the sign of that kitsch utopia, Graceland. It is not a single text, but a move in a long and powerful history. A transnational cultural studies will need not only to interpret *Graceland* but to write the global history of the intersection of novelists, filmmakers, and musicians with social movements.[14] In chapter four, I will explore one aspect of this alternative global culture, as it took shape in the novel.

There is of course no neat line dividing Nike and Bob Marley; nevertheless, I think it takes a kind of double vision to see them both as global culture, neither reducible to the other, neither existing without the other. Some writers on globalization simply choose one or the other as their avatar; others read both through a relatively ahistorical logic of global cultural flow, produced, commodified, consumed, homogenized, hybridized, co-opted, and resisted. To get beyond the antinomies of globalization, we need to attempt the foolhardy, to imagine the globe and its peoples in new ways, to write and teach a global history, to accept the risks of globaloney for the hope of a emancipatory transnational cultural studies, a critical globalization studies which restores the promise of the old internationalism. We have nothing to lose but our chains. We have a world to win.

3

A GLOBAL LEFT? SOCIAL MOVEMENTS IN THE AGE OF THREE WORLDS

As the twentieth century ended, an extraordinary street protest took place in Seattle, Washington, against the meeting of the World Trade Organization (WTO). With forms of nonviolent obstruction and blockade, protesters shut down the city and the WTO talks, triggering an enormous police response. Since then, the "battle in Seattle" has become a touchstone in conversations and debates over "the present crisis" and "the real movement" to abolish the present state of affairs. Did the Seattle protest mark the emergence of a new movement, a newer left? "Five years earlier," Naomi Klein wrote in 1999, "campus politics was all about issues of discrimination and identity – race, gender and sexuality, 'the political correctness wars.' Now they were broadening out to include corporate power, labor rights, and a fairly developed analysis of the working of the global economy."[1] Was this true? What did it mean? What kind of insurrection was the battle in Seattle, if indeed it was one? What kind of movement lay beneath it, if indeed there is one? In this chapter, I will take the WTO protest in Seattle as a starting point to make some preliminary, indeed speculative, arguments about social movements over the last half-century, during what we might call the age of three worlds, an age that emerged in the wake of the global Thirty Years War of the twentieth century, and which may have ended in 1989 with the "new times," our present crisis, an age when three worlds have seemed to resolve in one, an era of globalization. Put bluntly, despite the title of Alexander Cockburn and Jeffrey St. Clair's book on Seattle, *Five Days that Shook the World*, we know that it is no longer 1917. But is it still 1968?

This chapter will begin by looking at the ways social movement theory thinks about insurrections and movements; it will then turn to the social movements of the age of three worlds – the liberation movements of "1968"; in the final section, I will suggest that the WTO protest in Seattle represents a distinctly different form of social movement. However, it was not a movement that was inaugurated in Seattle. Rather Seattle marked the US manifestation of twenty years of popular insurrections against the global enclosures of the commons.

From Insurrection to Movement

My reflections grow out of teaching a seminar on social movements and subaltern insurrections, during which students made presentations on the militia movement, the occupation of Alcatraz by American Indians, the Watts riot of 1965 and the LA riot of 1992, the Iranian revolution, the Boston antibusing movement, the assassination of Harvey Milk and the gay rights movement, the abortion rights movement, and the Tompkins Square riots. Two theoretical issues recurred throughout our discussions. First, how do we understand the relation between insurrection and movement? How does one connect an event like a riot, a strike, or an occupation, and organizations like shop committees, neighborhood associations, informal caucuses, consciousness-raising groups, or publishing collectives. Second, how do we sort out and judge the range of social movements – new and old, good and bad, left and right?

The first question is, simply, how do we get from the event, the insurrection, to the movement? How do we interpret the five days in Seattle? It is the rare sociologist of social movements that invokes hermeneutics, the science of interpretation, but the relation between insurrection and movement raises the conundrums of the hermeneutic circle. For insurrections, uprisings, demonstrations, riots, general strikes that "shake the world" are always an enigma, lying somewhere between the hidden and invisible resistances of daily life and the regime-changing revolutions that make history. Even if they are apparently planned by some party, some network, some group of conspirators, organizers, or instigators, they tend to exceed their scripts, leaving instigators both claiming and disclaiming responsibility. Insurrections are unexpected interruptions, the site of the new, and as a result become social texts, open to competing interpretations; they are social dreams, the overdetermined manifestation of some subterranean content, a movement or a moment.

Social theory presents four main methods of interpreting insurrections. The first, which can be seen in Ranajit Guha's great work, *Elementary Aspects of Peasant Insurgency in Colonial India*, resists any narrative subsumption of insurrection. Surveying 110 insurgencies spanning a period of 117 years, he offers no linear narrative connecting or explaining them, no "making of the Indian peasantry," no "history of the Indian revolution." Insurrections, for Guha, are given narrative form not by the insurgents but by the magistrates, the officials and the police, by the prose of counterinsurgency. Against these narratives from above, the historian who takes the "rebel point of view" can only identify "common forms or general ideas in rebel consciousness."[2] This would lead us to a poetics of insurgency, a properly formalist reading of the battle in Seattle, noting the logic of the crowd's actions in the sign systems of its discrimination of targets, its inversions and desecrations (its "world turned upside down"), its popular conscience and its communal sanctions, its means of communication (particularly, following Guha, the role of rumor). This mode of interpretation comes particularly to the fore with insurrections whose political meaning and narrative seem obscure – think of the readings of the 1992 Los Angeles riots – but one can see it in several commentaries on Seattle, particularly the street diaries that proliferated across the Internet, and Alexander Cockburn's strenuous attempt to reject the narrativization – "myth-making" is his term – of the events by "lib-lab pundits, flacks for John Sweeney and James Hoffa. . . . middle-of-the-road greens, . . . [and] a recycle binful of policy wonks," in favor of the elementary forms of insurgency of the "street warriors."[3]

Most social movement theory, however, reaches for a narrative, an allegory, normalizing the uprisings – "movement-related events" – as part of an account of the way movement organizations mobilize resources, make alliances with different sections of the political elite, and thus link insurgent politics with institutional politics. The key question for this tradition of social movement theory – the "resource mobilization" tendency which, with various amendments and revisions, still dominates the sociological study of social movements – is that of the source of the resources.[4] From this standpoint, the source of the resources in Seattle was the non-governmental organizations (the NGOs), and they, despite Cockburn, are the victors. "The battle of Seattle," according to the *Economist*, "is only the latest and most visible in a string of recent NGO victories"; and it goes on to cite the 1992 Rio de Janeiro Earth Summit, the 1994 "Fifty Years is Enough" disruption of the World Bank, the 1998 defeat of the Multilateral Agreement on Investment (MAI), and the Jubilee 2000 debt reduction as victories of "the NGO swarm." In a curious reversal, the *Economist* correspondent argues that the "inter-governmental institutions such as the World Bank, the IMF, the UN agencies or the WTO have an enormous weakness in an age of NGOs: they lack political leverage." "No parliamentarian," the journalist manages to write with a straight face, "is going to face direct pressure from the IMF or the WTO; but every policymaker faces pressure from citizens' groups with special interests." The solution – and the *Economist* points to World Bank leader James Wolfensohn as a model – is to dilute these "mobilization networks" by making "a huge effort to co-opt" the NGOs.[5]

The dangers of such success and co-optation, of the move from insurgent politics to institutional politics, generate a third approach: the critique of movement organization in the classic *Poor People's Movements*, by Frances Fox Piven and Richard Cloward, one of the great books of US New Left thought, the New Left equivalent of Rosa Luxemburg's *The Mass Strike, The Political Party, and the Trade Unions*. Beginning from their own activism in the welfare rights movement and writing immediately after the demise of the National Welfare Rights Organization, Piven and Cloward see insurrections as the expression of particular concentrated historical moments. They stress the importance – and rarity – of brief insurrectionary moments when social change takes place; what is true of revolutionary change proves to be true even of so-called reform or evolutionary change. Social security and African-American civil rights were the results not of a long and patient working through the political system, but of brief insurrectionary moments, not of social movement alliances with sectors of the elite but of political crisis and weakness created by divisions among rulers:

> all of the labor, civil rights, and social welfare legislation of consequence in the industrial era [in the United States] was enacted in just two turbulent five-year periods: 1933–37 and 1963–67 . . . What was won was won all at once, as disruptive industrial strike waves, unemployed marches, and riots came to a head in the first period, and civil disobedience campaigns and riots came to a head in the second.

In such moments of upheaval, street heat and disruption – that is, the withdrawal of cooperation – should be continuous: "mass protest, not poor people's organizations, . . . wins whatever is won."[6] While only time will tell whether our moment is such a moment, this vision of a turbulent, disruptive moment can be seen in the "people's global action" understanding of Seattle as one event in a chronology and geography of "global action days": inaugurated not in the "acrid mist of Seattle's tear gas" but in the "humid mist of the Chiapas jungle" and echoing across M16 (May 16 1998 against the 2nd WTO Ministerial in Geneva with large demonstrations in Brazil and India), J18 (June 18 1999 against the G8 Summit with a large demonstration in London), N30 (November 30 1999 in Seattle), A16 (April 16 2000 with a Washington demonstration against the IMF and the World Bank), Mayday2K, S11 (in Melbourne), S26 (September 26 2000 against the World Bank/IMF meeting in Prague), and A20 (April 20 2001 in Quebec City).[7]

Nevertheless, Piven and Cloward's refusal to reduce the insurrection to the organization shares the curious ahistoricity of Guha's stress on the elementary forms of insurgency: in both cases, waves of social insurgency seem to recur in an almost cyclical manner, repeating an eternal repertoire of direct actions on the part of an always already subaltern, the "underothers," to translate that concept into the vernacular. Some social movement theorists have explicitly adopted this cyclical approach: Andre Gunder Frank tries to tie cycles of social movements to economic cycles. In this sense, it is always 1968, 1917, 1848, 1789, and so on.[8]

A fourth, more historical, alternative suggests that insurrection is a sign of long-term, underground, barely visible movements and movement cultures: this is, I would suggest, the lesson of E.P. Thompson's *The Making of the English Working Class*. *The Making* is a stranger and more interesting book than is often thought: its title, its bulk, its reputation, and its influence tend to obscure it. It is two different books, which are never resolved. The legendary book is the book of its title, its classic introduction and conclusion: a biography of a class imagined as a coherent subject, with all the metaphoric armature of a masculine biography or *Bildungsroman* – birth, formation, coming to consciousness, setbacks, maturity. This narrative has the linearity, sense of presence, and experiential fullness that is often associated with "Thompsonian social history from below;" and this made it the target of feminist, Althusserian, and post-structuralist critique. But the actual work never quite lives up to its title. On the contrary, the book is largely a history of an English revolution that didn't happen, a story of missed chances and lost revolutionary moments (particularly 1819 and 1832). A pioneering theorist of absence, Thompson argues that revolutions that *don't* take place are just as devastating as those that *do* happen.[9] The heart of the book is the attempt to understand the roots of an insurrection that did not succeed and thus did not become epic history. Thompson seeks to understand the meaning of a "*quasi-insurrectionary movement*": underground conspiracies that may or may not be the fantasies of police spies, episodes of machine breaking, massacres of unarmed demonstrators. The sources are clouded, Thompson reminds us, because working people meant them to be clouded. In an act of what he calls "constructive speculation," "we have to read, not only between the lines of the letters sent in, but also the letters which were never sent."[10] Here Thompson genuinely captures the hermeneutic dilemma facing every theorist of the relation between insurrection and movement. We must make connections between the occasional eruptions – machine breakings, store lootings, window smashings – and the longer *durée* movement cultures, connections that are often *denied* by the participants, connections of which they may be unaware. "It is scarcely possible to give a coherent historical account of an incoherent presence," he writes, "but some attempt must be made,"[11] as he reconstructs the popular radicalism that reaches from the revolutionary

1790s of Paine, Wollstonecraft, and Blake to the upheavals of 1832, an underground tradition or political unconscious that survives the deep freeze and repression of two decades of world war and English anti-Jacobinism. Does the battle of Seattle similarly inherit a popular radicalism, a movement culture? And if so, what is that legacy? Is it a legacy of the liberation movements of 1968, with Noam Chomsky as the Tom Paine of US popular radicalism? What, in fact, do we mean by 1968?

1968: Social Movements in the Age of Three Worlds

1968 stands as a shorthand for a moment of remarkable social and political upheaval and the appearance of a host of what were seen as new social movements. The very term "social movement" is resurrected in the period, and the emergence of social movement theory and research is both a product of and reflection on the politics of that moment. It is not an accident that the figures I invoked in the first part of this chapter – Ranajit Guha, E. P. Thompson, and Frances Fox Piven and Richard Cloward – are all significant intellectuals of 1968. The question of how to sort out and judge this remarkable range of popular mobilizations – among women and peace activists, fundamentalists and gays, environmentalists and white supremacists – has generated much controversy within social movement theory. The new social movements often insisted on their autonomy and distinctiveness, and most of the scholars of the new social movements have implicitly or explicitly accepted this understanding, studying the rise and fall, success or failure, of particular social movements in isolation from others. Social movement theory thus emerges as an analogue to sociological theories of institutions, groups, or parties, an abstract model of the dynamics of a particular social construction.

Those who have tried to find a common denominator among the social movements have been drawn to the relatively abstract categories of populism or identity. The first – I think of the work of Ernesto Laclau or of Michael Kazin's *The Populist Persuasion* – suggests that populist mobilizations are central to the mass politics of modernity, the age of parliaments, mass media, and urban crowds. Thus all social movements are versions of populism, invoking a rhetoric of we, the people; if one finds different accents of that populism – chauvinist and authoritarian at one time and place, egalitarian and democratic at another – it does not outweigh the substantial similarities between the movements as social phenomena. Those who suggest that social movements are "built around the trenches of specific identities," to quote Manuel Castells's *The Power of Identity*, are also willing to lump together movements of extraordinarily divergent ideologies and social characters. Castells brings together Mexico's Zapatistas, the US's militias and patriots, and Japan's Aum Shinrikyo as social movements against "the new global order." "*From an analytical perspective*," Castells writes, "there are no 'good' and 'bad,' progressive and regressive social movements. They are all symptoms of who we are." [12]

Neither of these views allows us to understand the historical specificity of the movements of 1968, nor to tell whether the Seattle protests mark a continuity or a break from those movements. I would suggest that the movements of 1968 must be understood not as versions of populism or identity politics but as liberation movements. Despite the common, retrospective use of the phrase "identity politics," I have found only one self-proclaimed identity movement – the white supremacist Christian Identity Movement. *Liberation*, not identity, was a key word of the movements: it was the women's liberation movement, the gay liberation movement, the black liberation movement. In the late 1950s, *Liberation* emerged as the title of the pioneering journal of the US New Left as well as the title of the journal of the African National Congress. By the early 1970s, it was the name of the major newspaper of the French New Left and of the US New Left's national news agency, and it was a central category in the work of thinkers as varied as Herbert Marcuse, Frantz Fanon, Shulamith Firestone, and Gustavo Gutierrez.

This is not merely a semantic issue. For the liberation movements were movements of a particular historical moment, the age of three worlds, a period dominated by a sense that the world was divided in three: the capitalist First World, the Communist Second World, and the decolonizing Third World. It is a moment that seems to have evaporated after 1989; the one thing globalization clearly means is that everyone thinks there is now one world. The most powerful account of the liberation movements of 1968 depends on this imaginative geography. Asserting that 1968 marked the second world revolution, Immanuel Wallerstein has argued that, in each zone of the world-system, the social movements of 1968 took aim at state regimes that had been the product of the century of struggle for state power that followed the world revolution of 1848: the First World's social democracies and their trade-union and labor party apparatuses, the Second World's people's democracies and their Communist Party *nomenklatura*, and the Third World's postcolonial states and their comprador nationalist elites.[13]

The liberation movements were the product of the new technical, educational, and occupational structures of capitalist, Communist, and nationalist "modernization," drawing on the vastly expanded world of students, technical intelligentsias, emancipated women, and white-collar and public sector workers: it was the first uprising of the knowledge proletariat, as Nick Dyer-Witheford puts it in *Cyber-Marx*.[14] And they fought the state: the welfare state, the warfare state, the interventionist state. The struggle of young women for sexual and reproductive freedom in the battle for the rights to divorce, contraception and abortion, and against sexual harassment and violence; the resistance to state accumulation of nuclear weapons and state prosecution of colonial wars; the wildcat strikes and self-organization of young public sector workers; the direct action for civil rights and welfare rights by ethnicized and racialized minority peoples: the state was the target and the stake of the struggle. From Althusser's analysis of ideological state apparatuses to Chomsky's attack on the new mandarins, from Piven and Cloward's critique of the welfare state to Foucault's genealogy of the prison, intellectuals of the liberation movements "brought the state back in" to social thought, often recovering themes from the anarchist tradition. In fact, in challenging the unfulfilled promises of Second International social democracy, Third International Communism, and Bandung nationalism, they came to question two fundamental assumptions of the earlier social movements of the "old left": the notion that the aim of social movement struggle was the seizure of state power, whether by parliamentary or insurrectionary means, and the notion that the party – whether mass or vanguard – was the central vehicle of the struggle. The century of the mass party – from the German Social Democrats to the African National Congress – seemed to fade into history.

There were often striking parallels between the liberation movements in the three worlds; George Katsiaficas has pointed to parallels in student movements in the First, Second and Third Worlds, and an illuminating dialogue between Daniel Cohn-Bendit and Adam Michnik points to the anti-authoritarian common ground between 68ers on either side of the Iron Curtain. But the genuine division in the world-system prevented all but the most fleeting of links across the three zones.[15]

Against these movements, there emerged the countermovements of 1968, movements against liberation. Just as the fascist countermovements of the early twentieth century adopted many of the forms and methods of proletarian socialism and communism, so the counter-liberation movements adopted the forms and tactics of the liberation movements, leading too many social movement scholars to deduce a substantive similarity from formal similarity. However, modernity has been, and continues to be, dominated by the left-right axis that emerged with the French Revolution. If one objects that this is a teleological conception, I would reply that movement and countermovement participants continue to see themselves in teleological terms, as part of a grand historical struggle, tied to the future or the past. Movements and countermovements continue to depend on philosophies of history, whether salvational histories of religious redemption, racial and national histories of Aryan nations and white supremacy, or indeed narratives of uncompleted revolution and eventual liberation.

If one accepts this account of the liberation movements of 1968, we can return, in my final section, to the question of Seattle. Is it still 1968?

Defund the Fund! Break the Bank! Dump the Debt!

The basic journalistic account of the Seattle coalition was that it was the uneasy alliance of four forces: direct action groups that train and mobilize people in forms of street protest from civil disobedience to street theater, including the Ruckus Society and the Direct Action Network; NGOs that have organized campaigns against the IMF, WTO, and World Bank, issuing publications, establishing internet networks and resources and nurturing the emerging movement intellectuals, including Global Exchange, the Naderite Public Citizen's Global Trade Watch, and the International Forum on Globalization; the AFL-CIO, under the New Voice leadership of John Sweeney which took over in 1995; and a small cluster of more or less anonymous anarchist tendencies including the NO2WTO network, the Black Clad Messengers, and the Anarchist Action Collective.[16] Though this picture accounts for the particular successes and tensions of the Seattle protest, and the more limited successes of subsequent actions where one or more of these forces were absent, it does not fully explain the conditions that created this curious alliance. For that, I think we have to look at the emergence of a new type of antisystemic action that has taken shape over the last quarter century, a form of social resistance which is remarkably different from the liberation movements of 1968.

This antisystemic tendency does not yet have a name, nor a recognized chronology. The literature on globalization often gestures to a moment of resistance, invoking a new transnational social movement, but it has rarely told its history. There are exceptions – my argument owes much to the excellent but rarely-cited work of John Walton and David Seddon, *Free Markets and Food Riots* – but for each exception on the forces of antiglobalization, there are a dozen on the forces of globalization. What follows is the beginning of a history, an attempt to give a coherent account of an incoherent presence. The antiglobalization movement erupted in three moments: a first wave of IMF riots in the late 1970s and early 1980s; a second earthquake in 1989 when history seemed to end; and a third, more visible, moment inaugurated by the uprising of the Zapatistas in Chiapas in January 1994.

The first moment of the antiglobalization movement begins with an unprecedented series of urban food riots. In the summer of 1976, mass demonstrations took place in Peru and in Poland (where the government tried to raise food prices by 60 percent); in January 1977, riots broke out in several Egyptian cities when the government raised food and gas prices in response to IMF austerity demands; three months later, demonstrations against price rises in Kingston, Jamaica, turned to looting.[17] These food and price riots broke out in the midst of the crisis of the three worlds in the wake of the world depression of the 1970s: what the Midnight Notes collective, one of the outstanding analysts of this turn, calls the crisis of the three deals – the Keynesian deal, the Stalinist deal, and the Third World nationalist deal.[18] Each was figured as a debt crisis: the fiscal crisis of the state echoed from New York City's default in the early 1970s to Mexico's threatened default of 1982. Over the next several years, austerity protests – "precipitated by drastic, overnight price hikes resulting from the termination of public subsidies on basic goods and services" – broke out in half of the debtor countries of the world (39 out of 80), reaching a peak in 1983–85, in wake of the Mexican debt crisis.[19]

These austerity protests came to be called IMF riots, since the IMF was the target of popular hostility for the "stabilization measures" it imposed on indebted states in the Second and Third World. By 1984, placards read "Out with the IMF" in the Dominican Republic where three days of street demonstrations and general strikes led to clashes with the police that left sixty people dead. In 1985, Sudanese women protesting rising food prices chanted "Down, down with the IMF."[20] Though these austerity protests had little success in reversing the "structural adjustment" – a term that emerges with the World Bank's "structural adjustment loans" in 1980 – they did play a role in the major social movements of 1979 and 1980: the street protests that triggered the revolution in Iran; the largest strike wave in Turkish history that was ended by a military coup in 1980; the Polish strikes of 1980, triggered by price rises, that resulted in the emergence of Solidarity and the subsequent military coup.

The second moment is less visible because the incidence of IMF riots seems to taper off in the late 1980s. However, the dramatic end of the age of three worlds – the collapse of Eastern European Communism, the fall of the apartheid regime in South Africa, and the transition to democracy as military dictatorships and one-party states in Latin America and Africa institutionalized opposition parties – owes more to IMF rioting than has been recognized, for the debt crisis and IMF stabilization destabilized states of the left and the right, Manley's social-democratic Jamaica as well as de Klerk's apartheid South Africa. The goulash Communisms of Poland, Hungary, and Yugoslavia and the military populisms in Brazil, Argentina, and Nigeria all depended on social contracts with workers and the urban poor, financed by international debt. The IMF's concerted assault on wages, on state subsidies for food and transportation, and on public sector employment – in short, on the moral economy of the global barrio – was also an assault on the legitimacy of those regimes. This was particularly clear in Yugoslavia's collapse into general war. Yugoslavia had contracted the largest foreign debt in Eastern Europe, and, beginning in 1981, the IMF had imposed conditions which led to soaring prices, reduced wages, and severe unemployment, generating the descent into the maelstrom.[21]

However, the new regimes of 1989 – in the South as well as the East – did not restore the earlier social contracts; rather we have seen a contradictory combination of popular uprisings and neo-liberal outcomes. By 1994, even the *New York Times* was writing that "the IMF and the bank now effectively oversee and supervise the economies of some thirty countries in sub-Saharan Africa."[22] The rise of political democracy has been accompanied by the global collapse of social democracy. If this has meant the savaging of social safety-nets, welfare systems and price subsidies, it has also been a global privatization of public lands, public industries, and public services, amounting to what the Midnight Notes collective called, in an increasingly influential manifesto of 1990, "the new enclosures."[23] The commons that had been won by the social movements of 1848 were being enclosed.

By the late 1980s and early 1990s, a new wave of uprisings took place: in Venezuela, a February 1989 increase in gas prices (felt as a huge increase in bus fares) triggered one of the largest austerity protests ever, as street barricades, lootings, and bus burnings were answered by military occupation and the killing of over three hundred people. The protests had been exacerbated because President Pérez had campaigned against the IMF, calling it "a bomb that kills people with hunger"; but then cut a deal with the IMF.[24] There was a nationwide general strike in Morocco in 1990, and general strikes in India in 1991 and 1992 against the adoption of IMF/World Bank austerity and liberalization measures. In 1992, a "postmodern food riot," as Mike Davis called it, rocked another global barrio: Los Angeles.

However, the third moment really begins with the uprising of the

EZLN in Chiapas, in early 1994. The Zapatistas were not an urban response to price rises, but a rural revolt against the enclosure of common land – the gutting of the communal land provision of Article 27 of the Mexican constitution. However, by staging their uprising to coincide with the North American Free Trade Agreement (NAFTA), they also articulated the revolt against what they called neoliberalism, and in calling for the support of a new civil society, they reshaped the discourse of the left. Whereas the IMF, structural adjustment, and the debt crisis had been seen as Second and Third World issues for most of the 1980s, the struggle over NAFTA – which in the United States had never fully broken from an older protectionist labor nationalism – and the protests against the creation of the WTO began to create a new common sense and new forms of analysis on the left, as a decade of battles over so-called identity politics began to vanish. The global public sector strike wave of 1994–97, the emergence of the New Voice AFL-CIO leadership in the US, the growth of student antisweatshop activism: all this lay behind the Seattle coalition. Many writers have remarked on the Seattle alliance of turtles and Teamsters, environmentalists and unions. But I was struck by a second, more unlikely, alliance: the emergence of the WTO, IMF, and World Bank as targets has allowed a remarkable concordat in the US between two halves of the left divided since the Vietnam war: the relatively nationalist and social-democratic labor left and the anti-imperialist solidarity left.

But the third wave is not simply the appearance of IMF riots/WTO protests in the G7 countries: May and June 2000 witnessed general strikes against government restructuring and austerity programs in South Korea, South Africa, Argentina, Uruguay, Nigeria, and India. The Nigerian strikes were provoked by fuel price increases resulting from IMF pressure; in India, where twenty million workers went out on May 11, a strike leader said that "the strike was aimed against the surrender of the country's economic sovereignty before the WTO and the IMF."[25] A decade after the uprisings in Venezuela, Hugo Chávez was elected Venezuela's president, becoming one of the first significant world leaders to be thrown up by the anti-IMF movements.

These disparate examples remind us that if they share a common foe, even a common struggle, they don't always share the same analysis, strategy, or even name for that foe. The third moment – the period since the EZLN in 1994 – has seen the development of new analyses, new theories, new movement intellectuals. Four overlapping tendencies stand out: first, the attempt by citizen and student groups and NGOs to set alternative rules for the world economy by fighting in world forums, a kind of global Keynesianism. Though there is a debate over which forums can be reformed – the "fix it or nix it" debate – this tendency includes the codes of conduct campaigns of the antisweatshop movement, the struggles for international standards for labor, women's rights, and the environment, and the creation of a tax on global financial transactions.

Second, the extraordinary proletarianization of millions of the world's peoples on a global assembly line – a doubling of the world working class – has generated a global syndicalism, a tendency looking to the social movement unionism pioneered in the 1980s by new unionisms in Brazil, South Africa and South Korea, and now looking to the new forms of organization and militancy of the young women in the world's *maquiladoras*, the export processing of toys, textiles and electronics. Third, a more distinctly Southern theorization of a moment of "recolonization" – what the Nigerian singer Fela called the "second slavery" – has generated a form of what used to be the "non-aligned movement." This new imagination of South-South connections can be seen particularly in the rhetoric of Hugo Chávez.

Finally, the analysis of the new enclosures has brought forth a remarkable reimagination of the commons, not only as a new land war, bringing the struggles of indigenous peoples to the fore in this movement, but also as a way of seeing the commodification and privatization of aspects of social life not imagined even a few decades ago – notably life and thought, or, as we now see them, genetic material and information.

This remains a sketchy attempt to give a coherent account of an inchoate and incoherent presence. Nevertheless, the effort is important because it would be wrong to see these apparently unconnected uprisings against recolonization, globalization, neoliberalism, the global assembly line, and the new enclosures as simply another cycle of instances of the elementary forms of insurgency or as versions of identity politics. For better or worse, the liberation movements of 1968 have gone the way of the three worlds, the three deals that they challenged. The rhetoric of a new politics of networks, links, a virtual commune, challenges not only the orthodoxies of social democracy and Leninism, but also the orthodoxies of 1968. "We do not," a young German wrote in the new times of the first world revolution of 1848, "tell the world: 'Cease your struggles, they are stupid.' . . . We merely show the world why it actually struggles."[26] That remains the task of a critical and emancipatory cultural studies, facing what may yet be a global left.

4

THE NOVELISTS' INTERNATIONAL

In the midst of the age of three worlds (1945–1989), the novel looked dead, exhausted. In the capitalist First World, it was reduced to increasingly arid formalisms alongside an industry of formulaic genre fictions. In the Communist Second World, the official conventions of socialist realism were ritualized into a form of didactic popular literature. Into the freeze of this literary cold war erupted Gabriel García Márquez's *Cien años de soledad* [*One Hundred Years of Solitude*] (1967), the first international bestseller from Latin America and perhaps the most influential novel of the last third of the twentieth century. In its wake, a new sense of a world novel emerged, with *Cien años de soledad* as its avatar, the Third World as its home, and a vaguely defined magical realism as its aesthetic rubric.[1]

Like world music, the world novel is a category to be distrusted; if it genuinely points to the transformed geography of the novel, it is also a marketing device that flattens distinct regional and linguistic traditions into a single cosmopolitan world beat, with magical realism serving as the aesthetic of globalization, often as empty and contrived a signifier as the modernism and socialist realism it supplanted. There is, however, a historical truth to the sense that there are links between writers who now constitute the emerging canon of the world novel – writers as unalike as García Márquez, Naguib Mahfouz, Nadime Gordimer, José Saramago, Paule Marshall, and Pramoedya Ananta Toer – for the work of each has roots in the remarkable international literary movement that emerged in the middle decades of the twentieth century under the slogans of "proletarian literature," "neorealism," and "progressive," "engaged," or "committed" writing. The African-American novelist Richard Wright captured the sense of political and literary enfranchisement that marked this "novelists' international" in his autobiography:

> It was not the economics of Communism, nor the great power of trade unions, nor the excitement of underground politics that claimed me; my attention was caught by the similarity of the experiences of workers in other lands, by the possibility of uniting scattered but kindred peoples into a whole. [. . .] Out of the magazines I read came a passionate call for the experiences of the disinherited, and there were none of the lame lispings of the missionary in it. It did not say: "Be like us and we will like you, maybe." It said: "If you possess enough courage to speak out what you are, you will find that you are not alone." [. . .] Out of step with our times, it was but natural for us [writers] to respond to the Communist party, which said: "Your rebellion is right. Come with us and we will support your vision with militant action."
>
> Indeed, we felt that we were lucky. Why cower in towers of ivory and squeeze out private words when we had only to speak and millions listened? Our writing was translated into French, German, Russian, Chinese, Spanish, Japanese. . . . Who had ever, in all human history, offered to young writers an audience so vast? True, our royalties were small or less than small, but that did not matter.[2]

This international of writers was allied to, and often organized by, the international Communist movement, and its failures and successes – "the horror and the glory" in Wright's phrase – echoed the checkered history of that movement in both the local Communist parties, legal and underground, and the revolutionary regimes ruled by Communist parties in the wake of 1917. Nevertheless, its history is by no means congruent with that of the official "socialist realisms" of the Communist regimes. And though the novelists of this movement were deeply influenced by the experimental modernisms of the early decades of the century, they rarely fit into the canonical genealogies of Western modernism and postmodernism. Though the royalties were small, the writers not all proletarians, and the audience often more a promise than a reality, the movement transformed the history of the novel. By imagining an international of novelists, it reshaped the geography of the novel. It enfranchised a generation of writers, often of plebeian backgrounds, and it was the first self-conscious attempt to create a world literature. From Maxim Gorky to Gabriel García Márquez, from Lu Xun to Pramoedya Ananta Toer, from Richard Wright to Ngugi wa Thiong'o, from Patrícia Galvão to Isabel Allende: the novelists' international spans the globe and the century.

To sketch the history of this novelists' international is a daunting task. First, literary histories usually focus on its dramatic and still controversial literary politics: the formation and splitting of writer's organizations and unions; the brief ascendency of the idea of a "proletarian literature" and the shift to "socialist realism" at the 1934 Soviet Writers' Congress; the famous writers' congresses in Kharkov (1930), Moscow (1934), Paris (1935), New York (1936), Lucknow (1936), Madrid (1937), Tashkent (1958), Cairo (1962), and Havana (1967); the struggles over the writers' place in revolutionary regimes from Stalin's Soviet Union to Mao's China and Castro's Cuba. One can easily collect the manifestos in which writers, critics, militants and bureaucrats tried to define the proletarian novel and the forms of a radical or revolutionary realism – critical, social, socialist – and announced their intention to produce a committed, engaged, and partisan writing. But the novels actually written under these literary charters rarely matched the manifestos and often provoked further controversy.

Second, though the aesthetic ideologies of proletarian literature, socialist realism, or engaged writing are found around the globe in the twentieth century, most literary histories focus on a single national tradition, and there is little comparative work that would indicate whether the novels share common modes, forms, and styles. Mainstream literary criticism has generally taken one of two stances: either arguing that proletarian or social realist novels share a transnational formula that marks them as less-than-literary outsiders to the national literature, or claiming that the finest left-wing writers transcend the generic formula and are thus best understood within the particular linguistic and cultural tradition that makes up the national literature. Moreover, the two leading transnational aesthetic terms, realism and modernism, were so embedded in the cultural Cold War that they became mere honorifics with little actual meaning. In the Communist world, favored writers were proclaimed realists; in the capitalist world, they were deemed modernists. The discovery that apparent modernists were actually realists (think of the cases of Picasso or Brecht) and the reverse claim that classic social realists were actually modernists (as in contemporary reinterpretations of Lu Xun) have regularly been part of the ideological battle conducted through these terms.

Third, the novel itself has an uncertain relation to politics and social movements. Radical writers have usually chosen shorter and more public forms, such as plays, poems, journalism, and short stories. Novels take time; as Gerald Martin notes in his history of Latin American fiction, "a great historical novel usually requires at least thirty years' distance from its subject matter. Great realist works will always exist . . . [but] they will not appear during the era to which they refer."[3] The great novels of the revolutionary movements that erupted around 1917 often did not appear until the 1950s and 1960s, when the political energies of the movements had receded. A history of this literary movement must thus move between two moments: the moment of the breakthrough books, the landmark "proletarian novels," short, sometimes crude, but electrifying works often written by figures who did not go on to careers as novelists; and the moment of fruition when writers shaped by the radical literary movement produced major works, long after the manifestos and polemics had been forgotten.

Thus, if proletarian literature came to world attention in the brief moment in the late 1920s and early 1930s when young writers like Wright founded Communist literary circles and magazines, and the fledgling Soviet regime attracted writers to literary congresses and published *Literature of the World Revolution* in several languages, its roots lay in the first alliances between writers and the socialist movement at the beginning of the twentieth century, and its legacies reach to the magical realisms and postmodernisms of the age of three worlds.

The First Socialist Realism

The massive historical presence of the Communist regimes and movements often screens out world socialism *before* the Bolshevik revolution. Though the phrase "socialist realism" is rightly linked to the 1934 Soviet Writers' Congress which formally adopted it as the new aesthetic (and thus as a central part of the consolidation of the Stalinist regime), the idea of a socialist realism was, as Régine Robin has argued, the culmination of decades of socialist debate over a new aesthetic.[4] Gorky's presence as the chair of the 1934 Writers' Congress was emblematic because he represented a generation of socialist realists who preceded the Bolshevik Revolution of 1917, a generation who came of age at the turn of the century just as the powerful labor movements and socialist parties of the Second International were forming. Preceding the experimental modernisms that exploded around the world in the 1910s, their slogans were realism and naturalism. Some affiliated themselves with the emerging socialist and labor parties, and others were adopted by them. If Gorky and the Chinese writer Lu Xun were to become international Communist icons (Gorky's *Mother* [1907] became a central book in this tradition), this generation would also include Europeans like H.G. Wells, George Bernard Shaw, Anatole France, Romain Rolland, Martin Anderson Nexo, Pio Baroja, and the authors of classic antiwar novels of World War I, Henri Barbusse and Jaroslav Hašek; North Americans like Theodore Dreiser, W.E.B. Du Bois, Upton Sinclair, and Jack London; and South Asians like Rabindranath Tagore and Prem Chand. By the 1920s and 1930s, they were "the grand old men of socialist literature," the classic fellow travelers.[5] Though several (including France, Dreiser, and Du Bois) were to join the Communist Party just before their deaths, it is worth emphasizing that the generation of Gorky marked the beginnings of an international socialist literary culture before 1917.

It was this generation that brought the novel to the forefront of socialist literary culture. In the latter half of the nineteenth century, the novel was not central to socialist cultural thought. Poetry and drama were the heart of socialist notions of *Bildung*, which stressed the appropriation and mastery of the classics by working people rather than the development of an independent, radical, or working-class art. Following the lead of Marx and Engels, socialist critics championed the classics of the epoch of an ascendent and revolutionary bourgeoisie – Lessing, Schiller, and Goethe – against the bourgeois culture of the time. The novel was generally seen as merely a form of entertainment, and socialists both criticized and tried to supplant the commercial dime novels and *Schundliteratur* that proliferated in working-class culture. The main exception to this disregard of fiction was provoked by the social novels of Zola and his naturalist followers. The Marxist debate over naturalism – now largely associated with the writings of Lukács in the 1930s – began among German socialists, including Franz Mehring, in the 1890s.[6]

By the turn of the century, the immense popularity of Zola's novels among working-class socialist militants and the emergence of the generation of Gorky brought the novel to the fore in socialist culture. The realists of the turn of the century were hailed as the heirs of Balzac and Tolstoy, and the first two decades of the twentieth century saw the hegemony of realism among socialists: this was the source of the notion of critical realism that Lukács would defend. Novels of turn of the century industrial cities like Gorky's *Mother* (1907, set in the shipworks of Nizhni-Novgorod), Sinclair's *The Jungle* (1906, set in Chicago's meatpacking plants), Nexo's *Pelle Erobreren* (*Pele the Conqueror*, four volumes from 1906–10, narrating the migration to working-class Copenhagen), and Baroja's *La Lucha Por La Vida* (*The Struggle for Life*, three volumes from 1903–05, set in Madrid) became internationally famous.

In the early 1910s, the first calls for a proletarian literature, that is, writing by workers, appeared among Russian social democrats in exile and Yiddish-speaking socialists in New York, and soon resonated with the younger "lefts" – syndicalists, maximalists, and Bolsheviks – who emerged in the strike waves of the 1910s. This marked a radical break with the classicism of Second International socialist *Bildung*, which had maintained a suspicion of both proletarian cultural iconoclasm and agitational or tendentious literature. In their rejection of received aesthetic canons, the young advocates of proletarian writing shared much with their dadaist, cubist and expressionist contemporaries.

Nevertheless, there were few attempts to organize left-wing writers before World War I; the socialist subcultures of newspapers, clubs, and party schools rarely brought together young worker-writers, and the Second International did not organize international writers' congresses. If an incipient socialist realism had taken shape, a novelists' international lay in the future.

1917: Toward a Proletarian Novel

The turning point was the world upheaval of 1917–1921. In the wake of the European slaughter, regimes and empires were challenged: there were revolutions in Czarist Russia and Mexico, brief lived socialist republics in Germany, Hungary and Persia, uprisings against colonialism in Ireland, India, and China, and massive strike waves and factory occupations in Japan, Italy, Spain, Chile, Brazil, and the United States. The "imaginative proximity of social revolution" electrified a generation of young writers who came together in a variety of revolutionary and proletarian writers' groups.[7] Three initiatives were particularly influential. The first was the formation of the first international writers' association, *Clarté*, in 1919 by Henri Barbusse, which symbolically enrolled many of the established writers of the prewar years including Gorky, Sinclair, and Tagore, and which led to a series of international writers' congresses. The second was the emergence of a proletarian culture movement in revolutionary Russia, a loose federation of clubs, educational societies, and workers' theaters which held its first national conference in Petrograd just a week before the storming of the Winter Palace, and which soon became known by the abbreviation "Proletkult." The Proletkult movement reached its peak in the Soviet Union in the early 1920s, spawning workshops, journals, and rival groups, and its example resonated around the world. By the time of the 1930 Kharkov conference of revolutionary writers, there were active unions of proletarian writers not only in the Soviet Union, but in Japan, Germany, Hungary, Poland, Austria, Korea, China, and the United States.

The third initiative was the Baku conference of 1920, which marked the turn by the Communist inheritors of European socialism to the anticolonial movements in Asia and Africa, generating the powerful alliance of Communism and anticolonialism that was to shape the global decolonization struggles of the twentieth century. The importance of the anticolonial movements for European radical artists did not register immediately; at the Kharkov conference, the delegates from Egypt and Brazil argued that "European revolutionary and proletarian writers do not pay sufficient attention to the colonial question" and to "one of the most important branches of world proletarian literature – the development of revolutionary literature in colonial countries."[8] In many ways, the proletarian literature movement was to have a deeper impact on the national literatures of the colonized countries than it would in Western Europe.

In the wake of the upheavals of 1917–1921, the slogans of revolutionary and proletarian literature were adopted by young avant-gardes around the world. The early Proletkult groups were usually organized around theaters or small magazines publishing poems, short stories, reportage, and workers' correspondence. However, by the late 1920s and early 1930s, just as the world plunged into economic depression, a group of landmark proletarian novels appeared, announcing a new form: among them were Feodor Gladkov's *Tsement* (*Cement*, 1925) in the Soviet Union; Mike Gold's *Jews Without Money* (1929), Agnes Smedley's *Daughter of Earth* (1929), and John Dos Passos's *The 42nd Parallel* (1930) in the United States; Kobayashi Takiji's *Kani Kosen* (*The Factory Ship*, 1929) and Tokunaga Sunao's *Taiyo no Nai Machi* (*The Street Without Sun*, 1929) in Japan; Alfred Döblin's *Berlin Alexanderplatz* (1929) and Willi Bredel's *Maschinenfabrik N&K* (*Machine Factory N&K*, 1930) in Germany; the controversial story collections *Los Que Se Van* (*Those That Leave*, 1930) by Ecuador's Guayaquil group of social realists and *Angarey* (*Embers*, 1932) edited by the radical Urdu writer Sajjad Zaheer; César Vallejo's *El Tungsteno* (*Tungsten*, 1931) in Peru; Patrícia Galvão's *Parque Industrial* (*Industrial Park*, 1933) and Jorge Amado's *Cacau* (*Cacao*, 1933) in Brazil; Lamine Senghor's *La Violation d'un pays* (1927) in French West Africa and Paul Nizan's *Antoine Bloyé* (1933) in France; Ding Ling's *Yijiu sanling nian chun Shanghai* (*Shanghai, Spring 1930*, 1930) and Mao Dun's *Ziye* (*Midnight*, 1933) in China; Yi Kiyong's *Kohyang* (*Hometown*, 1934) in Korea and Mulk Raj Anand's *Untouchable* (1935) in India; Jacques Roumain's *La Montagne ensorcelée* (1931) in Haiti and C.L.R. James's *Minty Alley* (1936) in Trinidad.

The polemics which tried to define the revolutionary or proletarian novel (did one define it by subject matter, by the writer's class origins, or by its implicit or explicit proletarian or revolutionary stance?) hardly illuminate this flowering of books, which were widely translated and read and which served as an inspiration to other radical writers. Some of the novelists, like Gold, Bredel, and Tokunaga, grew up in working-class families and found their literary vocation in the radical labor movement; others, like James and Anand, were the "talented tenth" of colonized peoples; still others, like Dos Passos, Galvão, and Döblin, were children of bourgeois families and elite schools who had come to the left from the ranks of the modernist avant-gardes: dadaism, German expressionism, French and Latin American surrealism, Brazilian antropofagia. Many had traveled widely: the plebeian writers as soldiers, migrant workers, or seamen; the young colonials as students in the imperial capitals; the modernists as artist expatriates, tourists, and journalists.

Their books were experiments in form, attempts to reshape the novel. Several challenges immediately presented themselves: the attempt to represent working-class life in a genre that had developed as the quintessential narrator of bourgeois or middle-class manners, kin structures, and social circles; the attempt to represent a collective subject in a form built around the interior life of the individual; the attempt to create a public, agitational work in a form which, unlike drama, depended on private, often domestic, consumption; and the attempt to create a vision of revolutionary social change in a form almost inherently committed to the solidity of society and history. The early novels are often awkward and un-novelistic. They had their roots in the reportage of worker correspondents, first-person testimonies of working life, and they adopted its plotless, loosely-linked sketches of shop floors and tenement neighborhoods. As Gorky had put it at the beginning of *Mother*: "it was clear that the life of working people was the same everywhere. And if this was true, what was there to talk about?"[9]

Thus, this emerging novelists' international and its proletarian novel is neither a sociological entity (all novels written by proletarians) nor a fully-formed genre, but is a continuing dialectic between a self-conscious literary movement and the literary forms it developed. In the three decades between the victory of the Russian Bolsheviks in 1917 and the victory of the Chinese Communists in 1949, this proletarian literature spread around the world, as both a movement and a mode, a formation and a form. In the midst of the Cold War, literary historians tended to read this as a single story, whether in the Soviet literary historian Ivan Anisimov's triumphant sense (in 1966) that the "literary movement set in motion by the Russian Revolution" marked "a new epoch in world literature," or in the German literary historian Jürgen Rühle's tragic judgment (also of the 1960s) that the "alliance between left-wing art and left-wing politics" was a complete failure.[10] More recent scholarship has focused on the place of these movements in national literary traditions, and we now have many fine revaluations of specific national proletarian literatures. However, a survey of these literary histories suggests that there were several common trajectories, and allows us to sketch a preliminary set of hypotheses about the movements and the forms.

Movements

Not surprisingly, the presence of a proletarian literary movement in a country usually correlates with the presence of a Communist movement, even though Communist parties were often skeptical, even suspicious, of their literary allies. But proletarian literary movements seem to have had their greatest impact in countries which experienced major cultural upheavals in these decades, conflicts that challenged the legitimacy of dominant cultural forms. Moreover, there seems to be an inverse relation between the impact of the proletarian novel on a culture and the earlier importance of the novel in a culture. In countries with a long-established tradition of the novel – and which did not see overwhelming cultural crises, England, for example – the proletarian novel left little mark. Thus, the most significant proletarian literary movements emerged in four types of situation: those in countries where Communist regimes came to power; those in countries where fascist or authoritarian regimes came to power; those in the creole countries of the Americas; and those in colonized regions of Asia and Africa.

The trigger for the proletarian literary movement was the Bolshevik Revolution of 1917, and subsequently the history of the Russian movement has cast a long shadow around the globe.[11] However, in a number of ways, the Russian proletarian literary movement was not typical but exceptional. The Russian writers of the proletarian movement had perhaps the most daunting literary inheritance, the prerevolutionary reinvention of the novel by Tolstoy and Dostoyevsky, not to mention the pioneering working-class novels of Gorky. It is not clear that any of the writers of the proletarian generation succeeded in creating a space of their own. Second, in Russia, the literary movement developed largely after the revolution, in alliance (in varying degrees) with the new regime, rather than as an oppositional avant-garde. As a result, proletarian novels were more about reconstructing the nation and building socialism than about struggling against capitalism or colonialism; the production novel – the tale of "how the plan was fulfilled or the project was constructed"[12] – not the strike novel dominated. Third, the early and often experimental proletarian novels of the Soviet cultural renaissance of the 1920s, like Gladkov's *Cement*, became canonized by the Stalinist state as models for a didactic and formulaic socialist realism. "Many forties classics," Katerina Clark notes, "read like reruns of either *Cement* or *How the Steel Was Tempered*."[13] In the Communist states established after World War II, works of the local proletarian literary movements were similarly canonized, and some of the writers became bureaucrats of an official socialist realism in state-run Writers' Unions: one can see this in the careers of Mao Dun in China, of Johannes Brecher in East Germany, and of Han Sorya in North Korea.[14]

The experience of fascism marked a second trajectory. The earliest proletarian literary movements to appear outside the Soviet Union, those in Japan and Germany, came to world attention in the mid-1920s before being crushed by fascist and authoritarian regimes in the early 1930s.[15] The vibrant left-wing cultural worlds of Weimar Germany and Taisho Japan had developed out of dramatic alliances between modernist intellectuals and young working-class writers, spurring passionate debates over the shape of a revolutionary or proletarian novel (like the debates in *Die Linkskurve* sparked by Lukács over the novels of Bredel and Ottwalt), and producing classic proletarian novels, like Tokunaga Sunao's *Taiyo no Nai Machi* (*The*

Street Without Sun, 1929), which was translated into German in 1930 and into Spanish in 1931. Fascism extinguished this culture – Kobayashi Takiji became a martyr of the international proletarian literature movement when he was arrested and tortured to death in 1933 – forcing it underground, and into exile. For these movements, the resistance to fascism became a central literary topos, displacing the factory and tenement novels of earlier years. One sees this in Anna Seghers' enormously popular novel of the antifascist underground, *Das Siebte Kreuz* (*The Seventh Cross*, 1942), written and published in exile.

After the defeat of fascism, the experience of the resistance, as well as the story of collaboration, haunted the work of left-wing writers who revived the energies of the proletarian literary movement under the new slogans of "neorealism," and "committed" or "engaged" literature. In Italy, where the early rise of fascism had prevented a proletarian literary movement from emerging out of the factory occupations of 1919, a neorealism in fiction and film – closely connected to the cultural prestige of the postwar Communist Party – created new modes of representing working-class life, in such works as Vasco Pratolini's *Cronache di poveri amanti* (*A Tale of Poor Lovers*, 1947) and Cesare Pavese's *La luna e i falò* (*The Moon and the Bonfire*, 1950). Neorealism had a powerful impact throughout the Mediterranean, on the Iberian peninsula, and in Latin America. For example, it was the mode of the early novels of the left-wing Spanish writer Juan Goytisolo during the Franco years of the 1950s and 1960s.[16]

The third trajectory of the proletarian literary movement was that of the creole nations of the Americas, where neither Communism nor fascism came to power, but where Communist movements of varying strengths found themselves facing nationalist, populist regimes ruling societies whose proletariats were colored by the ethnic and racial legacies of slavery, Indian conquest, and the recruitment of immigrant labor. American proletarian literary movements developed in the early 1930s, in the face of the great depression and political leaders like Roosevelt (United States), Cárdenas (Mexico), Vargas (Brazil), and Peron (Argentina), who attempted to incorporate insurgent labor movements into populist parties.[17] If left-wing writers of the Americas were at times bitterly hostile and deeply sympathetic to these New Deals and Estavo Nôvos, they also inherited the messianic exceptionalism and cultural inferiority complex that characterized settler societies. Thus, they, like the celebrated Mexican muralists, helped to constitute a national imaginary of "the people" by importing European modernisms, reviving American folk traditions, and adopting the proletarian musics of the New World metropolises: jazz, samba, son, and tango.

The proletarian novels of the young American radicals often proved indistinguishable from the emergence of regional or ethnic fiction. In his classic "Blueprint for Negro Writers," Richard Wright wrote, "Negro writers must accept the nationalist implications of their lives, not in order to encourage them but in order to change and transcend them."[18] The renaissance of African-American writing in the United States – from Claude McKay and Langston Hughes, through Richard Wright and Ralph Ellison, to Gwendolyn Brooks and Paule Marshall – grew out of a host of left-wing black writers' organizations, and created links with radical black writers in the Caribbean (Hughes translated and rallied support for the imprisoned Haitian Jacques Roumain). In the Andean republics, proletarian writing fused with the tradition of *indigenista* novels in works like César Vallejo's widely-read novel of Indian miners, *El Tungsteno*, and Jorge Icaza's *Huasipungo* (1934); in Brazil, Jorge Amado's cycle of six "novels of Bahia" ranged from cocoa plantations to the waterfront of Salvador and put black culture at the heart of Brazil: it included *Jubiabá* (1935), a popular tale of a black boxer who becomes the leader of a stevedores' strike.

The fourth kind of proletarian literary movement emerged in the Asian and African colonies of the European empires. Small left-wing, anticolonial writers' groups emerged among students in both imperial and colonial cities in the 1930s, as strikes and popular uprisings not only registered anticolonial ferment but became the subject of early novels like Mulk Raj Anand's *Coolie* (based on a 1935 Bombay textile strike) and Thein Pe Myint's *Thabeik-hmauk kyaung-tha* (*The Student Boycotter*, 1938), based on the 1936 Rangoon student strike. The imperial crisis created by World War II and the subsequent era of national liberation struggles – the age of three worlds – turned these small groups into major cultural movements. The All India Progressive Writers Association, conceived in London in the mid-1930s by the émigré writers Sajjad Zaheer and Mulk Raj Anand and founded at the 1936 Lucknow conference (addressed by Prem Chand,

South Asia's equivalent of Gorky or Lu Xun, just before his death), became a powerful force in post-independence Indian culture; though Anand's novels in English received the most attention outside India, the left-wing literary movement influenced writers in many South Asian languages throughout the age of three worlds, and was a major force for literatures in Bengali, Malayalam (particularly the figure of Thakazhi Sivasankara Pillai), and Urdu (including figures like Zaheer, Ismat Chugtai, Sa'adat Hasan Manto, and the poet Faiz Ahmad Faiz). Similarly, Indonesia's LEKRA (*Lembaga Kebudayaan Rakyat*, Institute for People's Culture), formed in 1950 and suppressed in 1965, was a key institution in developing a radical post-independence culture, figured in the novel by the work of Pramoedya Ananta Toer (who also translated Gorky's *Mother* into Indonesian in 1956).[19]

After the Bandung conference of 1955, these literary movements of decolonization began to create a new novelists' international – "the links that bind us," in the words of Ngugi wa Thiong'o – through a series of Afro-Asian writers' congresses and journals (particularly *Lotus*, published from Cairo beginning in 1967).[20] The novels by this generation of writers enfranchised by the proletarian literary movements often became the founding fictions of the new national literatures: for example, Pramoedya's *Perburuan* (*The Fugitive*, 1950), the tale of an underground fighter appearing as a beggar in his home village in the final hours of the struggle against Japanese occupation, adopts the outline of the traditional Javanese shadow puppet play to narrate an allegory of resistance and collaboration.

The culmination of the proletarian literary movements in the decolonizing world might thus be seen in the grand trilogies and tetralogies of the age of three worlds: Miguel Angel Asturias's banana trilogy, which encompasses the entire world of United Fruit, culminating in a banana workers' strike (Asturias won both of the competing prizes of the Cold War, the Nobel and the Lenin); Naguib Mahfouz's Cairo trilogy, a generational saga that narrates Egyptian society and politics from 1917 to 1944 through a single family, eventually divided between rival brothers, the Communist Ahmad and the Muslim Brother Abd al-Munim; and Pramoedya Ananta Toer's Buru Quartet, composed in prison, an epic of Indonesian nationalism in the early twentieth century, told through the life of Minke, a fictional portrait of the nationalist journalist, Tirto Adi Suryo.[21]

Forms

Given this diversity of proletarian literary movements, are there any common modes, forms, or genres? At first, it seems unlikely, given the multitude of linguistic, literary, religious, political, ethnic, and national traditions from which the proletarian or progressive writers came. On the other hand, unlike many novelists around the world, these writers held an explicitly internationalist aesthetic ideology; they sought links across continents and actively translated each other. The novelists' international certainly imagined the possibility of common forms and modes, and attempted to develop them. Nevertheless, here my conclusions are tentative, based on a mere sampling of the novels, mostly in translation, and on a survey of the critical studies of proletarian literature traditions.

It is fair to say that if the master plot of Soviet socialist realism – the production novel with its heroic militants – informed the officially sanctioned literatures of the Communist states, it had little presence in the genealogies of proletarian or engaged fiction elsewhere. Indeed, novels of militants and organizers were relatively rare, and those written were not particularly successful. Could one synthesize the realism of the novel with an engaged, agitational stance? The classical Marxist tradition, represented in these years by Lukács, was skeptical, and argued for realism at the expense of agitation. Gorky had pulled it off in *Mother*, making revolutionary organizers central characters, but perhaps it only worked if working-class or anticolonial struggles reshaped a society's history, if the organizers and militants became, in Lukács's sense, typical. It was more common for militants and organizers to be secondary characters, providing guidance like the donor in folk tales.

Rather, two kinds of works quickly emerged: novels of, to use the capitalized personifications of Pietro di Donato's *Christ in Concrete*, Job and Tenement.[22] Representing the factory and its collective laborer was not only a central formal, and political, challenge, but it offered a microcosm, a knowable community that might found a new realism. "There are no heroes in this work – no leading characters or persons such as you would find in works dealing with the lives of individuals," Kobayashi Takiji wrote about his *Kani kosen*, a landmark of Japanese proletarian literature that was banned in Japan and translated around the world. "The collective hero is a group of laborers. . . . I have rejected all attempts at depicting character or delving into psychology."[23] The narrative is a sequence of incidents in the daily life of the factory ship, culminating in a strike.

The strike narrative becomes, not surprisingly, a core element in these works, representing the interruption in daily life – a festival of the oppressed – that creates a story. Certain actual historical strikes – the 1927 Shanghai strikes and the 1929 Gastonia (US) textile strike, for example – became the subject of a cluster of novels. If the strike is often defeated, it is because it stands as a figure for a promised revolution. In the early, simpler novels, the strike serves as the climax, often meriting only a few pages; by Sembene Ousmane's *Les Bouts de Bois de Dieu* (*God's Bits of Wood*, 1960), the strike (a fictional account of the 1947–48 railway strike in French West Africa) becomes the subject of the entire novel, its own form of daily life and struggle, a totality that encompasses not a single workplace but an entire land connected by the railway.

The other formal option was to represent the tenement, the crowded and chaotic collective households of urban workers which spilled out into the streets of the proletarian quarter. "When I think," Michael Gold wrote, "it is the tenement thinking."[24] A few of the radical writers – following the celebrated examples of Dos Passos and Döblin – attempted to write what might be called the novel of the metropolis by juxtaposing the workers' districts to the city of the bourgeoisie. In Mao Dun's sprawling portrait of Shanghai, *Midnight*, an omniscient narrator tries to weave together the family sagas of silk factory owners and workers; in Patrícia Galvão's brief and staccato montage of São Paulo street life, an omniscient editor splices together maps, statistics, conversations, and speeches under chapter headings like "In a Sector of the Class Struggle," "Where Surplus Value is Spent," and "Where They Talk About Rosa Luxemburg."

But the novel of the metropolis was far outnumbered by the novel of the ghetto, the tale of working-class districts isolated from the city, that is to say, the commercial districts whose department stores, skyscrapers, and theaters served as emblems of modernity. Early twentieth-century socialist and Communist subcultures were usually found in class-isolated mining and textile towns, and the class-segregated urban waterfronts and metal-working districts, and this became the characteristic landscape of the proletarian novel: Johannesburg's Malay Camp in Peter Abrahams' narrative of a South African miner, *Mine Boy*; the immigrant patchwork of New York's Lower East Side in the novels of Michael Gold and Henry Roth; or a single street like Florence's Via del Corno ("fifty yards long and five wide") in Vasco Pratolini's *A Tale of Poor Lovers*. Often, the protagonist of these novels was not an adult worker, but a child growing up in the streets and tenements. Equally common were accounts of the intellectual outsider watching and learning from the life of the "barrack-yards," as in C.L.R. James's *Minty Alley*.

Both of these modes were forms of subaltern modernism, as writers abandoned established family plots and the individual *Bildungsroman* to create an experimental collective novel based on documentary and reportage (terms both coined in this period). This impulse continued throughout the age of three worlds, manifesting itself in the aesthetic of neorealism, in fiction and film, at mid-century, and then in the testimonial literature of the 1960s and 1970s.[25] However, these often powerful documentary portraits of factories and tenements were, like many modernist fictions, curiously ahistorical, and rarely produced the temporal and spatial sweep of grand historical fiction or generational epics. A larger historical sensibility first emerged among the proletarian writers with the resistance narratives of antifascist and anticolonial wars, but it fully developed in the novels that grew out of the recognition that the new proletarians of the century were not simply factory workers and tenement dwellers, but were migrants from the countryside.

The worldwide migration from country to city was one of the central historical events of the age of three worlds: as Eric Hobsbawm writes, "the most dramatic and far-reaching social change of the second half of this century . . . is the death of the peasantry. . . . With the exception of Britain, peasants and farmers remained a massive part of the occupied population even in industrialized countries until well into the twentieth century." In 1940, Hobsbawm notes, there were only two countries – England and Belgium – where farmers were less than twenty percent of the population; in Latin America, peasants were a majority at the end of World War II. But by the 1980s, farmers were less than ten percent in almost all the countries of western Europe, and peasants were a minority throughout most of Latin America. "In Japan . . ., farmers were reduced from 52.4 percent of the people in 1947 to 9 percent in 1985."[26] Like the Leninist Communisms of the twentieth century which inspired them, the proletarian literary movements were hybrid concoctions, at once peasant and proletarian, completely entangled in this worldwide migration. Many of the novelists were themselves products of the migration, peasant children who moved to cities for work or education, or the city-bred children of peasant migrants.

Thus, in the decades after the initial factory novels of the proletarian avant-garde, the social and cultural uprooting that accompanied the migration from rural villages to the vast proletarian metropoles became the key historical experience behind the works of the novelists' international. At times, it took the form of a quasi-autobiographical tale of a young man, as in the trans-Pacific migration of the Filipino proletarian novelist Carlos Bulosan, recounted in his *America is in the Heart* (1944), or the migration of the student nationalist Minke from a Javanese village to the port city of Surabaya and the capital city of Batavia that structures Toer's Buru Quartet. At other times, it becomes the quasi-epic saga of a migrant family: John Steinbeck's *The Grapes of Wrath* (1939) narrates the exodus of a southwestern Dust Bowl family to California's "factories in the fields," and Harriette Arnow's *The Dollmaker* (1954) follows an Appalachian hill family to the war plants of Detroit. The migration was present even if it was not directly represented: it was the subtext to the contemporary murder mysteries that structure Richard Wright's *Native Son* and Ngugi wa Thiong'o's *Petals of Blood*.

The contemporary experience of migration is one reason why many of the earliest proletarian novels were actually novels of the peasantry, like Jacques Roumain's *Gouverneurs de la rosée* (*Masters of the Dew*, 1944) or the Brazilian novels of the "Northeast." "The urban masses are, on the whole, only rarely the central focus of Latin American narrative," one literary historian notes, and even the radical self-consciously proletarian writers often represented those who, metaphorically, stood between the peasantry and the urban working classes: rural proletarians like miners, plantation workers, sharecroppers, and tenant farmers. Mining novels, sugar novels, banana novels (including Asturias's classic banana trilogy) became entire genres in the middle decades of the twentieth century.[27]

When the radical writers turned to historical fiction, they also returned to the countryside, writing narratives of the epoch Marx had called "primitive accumulation." In his classic *Terras do sem fim* (*The Violent Land*, 1942), Jorge Amado turned away from the proletarian naturalism of his early novels to fashion a historical romance of the founding of the cacao plantations, a "land fertilized with human blood":

> It was the last great struggle in connection with conquest of the land, and the most ferocious of them all. For this reason it has remained a living reality down the years, the stories concerning it passing from mouth to mouth . . . at the fairs in the towns and the cities blind musicians sing of these gun-frays which once upon a time drenched with blood the black land of cacao.[28]

Out of the clash of peasant and proletarian worlds came the most powerful new form to emerge from the proletarian literary movements: magical or marvelous realism. Though magical realism is often considered as a successor and antagonist to social realism, its roots lay in the left-wing writers' movements. The idea and practice of magical realism was developed by two left-wing novelists from the Caribbean and Central America, the Cuban Alejo Carpentier and the Guatemalan Miguel Angel Asturias, both of whom had been briefly imprisoned as young radicals in their native countries and both of whom were influenced by the Communist surrealists during periods of exile in Paris. Carpentier's notion of "*lo real maravilloso*" was an explicit attempt to capture the temporal dislocations, the juxtaposition of different modes of life – the mythic and the modern – that had resulted from a history of conquest, enslavement, and colonization. "What is the entire history of America if not a chronicle of the marvelous real?", he asked in the 1949 preface to *El Reino de Este Mundo* where he coined the phrase. The novel that followed was a tale of the Haitian revolution, a central turning point in that history, and a narrative that the proletarian writers often retold.[29]

The magical realism of Carpentier and Asturias is perhaps best seen as a second stage of the proletarian avant-garde. If the first moment in the wake of the upheavals of 1917–1919 was dominated by a paradoxically ahistorical modernism that tried to document the lived experience of the radically new factory and tenement, the magical realism of 1949 is the return of the repressed history, lived and witnessed by the exiles and migrants, and the consequent insistence on the specific reality of the colonized world at the moment of liberation in India, Indonesia, and China, a moment that finds its historical precursor not in the French Revolution (as the Bolsheviks did) but in the Haitian Revolution.

If this is true, then one can see why the notion of magical realism resonates far beyond the Caribbean islands and coasts where it began. The term comes to represent a larger shift in the aesthetic of the novelists' international, from the powerful censoring of desire in the early novels (the works of the epoch of worldwide depression are novels of lack and hunger, and the utopian novel is rare) to an unleashing of desire and utopia, foreshadowing the liberation ideologies of the New Left. This is why it is common to see magical realism as the antithesis of an earlier social realism. One can see the shift in individual writers: in Brazil, Amado remains loyal to the Communist left while creating a fictional equivalent of carnival, beginning with *Gabriela, carvo e canela* (*Gabriela, Clove, and Cinnamon*, 1958); in Egypt, Naguib Mahfouz turned from the urban realism and generational saga of his Cairo trilogy to a series of allegorical tales on the betrayal of the revolution of 1952, beginning with *Awlad haratina* (*The Children of our Quarter*, 1959). It is also evident in the work of the left-wing writers of the postfascist Iberian peninsula, Juan Goytisolo and José Saramago, in the turn to surrealism and magical realism in the post-1965 Indonesian novel of figures like Iwan Simatupang, and in the work of the contemporary English-language inheritor of the Marxist traditions of India's Kerala, Arundhati Roy.[30]

Magical realism finds its most celebrated avatar in Gabriel García Márquez's *Cien años de soledad*. The 1967 novel, part of the celebrated boom in Latin American fiction, came to stand for the moment of Third World hopefulness in the wake of decolonization, the 1955 Bandung conference, and the 1959 Cuban revolution, peaking at the Havana cultural congress of 1967, a moment that died with the coups in Brazil (1964), Indonesia (1965), and Chile (1973). The literary analogue of the 1960s dependency theory of Latin American Marxists, *Cien años de soledad* is a tale of primitive accumulation and desire, of the origins of the capitalist world system with its wonders and its monsters; the house of the Buendías is neither a factory nor tenement. Nevertheless, it could be said to contain the classic proletarian novel, for at its heart lies a strike story. The climax of the novel – "the events that would deal Macondo its fatal blow" – is directly based on the 1928 strike by Colombian banana workers against United Fruit, and the subsequent massacre of the workers by government troops. The curious nature of García Márquez's strike sequence suggests that *Cien años de soledad* is both the culmination and overturning of the half-century of proletarian literary movements.[31]

In 1928, the strike might have inspired one of the original proletarian novels. For García Márquez, a generation later (he was born the year of the strike), it is a history suppressed by the "official version . . .: there were no dead, the satisfied workers had gone back to their families." The strike stands not as a figure for future revolution, but for social amnesia, as it is swept away in the torrential five-year rains that bring ruin to Macondo: "Nothing has happened in Macondo, nothing had ever happened, and nothing ever will happen." Indeed, the strike has a contradictory place in the novel, at once central and marginal, memorialized in a single brief chapter, a climax which is forgotten by nearly every character. There is no preparation for the strike, and the massacre seems to take its place among the myriad of magical events that constitute Macondo's reality. Unlike Asturias in his banana trilogy, García Márquez makes no effort to represent either United Fruit or the banana workers. The only link between the strike and the novel's larger narrative is that one of the more "colorless" and anonymous Buendías – José Arcadio Segundo – becomes one of the leaders of the strikers and the sole survivor of the massacre, keeping its memory alive.[32]

Thus, *Cien años de soledad* stands as both a sign of the crisis in the literary desire to represent workers that had animated a generation of plebeian writers and as an attempt to bear witness to that desire. On the one hand, not only does García Márquez not represent the banana workers; he testifies to the "hermeneutical delirium" in which "by a decision of the court it was established and set down in solemn decrees that the workers did not exist." On the other hand, García Márquez, like the child witness to the massacre, continues to recount the tale "to the disbelief of all."[33] Nearly a century after the first calls for an international proletarian literature and socialist realism, that desire seems not only defeated, but nonexistent and unimaginable. Yet like the strike story in *Cien años de soledad*, the aspirations and aesthetics of the novelists' international remain the forgotten, repressed history behind the contemporary globalization of the novel.

PART TWO

WORKING ON CULTURE

5

THE SOCIOANALYSIS OF CULTURE: RETHINKING THE CULTURAL TURN

Perhaps the central concept in the humanities over the last several decades has been the concept of culture. Raymond Williams, who was as responsible as anyone for the centrality of the term, once told an interviewer that he sometimes wished he had never heard the damn word. I know the feeling. After looking around my office, a student once joked that every book in it had the word culture in its title – an exaggeration, but not by much. Over the last fifteen years, the ostensibly innocuous phrase "cultural studies" has become a divisive slogan, celebrated or denounced for either rescuing or destroying the humanities.

How did a term which was almost entirely the property of mainstream scholarship and conservative criticism in 1950 become the slogan of the left, the postmodern, and the avant-garde in 2000? There is little doubt that the concept of culture was generally conservative at mid-century, tied to notions of consensus and organicism. As Warren Susman has argued, the "general and even popular 'discovery' of the concept of culture" in the 1930s "could and did have results far more conservative than radical, no matter what the intentions of those who originally championed some of the ideas and efforts." Why did this change?[1]

One answer is that it didn't change. A number of recent writers on the left have argued that, despite the intentions of those who champion cultural studies, the cultural turn continues to have conservative results, marking a slide away from politics and an uncritical embrace of the market's own infatuation with the popular. Despite the apparent shift from worshipping high art to wallowing in cheap entertainment, several writers argue that there are deeper continuities between earlier notions of culture – and of cultural criticism – and the postmodern cultural studies.[2] I disagree.

In this chapter, I will examine the socioanalysis of culture that emerged in the age of three worlds. I will begin by looking at the sea-change in the concept of culture, distinguishing modern from postmodern definitions; I will then try to sort out the antinomies of the form of New Left thought that came to be called cultural studies, the critical reflection on the culture industries and the state cultural apparatuses; and finally, as an imaginary resolution to no doubt real contradictions, I will outline the lineaments of a labor theory of culture.

Updating the History of the Concept of Culture

The history of the definitions of culture is an old genre which goes back at least to 1782. Culture was a word of Latin origin which, it seems, the English adopted from the Germans who had adopted it from the French who thereupon abandoned it even in translation: E.B. Tylor's *Primitive Culture* was translated as *La Civilisation primitive* in 1876–78, and as late as 1950 Ruth Benedict's *Patterns of Culture* was translated as *Échantillons de civilisations*. Let me pick up the story at mid-century with two once canonic and now more rarely cited openings. "My purpose in writing the following chapters," T.S. Eliot wrote in 1948, "is not, as might appear from a casual inspection of the table of contents, to outline a social or political philosophy; nor is the book intended to be merely a vehicle for my observations on a variety of topics. My aim is to help define a word, the word *culture*." Four years later, A.L. Kroeber and Clyde Kluckhohn wrote that

> The "culture concept of the anthropologists and sociologists is coming to be regarded as the foundation stone of the social sciences." . . . few intellectuals will challenge the statement that the idea of culture, in the technical anthropological sense, is one of the key notions of contempor-

> ary American thought. In explanatory importance and in generality of application it is comparable to such categories as gravity in physics, disease in medicine, evolution in biology.

Between Eliot's modestly-titled *Notes towards the Definition of Culture* and Kroeber and Kluckhohn's confident and encyclopedic *Culture: A Critical Review of Concepts and Definitions* stood the mid-century culture concept.[3]

Despite their prominence in the 1950s, neither Eliot nor Kroeber and Kluckhohn are the source of contemporary cultural studies; in retrospect, they now seem more an end than a beginning. Why? Both Eliot and Kroeber and Kluckhohn look back eighty years and find the same landmarks: Matthew Arnold's *Culture and Anarchy* of 1869 and E.B. Tylor's *Primitive Culture* of 1871. Between Arnold and Eliot, Tylor and Kroeber and Kluckhohn, we see what we might broadly call the modernist conceptions of culture: the literary and humanistic notion of culture as an ideal, the arts and letters, the "study and pursuit of perfection," combining "sweetness and light" with "fire and strength," to use Arnold's words; and, on the other hand, the anthropological notion of culture as a whole way of life, the "complex whole," in Tylor's words, of "knowledge, belief, art, law, morals, custom" and other capabilities and habits. Though aspects of Arnold and Tylor seem more Victorian than modern, their concepts of culture came to prominence in the modern era. Kroeber and Kluckhohn note a dramatic gap between Tylor's use of culture and its widespread adoption after 1920. Similarly, Raymond Williams's *Culture and Society* jumps quickly from Arnold over an "interregnum" to the clearly modernist figures of Eliot, Richards, and Leavis. It is striking, for example, that neither Marx nor Engels used it, even though the modern concept of culture has some roots in mid-nineteenth-century Germany (in 1857 Marx did note that he should not forget "so-called cultural history").[4]

These modernist conceptions of culture dominated the first half of the twentieth century, until, beginning in the 1950s, new postmodern definitions of culture emerged that broke decisively from both the Arnoldian *sweetness and light* and the anthropological *customs and morals*, giving both Eliot and Kroeber their retrospective air. *Culture and Society*, Raymond Williams's key intervention in the history of the culture concept, stands as a vanishing mediator. It borrowed from the Arnoldian and Tylorian traditions while burying them.[5]

How do we account for this history? Why did the concept of culture appear and why did its meaning change? In a classic analysis of the meaning of the abstraction "labor," Marx argued that the concept of a generalized, unspecified labor did not emerge until certain social relations created an equivalence between the many different activities which were henceforth labor: "It was a prodigious advance of Adam Smith," Marx wrote, "to throw away any specificity in wealth-producing activity – labor pure and simple, neither manufacturing nor commercial nor agricultural labor, but the one as much as the other." "The most general abstractions," Marx suggested, "generally develop only with the richest concrete development, where one [abstraction] appears common to many, common to all." One might pursue a similar inquiry about the concept of culture. What concrete development enabled the "general abstraction" of culture? What allowed the reduction of such a wide range of human activities to the peculiar common denominator we call culture? We often forget the strangeness of the category, a strangeness that led Adorno and Horkheimer to refuse it: "to speak of culture was always contrary to culture. Culture as a common denominator already contains in embryo that schematization and process of cataloguing and classification which bring culture within the sphere of administration." Why did the modernist concept of culture emerge in 1870? And why did it undergo a sea-change in 1950?[6]

A rereading of Arnold and Eliot, Tylor and Kroeber and Kluckhohn, offers a plausible hypothesis: the modernist notion of culture is largely the product of a crisis in religious thinking. For both Arnold and Eliot, culture was less a canon of great books than the historic dialectic between Hellenism and Hebraism, classical antiquity and Biblical revelation. Moreover, both Arnold and Eliot understood culture in relation to the battles between the established church and the dissenting sects. Sharing the peculiarities of Anglicanism – a Catholicism without a Pope, an established Protestantism – they both imagined culture as an ideal whole that incorporates the social cement of religion without its doctrinal controversies. The two errors, Eliot tells us, are either to see religion and culture as identical; or to see a relation between religion and culture. Searching to solve this conundrum, he arrives at a metaphor: culture is the "incarnation" of religion.[7]

Similarly, the anthropological "science of culture" emerged largely in the imperial encounter with "savage" religion, recoding religious difference – which is to say paganism – as "primitive culture." Though the science of culture, like the Arnoldian tradition, continued to draw a line between the sacred and the profane, culture, the science of the complex whole no less than the study of perfection, was able to cross that line with relative ease, seeing all the particular forms of worship as means, not ends.

The modernist notion of culture thus takes shape as an abstract realm of generalized spirituality or religiosity. Thus, culture, one might say, emerges only under capitalism. Though there appears to be culture in precapitalist societies, the concept is invented by Tylorians and Arnoldians alike to name those places where the commodity does not yet rule: the arts, leisure, and unproductive luxury consumption of revenues by the accumulators; and the ways of life of so-called primitive peoples. The world dominated by capital – the working day, the labor process, the factory and office, machines and technology, and science itself – is thus outside culture.

These two complementary modernist notions of culture had remarkable success and influence in the first half of the twentieth century, particularly, as Kroeber and Kluckhohn noted, in the societies of the European semiperiphery, the United States and Russia. Even the Marxist tradition adopted aspects of both the anthropological definition, particularly in theorizing the national question, and the high culture definition, particularly in the social-democratic tradition of appropriating and popularizing the classics. The latter was the cultural history that was the object of Walter Benjamin's brilliant critique in his essay on Eduard Fuchs. Marxism's major addition was the concept of cultural revolution which came out of the Russian Marxist tradition, particularly in the work of Lenin and Trotsky. This would deeply influence Gramsci and Lukács (particularly in his path breaking essay, "The Old Culture and the New Culture" of 1920). Nevertheless, by 1950, it would be odd to think of a specifically Marxist theory of culture, the way there was, from Mehring and Plekhanov to Christopher Caudwell and Ernst Fischer, a Marxist aesthetics.

Once we reach the work of Raymond Williams, culture emerges as a very different kind of abstraction. Williams's carefully constructed index of "Words, Themes, and Persons" in *Culture and Society* has entries for "Ideology" and "Panopticon," but none for "Religion." Arnold and Eliot's concern for the controversies of establishment – the disestablishment of the Irish church, Arnold's thoughts on the "great sexual insurrection of our Anglo-Teutonic race" figured by the Shakers and the Mormons, or Eliot's use of the term "sub-culture" to refer to the divided parts of Christendom, Roman Catholics in England – are replaced in Williams's *The Long Revolution* by the grand chapters on education, the growth of the reading public, and the rise of the popular press.

Williams's culture thus echoes the dramatic explosion throughout the world of what was called at the time "mass culture" – a culture that seemed as far from customs and morals as from the pursuit of perfection, as far from "folk" culture as from elite culture.[8] The postmodern concept of culture was the result of the generalization of the commodity form throughout the realm the moderns had called culture. What had been an elite culture became, as Pierre Bourdieu was to argue, simply a cluster of cultural commodities of distinction; and what anthropologists had seen as distinctive noncapitalist ways of life became different lifestyles, ways of purchasing. Religion was transformed less by a process of secularization than by a process of commodification.[9]

Far from marking the places outside capital's empire, culture was itself an economic realm, encompassing the mass media, advertising, and the production and distribution of knowledge. Moreover, it came to signify not only the cultural industries and state cultural apparatuses but the forms of working-class subsistence and consumption, both the goods and services supplied by the welfare state or purchased in the market, and the time of leisure and social reproduction outside the working day.

The shape of this new postmodern culture concept – the culture of entertainment industries and welfare states – can be seen in the essays of the 1940s and 1950s that have lasted longer than those of Eliot or Kroeber and Kluckhohn: Adorno and Horkheimer's "The Culture Industry," Dwight Macdonald's "Theory of Popular Culture," later revised as "Theory of Mass Culture" and then as "Masscult and Midcult" (it is interesting to note that Eliot himself wrote that "Macdonald's theory strikes me as the best *alternative* to my own that I have seen"), Roland Barthes's *Mythologies*, Richard Hoggart's *The Uses of Literacy*, C. Wright Mills's unfinished book on *The Cultural Apparatus*, Williams's own *The Long Revolution*, C.L.R. James's turn from an Arnoldian Trotskyist cultural politics to a new engagement with popular or mass culture in *American Civilization* and *Beyond a Boundary*, and the American Studies movement associated with figures like Leo Marx, whose "Notes on the Culture of the New Capitalism" was published in *Monthly Review* in 1959. It is perhaps not an accident that one of the first uses of the term "postmodern" appears in the landmark anthology of 1957, *Mass Culture*, which collected essays by Adorno and Macdonald, among others. By 1959, Daniel Bell was noting that the new journals of the left, *Dissent* and *Universities and Left Review* (soon to become *New Left Review*) "are full of attacks against advertising, the debaucheries of mass culture and the like. . . . these problems are essentially cultural and not political," he argued, "and the problem of radical thought today is to reconsider the relationship of culture to society."[10]

The four decades since Bell wrote have seen an extended reconsideration of the relationship of culture to society, as both Arnoldian cultural criticism and Tylorian cultural anthropology have been displaced by the postmodern notion of culture and cultural studies, what one might call socioanalytic theories of culture.[11]

The Antinomies of Cultural Studies

One could begin to sort out the kinds of socioanalytic theories of culture by intellectual histories and national traditions – British cultural studies, French structuralism and post-structuralism, German critical theory, North American theory, canon revision, and new historicism, Latin American dependency theory, South Asian subaltern studies, among others. No term captures all of these trends: postmodern theory is too broad; cultural Marxism misses the often antagonistic relation to the Marxist tradition; New Left theory sounds too narrowly political. Nevertheless, a generation of New Left intellectuals around the globe did seem to turn to culture in order to reshape radical thought (see Table 2).

Table 2
New Left Generation (the year they turned 20)

Roland Barthes 1935	Richard Ohmann 1951
C. Wright Mills 1936	Samir Amin 1951
Louis Althusser 1938	Stuart Hall 1952
Leo Marx 1939	Alexander Kluge 1952
Doris Lessing 1939	Antonio Negri 1953
Harry Braverman 1940	Susan Sontag 1953
Raymond Williams 1941	Stanley Aronowitz 1953
Betty Friedan 1941	Fredric Jameson 1954
E.P. Thompson 1944	Amiri Baraka 1954
Lucio Colletti 1944	Edward Said 1955
Amilcar Cabral 1944	Armand Mattelart 1956
André Gorz 1944	Nicos Poulantzas 1956
Frantz Fanon 1945	Wolfgang Haug 1956
Michel Foucault 1946	Frigga Haug 1957
John Berger 1946	Perry Anderson 1958
Gustavo Gutiérrez 1948	Ngugi wa Thiong'o 1958
Jürgen Habermas 1949	Roberto Schwarz 1958
Noam Chomsky 1949	E. San Juan 1958
Hans Magnus Enzensberger 1949	Juliet Mitchell 1960
Andre Gunder Frank 1949	Régis Debray 1960
Jean Baudrillard 1949	Etienne Balibar 1962
Immanuel Wallerstein 1950	Walter Rodney 1962
Pierre Bourdieu 1950	Gayatri Spivak 1962
Jacques Derrida 1950	Ariel Dorfman 1962
Roberto Fernández Retamar 1951	Angela Davis 1964

Not surprisingly, many of the most important New Left intellectuals were not themselves students during the great student uprisings of the late 1960s and early 1970s (the meaning and shape of the intellectual work produced by the New Left student cohort – those who turned twenty between, say, 1965 and 1975 is a somewhat different story). Rather they were the teachers, literally or symbolically, of those students, having come of age in the 1940s and 1950s. Usually too young to have shared in what was henceforth the old left – the depression-era Stalinisms, anti-Stalinisms and antifascisms – they sought some new left, *nouvelle gauche*, *neue Links*, in the face of the crisis of Stalinism, the triumphalism of the American century, and the electrifying new politics of the national liberation movements. In retrospect, it was a generation as striking as the classic modernist generation of Western Marxists – the generation of Lukács, Gramsci, Benjamin, Mariátegui, de Beauvoir, and C.L.R. James.

The turn to culture by the New Left generation was not a turn back to Arnold or Tylor; rather it was, as Bell put it, a turn to "advertising" and the "debaucheries of mass culture," the very aspects of the "new capitalism," as Leo Marx called it, that generated this new abstraction "culture" and seemed to leave both arts and customs behind. The most visible manifestation, the phenomenal appearance, of this new world was the new means of communication. I use this phrase "means of communication" in part because the word "communication" was a key word for this generation (perhaps, as Kenneth Burke suggested in the early 1950s, the word was a displacement, carrying some of the libidinal energies invested in the now-disgraced master concept "communism"[12]). *Communications* was the title of Raymond Williams's major programmatic work. I also use the phrase because it captures the first key antinomy of cultural studies, the hesitation between the means of communication as the mass media and the means of communication as the forms and codes by which communication takes place. On the one hand, the means of communication understood as a set of instruments and technologies – the mass media – was a constant temptation toward versions of technological determinism, from McLuhan's *The Mechanical Bride* and *Understanding Media*, to the enormous prestige of Benjamin's rediscovered "The Work of Art in the Age of Mechanical Reproduction." This line culminates in Armand Mattelart's genealogy of communications, *Mapping World Communication*, which is both an "itinerary of technical objects" and a history of the theories that accounted for them.

On the other hand, the means of communication understood as the forms and codes of symbolic action led to a resurrection of the ancient sciences of rhetoric and hermeneutics, with their concern for the tropes and allegories of social discourse, and the invention of the new sciences of signs and sign systems, semiology and semiotics. The influential work of Roland Barthes captured both the rhetorical and the scientistic sides: the playful decodings of detergents and plastics, of the brain of Einstein and a photograph of a saluting black soldier, in *Mythologies*, set along the quasi-mathematical rigor and forbidding jargon of *Elements of Semiology*. The last half-century has seen the rise and fall of several of these new "sciences" including deconstruction and discourse analysis. Nevertheless, their central object, what Stuart Hall has called the "relations of representation," remains at the heart of cultural studies.[13]

These new analyses of the means of communication, of what came to be called "mass culture," were not simply added to an already established social or political theory. Rather, as is implied by the echo between means of communication and means of production, the mass media often appeared to be the central terrain, the dominant level, of a postindustrial, consumer order. The new cultural materialisms were not simply a reassertion of the importance of the superstructure, but a rethinking of economy and politics in cultural terms: one can see this even in the least cultural of the New Left Marxists, the *Monthly Review* tendency, who placed a powerful explanatory emphasis on the role of advertising and the sales effort in monopoly capitalism.[14]

In a way, this was not surprising, for the new mass culture, the means of communication, were themselves closely tied to the power of the market and the state. The division between market and state echoes throughout the postwar years, and shapes the second fundamental antinomy of cultural studies – spectacle or surveillance, shopping mall or prison. This antinomy between market-oriented and state-oriented cultural studies developed out of the great conundrum facing the 1960s New Left: how to invent a Marxism without class. How could one maintain the insights and political drive of historical materialism in an epoch when left, right, and center generally agreed that the classes of Fordist capitalism were passing from the stage of world history, when the "labor metaphysic," as C. Wright Mills put it in his influential "Letter to the New Left" (published in New Left magazines on both sides of the Atlantic), seemed irrelevant?[15]

One powerful solution lay in the resurrection of the secret history of the commodity, from Lukács's long-forgotten *History and Class Consciousness* with its analysis of reification, to Benjamin's archaeology of the "universe of commodities" in the arcades and world exhibitions of nineteenth-century Paris, to Adorno and Horkheimer's account of the "Culture Industry," where the commodity form reduces all art to the eternal sameness of radio jingles, to the "sexual sell" that lay at the heart of the emptiness Betty Friedan called "the problem with no name," the "feminine mystique." It was a short step from the Paris arcades of Benjamin to the Bonaventure Hotel of Fredric Jameson; and one can take Guy Debord's Situationist pamphlet of 1968, *The Society of the Spectacle*, as the quintessential denunciation of a world where we don 3-D glasses in the cinema of daily life. In Latin America, where political independence coincided with economic and cultural dependence, cultural imperialism was also cast in commodity terms, as in the 1971 Chilean classic by Armand Mattelart and Ariel Dorfman, *How to Read Donald Duck: Imperialist Ideology in the Disney Comic.*[16]

The contradictions of this commodity Marxism are well known, as we veered from advertising dystopias to rock and rap utopias. Few of us have been immune to either the despair induced by more and more genuinely mindless entertainment or the hopes inspired by the occasional eruption of a genuinely popular and liberatory art. As long as capitalist culture presents itself as an immense accumulation of commodities, displayed in the multimedia emporia of Barnes and Noble, Tower Records, and Blockbuster Video, no escape from the antinomies of consumer culture is likely, and Jameson's dialectic of reification and utopia stands as one of the richest, if necessarily failed, imaginary resolutions of that contradiction.[17]

Moreover, it is worth recalling that the power of commodity theories of culture goes beyond the analysis of popular cultural commodities themselves. Together, the theory of reification (the transformation of relations between people into relations between things as a result of the generalization of the commodity form) and the inverse but complementary theory of the fetishism of commodities and the fetishism of capital (the transformation of the products of human labor into godlike creatures with the power to dictate the terms of daily work) constitute an entire aesthetic, a theory of the history of the senses, in which the aspects of daily life which had been a "complex whole" – food, worship, art, song, sport – are divided and taylorized into the disconnected jargons, subcultures, and specializations of postmodern daily life. The results of this instrumentalization of human culture are powerfully analyzed in the work of Pierre Bourdieu, where culture emerges not simply as consumption but as productive consumption, that is to say, as an investment in the creation of a specifically cultural capital. It is a small capital, to be sure, always dominated by economic capital: but, nevertheless, in the symbolic violence of the fields and habitus of capitalism, human choices in food, clothing, and the arts become badges of distinction, the stakes and weapons in class struggle.

The major alternative to these commodity theories of culture have been those that begin from the state rather than the market, from the exercise of power and domination rather than the buying and selling of goods and labor, and from theories of ideology rather than theories of fetishism.[18] "Our society is one not of spectacle, but of surveillance," Michel Foucault wrote in *Discipline and Punish*, and he implicitly replaced the nineteenth-century Parisian arcades of Benjamin with the nineteenth-century French penitentiaries, as Mike Davis would later replace Jameson's Bonaventure Hotel with the Metropolitan Detention Center as the emblem of postmodern Los Angeles. The prison – or what Foucault called the "carceral archipelago," the network of prison, police, and delinquent – held a central place in New Left politics and imagination.

> Sometimes I think this whole world
> Is one big prison yard
> Some of us are prisoners,
> The rest of us are guards,

Bob Dylan sang after the shooting of George Jackson. *Discipline and Punish* itself had its origins in the prison revolt at Attica, New York. However, the power of *Discipline and Punish* lay not simply in the horrifying, if static, diptychs of premodern and modern punishment – the torture of the regicide juxtaposed to the timetable of the house of young prisoners, the chain gang set against the police carriage – nor even in its alleged theory of power. Rather it lay in the long digression of Part Three which outlined "the formation of a disciplinary society," and what we might call a "discipline theory of culture." Discipline became another name for culture itself, now defined as the articulation of knowledge and power. Discipline produces docile and useful bodies through elaborate techniques. Discipline indeed has the same productive double meaning we saw in "means of communication." The disciplines are at once the institutions and apparatuses of cultural knowledge, the human sciences, and the particular forms and codes by which that knowledge is transmitted. Just as Marx dissected the simple forms of value, so Foucault anatomized the simple forms of discipline: hierarchical observation, normalization, examination.[19]

The analysis of these articulations of power and knowledge, these disciplines, offers a remarkable contrast to the commodity theories of culture. The fascinating world of consumer desire – the fetishism and fashion of world's fairs and shopping malls, what Benjamin called the "sex appeal of the inorganic," fades before the relentless surveillance and policing of desire by what are the state and quasi-state institutions of the Western social democracies and the Eastern people's democracies (prisons, armies, schools, hospitals) and, as elaborated in Edward Said's *Orientalism* and *Culture and Imperialism*, by the disciplines, discourses, and apparatuses of the colonial state.[20]

For if the New Left was in part a rebellion against the consumer capitalism of the affluent society, it was also a revolt against the institutions of what Louis Althusser called the "ideological state apparatuses" (the ISAs). The ISAs were, one might say, the state counterpart to Adorno and Horkheimer's culture industry. Like the disciplines, the ideological state apparatuses created – interpellated, in Althusser's jargon – subjects. We recognize who we are in being addressed by the institutions we live in. However, though the discipline/apparatus theories of culture depended on the double meaning of subject – one was subjected to power and domination, but one was also a subject, an agent capable of action – for the most part the docile body overshadowed the useful body. The disciplines and the apparatus were like the Borg on *Star Trek*: resistance was futile.

The other major political, or state-oriented, theory of culture – what I will call the "hegemony theory of culture" – developed as a response to the imprisonment of the subaltern in the disciplines and apparatuses of the state. Like the discipline theory, the hegemony theory stressed the complexity of the modern state, a state which is, in Gramsci's words, educative, ethical, cultural: it "plans, urges, incites, solicits, punishes." But the source of the hegemony argument was not the epochal history writing that underwrote the formation of a disciplinary or commodity society. Rather it was the conjunctural analyses found in Marx's famous pamphlet on the defeat of the revolutions of 1848 and the rise of Louis Napoleon, *The 18th Brumaire*, and in Gramsci's notes on the defeat of the Italian factory councils and the rise of Mussolini, both of which shaped Stuart Hall's brilliant articles on the defeat of social democracy and the New Left and the rise of Margaret Thatcher. All three interventions on the defeat of the left and the rise of an authoritarian populism set the economic narrative in the background, insisting on the relative autonomy of state and social movement politics. However, all three were less interested in power or domination than in the relations of force of particular moments. The argument of all three was, in essence, that politics worked like poetry, that the relations of force were intertwined with the relations of representation. The struggle for hegemony was not merely the disciplining of docile/useful bodies, nor was it simply the cheap bread and circuses of a McDonald's happy meal; rather it depended on the work of representation, on the summoning up of the ghosts and costumes of the past to revolutionize the present. Just as Marx called Louis Napoleon "an artist in his own right," a comedian who saw his own comedy as world history, so Hall argued that Thatcher, "our most-beloved Good Housekeeper," succeeded by representing – depicting and speaking for – the Thatcherite man and woman in us all.[21]

"The question of hegemony," Hall wrote, "is always the question of a new cultural order. . . . Cultural power [is] the power to define, to 'make things mean'." This politics of representation extended beyond the state and political parties to what Gramsci called "the forms of cultural organization," schools, churches, newspapers, theaters, literary quarterlies, serial novels, and the intellectuals who staffed them. Neither shopping mall nor prison, culture appeared as a giant school system, its product less spectacle or surveillance than the school recital of the Pledge of Allegiance, the articulation of that hybrid of nationalism and populism that Hall, following Gramsci, called the "national-popular." The emergence of this hegemony theory of culture was closely connected to the upheavals in mass education, which ranged from the formation of the postwar US "multiversity" and the labor-oriented adult education at the base of British cultural studies, to the international student revolts of 1968, to the battles over affirmative action and curricular reform of the last two decades.[22]

Hall's attention to the national-popular, and to the place of racisms in its formation, was part of a dramatic shift in the relations of force in cultural studies generally, a shift that took place in the late 1970s and early 1980s. The post-World War II fascination with mass culture, with culture as the means of communication, began to be displaced by the notion of culture as communities, as peoples. Cultural theory increasingly took up the question of how peoples are produced. It focused on the concepts that produce a people – nation, race, ethnicity, colony, color, minority, region, diaspora, migrant, post-colonial – and the national and imperial discourses that underlay these fantasies of racial and ethnic identity.

There were many symptoms and markers of the transformation: the great debate about the canon, which proved not to be about high and low culture, but about the lineaments of a national language, literature and education system; the trajectory of the post-structuralists Gayatri Spivak and Edward Said from their early meditations on *différance* and beginnings to their critiques of the discourses of colonial and postcolonial regimes; the remarkable success in the humanities of Benedict Anderson's little book on nationalism, *Imagined Communities*; the relative waning of Raymond Williams as the emblem of British cultural studies largely because of his apparent blindness to questions of nation, race, and empire; the emergence of the leading intellectuals of the decolonizing national liberation movements, figures like Du Bois, Fanon, and James, into the mainstream of North Atlantic cultural theory; the re-emergence of Etienne Balibar, an architect of the Althusserian rereading of *Capital*, as a theorist of racism and nationalism; and the revival of American studies, the original identity discipline.

One *could* see this national turn in cultural theory as the resurrection of the pluralist anthropological notion of culture as the ways of life of particular peoples, the foundation for the studies of national character. Indeed both defenders and critics of multiculturalism have seen this as an "identity theory of culture," implicitly adopting Immanuel Wallerstein's definition of culture: "when we talk of traits which are neither universal nor idiosyncratic we often use the term 'culture'. . . . Culture is a way of summarizing the ways in which groups distinguish themselves from other groups." For me, this definition misses precisely those aspects of postmodernity that had rendered the "mores and customs" notion of culture inadequate: the mass culture of market and state. Actually, the radical core of so-called identity theories of culture lies in the fact that they are not pluralist group or ethnic theories, but what I will call, borrowing from Nancy Fraser's work, "recognition theories of culture." They find their inspiration in the Hegelian/existentialist theories of culture that emerged alongside the mass culture debates of the 1950s in Sartre's *Anti-Semite and Jew*, de Beauvoir's *The Second Sex*, Fanon's *Black Skin, White Masks*, and even, I think, in Hoggart's *The Uses of Literacy*. In all of these works, the culture of the subaltern is a product of a dialectic of self and other, where the self is objectified as the other and denied any reciprocity of recognition. The politics of recognition range from Fanon's attack on the illusions of any national or identity culture and his defense of the cleansing violence of the colonial subject in *The Wretched of the Earth*, to the consciousness raising which sought to exorcise the ideologies of inferiority and inessentiality inscribed on the self, to the claim – on the state and the market – for cultural justice, for "affirmative action" in the woeful bureaucratic language we must defend. A "recognition theory of culture" is *not* built on the plurality of a multiculture, but on what Gayatri Spivak has seen as the radical emptiness of the category of the subaltern, the "underother."[23]

From Text to Work: Toward a Labor Theory of Culture

If the New Left's postwar socioanalytic theories of culture – cultural studies for short – were the product of a new attention to the means of communication dominated by the forces of the market and the state, it is not surprising that Marx's theories of fetishism and ideology were resurrected. And it should be clear that this turn to culture was not a turn away from political economy or politics, but a dramatic reconceptualization of them. However, the cultural turn rarely reclaimed Marx's analysis of the labor process, and it was a turn away from the classic Marxist concerns with work and production. Here it shared the New Left's aversion to the "labor metaphysic."

Thus cultural theorists were more likely to reach for Foucault's *Discipline and Punish* than for Harry Braverman's landmark analysis of the labor process, *Labor and Monopoly Capital* (1974). If Foucault began from the prison, Braverman began from the factory and the office; what Foucault called discipline, "movement in a resistant medium," Braverman called by two names: management and craft. Against the scientific management of Taylorism, he defended a scientific workmanship. If Foucault offered an outline of a discipline theory of culture, Braverman offers the lineaments of a labor theory of culture.

To call for a labor theory of culture may seem odd, a perverse return to the "labor metaphysic." If anything remains of Marxism in our post-Fordist, postindustrial cyber-economy, one would not think that it was its emphasis on work and production. Capitalism, we are told, is not about work but about the market. None of us really work, we simply sell our weekdays in order to buy our weekends. The capitalist dream of complete automation never dies – robotic assembly lines, desktop publishing, and money breeding money on an eternally rising stock exchange. Bill Gates's Microsoft mansion is the latest rewiring of a utopia without work. Even the left often seems to have given up on production; virtually all liberal and radical critiques of capitalism focus, as Harry Braverman noted, on capitalism as a mode of distribution rather than as a mode of production. Many radical anthropologists, ecologists, and feminists have explicitly argued that Marxism is, in Baudrillard's famous phrase, a "mirror of production," a captive of the nineteenth-century desire to dominate nature with a spiraling and self-destructive exploitation of energy and resources.

Moreover, work and culture seem to be opposites in a number of ways. Culture is seen as the equivalent of leisure, not labor; the symbolic, not the material; shopping and tourism, not jobs; sex, desire, and fantasy, not work. It is a commonplace to note our reluctance to represent work in our popular stories. A Martian who hijacked the stock of the average video store would reasonably conclude that humans spent far more of their time engaged in sex than in work. And most work remains invisible: we have all seen more different places of consumption than places of production: The Gap in the mall, not the garment sweatshops; the Honda showroom, not the auto factory; Perdue chickens in the supermarket, not the chicken processing plants. These places of consumption are, of course, places of work; but it is not an accident that we tend to see front-line service workers – the UPS drivers in the 1997 strike, for example – as the most characteristic kinds of workers.

However, Braverman reminds us that work and culture are synonyms, not antonyms. Culture is the product and result of labor, a part of the same process. Quoting the famous passage in *Capital* – "what distinguishes the worst architect from the best of bees is this, that the architect raises the structure in imagination before he erects it in reality. At the end of every labor process we get a result that had already existed in the imagination of the laborer at its commencement" – he notes how Marx's definition of human labor echoes Aristotle's definition of art. Human work and culture is purposive, conscious, and directed by conceptual thought.[24]

Thus, the fundamental divide in this theory of culture is not that between state and market, nor that between self and other, men and women, Jews and Goyim, Greeks and barbarians, cowboys and Indians. Rather it is the line between conception and execution, between, to use a musical analogy, composition and performance. The fundamental aspect of human labor, Braverman argues, is that the unity of conception and execution can be broken in time, space, and motive force; it is this that produces human culture. One person can conceive and another can execute. This is both the power and tragedy of human labor. A conception can be communicated from one place and time to another by sophisticated means of communication: writing and the means of mechanical and electronic reproduction. It can be saved in a variety of means of storage – books, blueprints, machines, computer programs – to be executed later, even centuries later, as we stage new productions of Shakespeare's plays and Beethoven's symphonies. But this very separation allows the de-skilling of the crafts that make up the arts, and the appropriation of art and culture to a spiritual realm apart from the world of manual labor.

The unity and division between mental and manual labor is thus the starting point of any labor theory of culture. Of course, we are more aware of their separation than their unity, since, as Braverman argued,

> the separation of hand and brain is the most decisive single step taken in the division of labor by the capitalist mode of production. . . . The unity of thought and action, conception and execution, hand and mind, which capitalism threatened from its beginnings, is now attacked by a systematic dissolution employing all the resources of science and the various engineering disciplines based upon it.

Though there remains a mental element to all manual labor, and a manual element to all mental labor – even Lt. Troi in *Star Trek* gets exhausted exercising her Betazoid telepathy as the ship's counselor – the illusion of their separation is a *real* illusion. All people are intellectuals, Gramsci writes in a classic version of this theory, but not all have the function of intellectuals in a given society. Thus culture appears simultaneously as something we all have (unlike the Arnoldian culture), and as something in which a few are specialists. Culture appears to us as a vast store of accumulated mental labor – the history of consciousness as one metaphor puts it. This accumulated mental labor appears to be the property of separate classes, leisured or cultured or intellectual classes, or of a separate time, a leisure time: hence the centrality of the struggles for the eight-hour day, the weekend, the paid vacation, and the rights to adolescent education and adult retirement.[25]

Just as the antinomies of public and private, liberty and equality, haunt liberal thought, the paradoxical unity and division of mental and manual labor haunts all socialist theories of culture. It lies behind a number of classic debates which liberal thinkers rarely, if ever, even enter: those of the the relation between base and superstructure in social thought and of the relation between workers and intellectuals in political organization. It is not surprising that many of the most powerful utopian images in the socialist tradition are images of the union of mental and manual labor: Marx's self-mocking vision of a society where one may "hunt in the morning, fish in the afternoon, rear cattle in the evening, criticize after dinner . . . without ever becoming hunter, fisherman, shepherd or critic," William Morris's craft ideal, the slogan of workers' self-management, and the various communitarian experiments from Brook Farm to Dorothy Day's Catholic Worker.[26]

All very well, you may say, but what are the consequences of such a labor theory of culture? It is not meant as a replacement for the cultural theories I have outlined. We live in a divided and reified culture, and each of the New Left socioanalyses of culture – commodity, investment, discipline, hegemony, and recognition – has its interpretative power and, as we used to say, its relative autonomy. However, a labor theory of culture does address a number of weaknesses and false problems in these other conceptions.

First, a labor theory of culture can take us beyond the noisy sphere of the market in the analysis of mass culture, reminding us that the apparent confrontation between cultural commodities and cultural consumers obscures the laborers in the culture industry. If no reading is uncontested, neither is any composition or performance. The fundamental contradiction in the culture industry is that it is not an automaton, but depends on the sale of the products of particular labor powers. As a result, as I argued at length in *The Cultural Front*, the struggles of the "hacks" and "stars" of the culture industries are fundamental to any understanding of mass culture. With the digitization of cultural skills – think of the effect of synthesized and sampled musics on contemporary instrumentalists – Braverman's model grows more and more relevant to cultural studies. Moreover, by reminding us of the important analytic distinction between the labor process and the valorization process, between the material content of purposive human activity and the specific form labor takes under capitalism, a labor theory of culture guards against the reduction of culture to commodification.

Second, a labor theory of culture avoids a fundamental weakness of the political theories of culture – again, using political in the narrow sense. One reason I hold on to the concept of culture rather than switching to the classical concept of ideology – there are many days when I would be happy to call what I do ideological studies rather than cultural studies – is that the concept of ideology remains a political term, having to do with power, domination, and legitimation. And a fundamental weakness of both the discipline and hegemony theories of culture is the tendency to see all of culture as first and foremost a weapon, a tool for constructing subjects of one sort or another. This has led some in cultural studies, including Eric Lott, to call for a revival of the aesthetic. Ironically, Lott's own early work was a brilliant example of, in his words, "the definition of culture as 'a whole way of conflict'," looking at "the role of culture in . . . political development." I think that what Lott wants is less the aesthetic than a sense that culture is a kind of work, rooted in our senses as well as our politics, and in its own materials and instruments; it thus always goes beyond the ideological functions emphasized in the political definitions of culture.[27]

In this way, a labor theory of culture also enriches Fredric Jameson's influential argument for the utopian elements of cultural productions. For Jameson, utopia is represented not by private desire and pleasure but by collective wish fulfillment, the imagination of community. But one needs to add to this a legacy of classical German aesthetics, the promise of play, of unalienated labor. How does labor get turned into beauty, particularly since we usually don't want to look at it? Performance is always tied to a strict economy of when and when not to show them that you're sweating. How do the rhythms of work become the rhythms of art? The hypothesis of a "labor unconscious" would mean that cultural historians and interpreters might explore the relations between forms of work and forms of art not only in those classic folk genres – quilts, sea chanteys, and field hollers – where the connections seem immediate, but in the arts and entertainments that seem most distant from the world of work.

Finally, the labor theory of culture reminds us that the cultures of the subaltern, the underothers, which demand recognition and cultural justice are not simply the expression of some pre-existing identity; their unities and divisions are the mediated products of the forms of labor – childbirth, slavery, sweatshop, assembly line – to which subalterns have been subjected. It is worth recalling that one of the most powerful works in what I have called the "recognition theory of culture," Tillie Olsen's *Silences* of 1978, was also an expression of a labor theory of culture, seeing work and art as two sides of the same reality. "For our silenced people," the dedication of *Silences* reads, "century after century their beings consumed in the hard, everyday essential work of maintaining human life. Their art, which still they made – as their other contributions – anonymous; refused respect, recognition; lost."[28]

If the revolutionary explosion of the means of communication – the vast culture industries and state cultural apparatuses – set the agenda for cultural studies in the second half of the twentieth century, perhaps their very ordinariness today can lead us back to their place in daily life, to a sense of culture not simply as the peculiar ways of life of small and distinctive communities of identity nor as the new high arts of the studios of Disney or Nintendo, but as the means of subsistence of mobile and migrant global workers. In the circuit of labor power, the working day is the moment of consumption; culture is the labor which produces labor power. "Marx's rather surprising failure to undertake any systematic study of the processes governing the production and reproduction of labor power itself" was, as David Harvey has argued, ". . . one of the most serious of all the gaps in Marx's own theory, and one that is proving extremely difficult to plug if only because the relations between accumulation and the social processes of reproduction of labor power are hidden in such a maze of complexity that they seem to defy analysis." For labor power remains a curious commodity in that it is, unlike other commodities, not produced as a commodity.[29]

Culture is a name for that habitus that forms, subjects, disciplines, entertains, and qualifies labor power. In it lies the very resistance to becoming labor power. It is the contradictory realm of work in the shadow of value, the unpaid and "unproductive" labor of the household and what the autonomous Marxists called the "social factory"; but it is also the contradictory realm of the arts of daily life, of what Marx called "the pleasures of the laborer," the "social needs and social pleasures" that are called forth by the "rapid growth of productive capital." That maze of complexity – the labyrinth of capital, labor, and culture – remains the challenge of an emancipatory cultural studies.[30]

6

THE END OF MASS CULTURE

Reification and Utopia in the Reagan Years

The era of Reaganism and Thatcherism, running roughly from the late 1970s to the early 1990s, produced a renaissance in the study of popular or mass culture in the universities of the United States and the United Kingdom. Though this discovery by intellectuals of the "culture of the people" was by no means unprecedented (indeed, a key text in this renaissance, Peter Burke's *Popular Culture in Early Modern Europe* [1978], opened with an account of the first modern discovery of popular culture), it stood both as a symptom of the political and cultural situation and as a distinctively new interpretation of the terrain called variously popular, mass, commercial, or vernacular culture. This interpretation began from an impasse, a sense of an intractable antinomy in cultural criticism. Choosing one's term – "mass culture" or "popular culture" – was choosing a side. In the United Kingdom, the opposition was coded as one between structuralism and culturalism;[1] in the United States, between the Frankfurt critique of the culture industry and populism.[2] The attempt to transcend these oppositions dominated theoretical, historical, and interpretative arguments.

Perhaps the most influential formulations of the new interpretation were two essays from 1979: Fredric Jameson's "Reification and Utopia in Mass Culture" and Stuart Hall's "Notes on Deconstructing 'The Popular'."[3]

Their central arguments – that mass cultural artifacts are at one and the same time ideological and utopian, and that popular culture is neither simply a form of social control nor a form of class expression, but a contested terrain – became commonplace, the opening moves in many discussions of popular culture. The fixed poles of the late 1970s lost their magnetic force; few leftist cultural critics or historians were driven to denounce or celebrate mass culture. No longer were considerations of popular culture merely occasions for jeremiads on cultural degeneration or a self-conscious cultural slumming. Rather the study of popular culture, understood as that contested terrain structured by the culture industries, the state cultural apparatuses, and the symbolic forms and practices of the subaltern classes, became the center of cultural studies generally.

In this chapter, I want to consider the consequences of this shift. Was it simply the establishing of a new academic paradigm, a way of producing new research on formerly despised materials? Did it retain any connection to a wider critique of culture, let alone to a project of cultural reconstruction? Or was it, as skeptics and cynics put it, a way for leftist academics to find resistance and subversive moments in *Dallas* and *Dynasty*?[4] What was the relation of this rethinking of mass culture to considerations of working-class history and culture? I will begin by reconsidering the arguments of Jameson and Hall, and suggesting some reasons why these arguments found wide acceptance; I will then argue that we can best avoid the caricatures of the critics by integrating the analysis of commodity forms with that of class formations, and by resituating the study of popular or mass culture in a more comprehensive cultural studies.

At first glance, the essays of Jameson and Hall appear very different. Jameson's essay, a centerpiece in the launching of the journal *Social Text*, was addressed to literary, film, and cultural critics, while Hall's essay was first delivered at a *History Workshop* gathering to historians. Jameson's concerns revolve around the interpretation of cultural texts; Hall begins with the issue of periodizing cultural transformations. Moreover, at the time, leftist cultural discourse in the United States was largely bound by the relatively recent translations of Frankfurt critical theory and Derridean post-structuralism; the quite different formation in the United Kingdom was symbolized by the furor over E. P. Thompson's attack on British

Althusserianism. Nevertheless, despite the differences in address and situation, the essays by Jameson and Hall shared several key arguments. First, both stressed the political centrality of culture. They both claimed that one misunderstood contemporary society if one thought of culture as leisure, entertainment, or escape, that is, all that was not "real life." For, as Jameson put it,

> we must ask the sociologists of manipulation . . . whether they inhabit the same world as we do. . . . culture, far from being an occasional matter of the reading of a monthly good book or a trip to the drive-in, seems to me the very element of consumer society itself. . . . everything is mediated by culture, to the point where even the political and the ideological "levels" have initially to be disentangled from their primary mode of representation which is cultural.

Similarly, Hall's argument depended on his sense that popular culture was not simply "those things the 'people' do or have done. . . . Pigeon-fancying and stamp-collecting, flying ducks on the wall and garden gnomes." Rather "popular culture is one of the sites where [the] struggle for and against a culture of the powerful is engaged. . . . it is one of the places where socialism might be constituted." "That," Hall concludes, "is why 'popular culture' matters. Otherwise, to tell you the truth, I don't give a damn about it."[5]

Second, Jameson and Hall sought to transcend the antinomies of social control and class expression, containment and resistance, incorporation and autonomy, manipulation and subversion, which had structured most ways of seeing popular culture. They did this not by ignoring the opposition but by relocating it. Thus, not only did they argue against the mutually exclusive positions that mass culture was *entirely* a manipulative industrial product or *entirely* an authentic cultural creation, but they also refused the proverbial separation of sheep from goats, of the progressive popular culture from the reactionary mass culture. Indeed, they argued that *neither* pole existed, that all cultural creation in capitalist society was divided against itself. As Hall writes, "if the forms of provided commercial popular culture are not purely manipulative, then it is because, alongside the false appeals, the foreshortenings, the trivilisation and shortcircuits, there are also elements of recognition and identification, something approaching a recreation of recognisable experiences and attitudes, to which people are responding." Jameson also suggests "that the works of mass culture cannot be ideological without at one and the same time being implicitly Utopian . . . they cannot manipulate unless they offer some genuine shred of content as a fantasy bribe to the public about to be so manipulated . . . such works cannot manage anxieties about the social order unless they have first revived them and given them some rudimentary expression."[6]

But this does not merely "rescue" commercial culture; it throws into question any notion of a purely authentic popular culture. "There is no separate, autonomous, 'authentic' layer of working class culture to be found," Hall argues. "Could we expect otherwise?" he asks in a brief consideration of popular imperialism. "How could we explain . . . the culture of a dominated class . . . which remained untouched by the most powerful dominant ideology . . .?" Jameson too argues that "the 'popular' . . . no longer exists," that even a "political art" is more a question than a prescription.[7]

It is the dialectic of containment and resistance, of reification and utopia which defines popular or mass culture for Jameson and Hall, though Hall emphasizes the battle surrounding the texts, artifacts, and performances – the "continuous and necessarily uneven and unequal struggle, by the dominant culture, constantly to disorganise and reorganise popular culture" – and Jameson emphasizes the conflict within the symbolic forms themselves.[8]

Finally, both Hall and Jameson throw into question the separation of high culture from popular culture, not by reversing the valuation or dissolving the distinction, but by moving beyond what Jameson calls "the false problem of value." Jameson argues that mass culture and modernism are, in Adorno's famous phrase, "torn halves of an integral freedom, to which however they do not add up;" they share a social and aesthetic situation, and their responses to the dilemmas of form and of audience are complementary. Hall, on the other hand, focuses attention on the process of boundary construction, on the way that the dividing of Culture from non-culture is an exercise of cultural power that should itself be the object of scrutiny.[9]

All of these are powerful and controversial arguments. My interest here is less in elaborating or defending them (or in discriminating between Jameson and Hall) than in suggesting several reasons why they won consent among socialist intellectuals in the 1980s and 1990s. First, the regimes of Reagan and Thatcher closed the door on the period of boom and upheaval that followed World War II, the period that is now named postmodernism, the Sixties, and the American Century. Of course, the end had been in sight with the depression of 1973–74 and the collapse of the insurgencies of the late 1960s; nevertheless, the 1970s were marked by the continuing legitimation crisis that led to the fall of a second US president – and a third if one counts the failure of Jimmy Carter to establish a hegemonic bloc – and saw victories to national liberation and socialist movements in Vietnam, Angola, Mozambique, Jamaica, Grenada, and Nicaragua. The success of the Reagan regime in constructing a new historical bloc, in giving new life to authoritarian regimes and counterrevolutionary forces, and particularly in forging a new national-popular ideology, a distinctive populism, often perplexed leftist critics. The peculiar powers of the "Great Communicator," who seemed less Hollywood actor than broadcast host or television evangelist, demanded a cultural explanation. Whereas Richard Nixon's success seemed sufficiently explained by media debunkers detailing the "selling" of a president, Reagan confounded manipulation theory. There was that utopian promise in the Reagan narrative, that fantasy bribe, that element of recognition, and it is not surprising that the two finest interpretations of Reagan's regime (Garry Wills's *Reagan's America* and Michael Rogin's *Ronald Reagan, The Movie*) turn on the dialectic of ideology and utopia in popular culture. Similarly, Stuart Hall's theoretical discussion of popular culture gained its power by informing his influential account of the authoritarian populism of Thatcher's (and Reagan's) "Great Moving Right Show."[10]

The crisis in feminism also provoked a reassessment of popular or mass culture. Like many insurgent movements, the women's movement emerged with an intransigent hostility to mass culture, denouncing, satirizing, and criticizing the popular paraphernalia of the feminine – beauty pageants, fashion, Hollywood cinema, and advertising. Feminist culture was avant-garde in sensibility, seeking new forms, new languages, new images for women's experience, and constructing new public spheres. By the 1980s, however, the political crises and successes of the women's movement – the mobilization of anti-feminist women by the right; the dividing lines of race, class, and generation; and the popularization of an economic feminism among newly-organized working-class women – led to a reassessment of commercial culture for women. Perhaps the most striking critical work in the renaissance of popular culture studies emerged in the debates over popular romance novels and over Hollywood melodrama.[11]

Third, the interest in the essays of Jameson and Hall was a symptom of the recognition, naming, and acceptance of postmodernism. Postmodernism could be defined as the reevaluation of mass culture by artists, writers, critics, architects: a learning from Las Vegas. In this light, Jameson might be seen not only as an analyst of postmodernism, but as an exemplary postmodernist theorist. If modernism and mass culture emerge together, "as twin and inseparable forms of the fission of aesthetic production under late capitalism," perhaps they come to an end together, recognizing their kinship, ceasing their hostilities, and fusing into the cassette tapes and digital disks that dominate postmodern culture.[12]

The changes in the culture industry in the last decades of the century bolster this sense. Though the capital invested in culture is more concentrated than ever, cultural commodities appear less centralized, less concentrated, as the heyday of network television and the Hollywood studio system has passed. The technology of the cassette and the disk changed American habits in consuming films, broadcast programs, and popular music, making contemporary capitalist culture look less like a mass culture and more like a series of elaborate, interlocking subcultures, each with their own market share. Though this vision of cultural pluralism is a far cry from a democratic or socialist culture, it did lead to a reduction in the overt hostility to and fear of mass culture. However, the cultural battles did not cease: one need only look at the battle over mass university education that was waged over the slogan of the canon and the jeremiad of that typical product of American mass culture, Allan Bloom, or at the intense battles throughout the Reagan era over vernacular musics – like the attempts to censor rock lyrics and the moral panics over disturbances at rap concerts –

which were regularly reported by one of the best "little magazines" of the 1980s, Dave Marsh's *Rock and Roll Confidential* (later, *Rock and Rap Confidential*).

But the fact is that mass culture has won. There is nothing else. The great powers of broadcasting and mass spectacles are second nature. Think for a moment about the earlier moments of the mass culture critique. It began as a reaction to the novel and threatening powers of broadcasting and film – emblemized by the notorious panic provoked by Orson Welles's radio broadcast of *The War of the Worlds* on the eve of World War II – and thought through the concepts of propaganda and manipulation. The second wave of mass culture critique was largely orchestrated around the postwar critique of Popular Front culture, the sense among the New York Intellectuals that the experiments in the popular arts that characterized the Popular Front were an integral part of a Stalinist (and capitalist) reduction of culture to kitsch. The third and most recent wave of hostility to mass culture largely derived from a hostility to the New Left and the counter-culture. The post-New Left flowering of popular culture criticism was not the result of an academization of popular culture, for the academic industry – symbolized by the *Journal of Popular Culture* and the Popular Culture Association which emerged in the early 1970s – has largely been a failure, never providing the theoretical or historical breakthroughs. Rather the breakthrough came out of the cultural criticism of the New Left, and particularly from the writers and readers associated with three journals: *Working Papers in Cultural Studies*, which was published by the Birmingham Centre for Contemporary Cultural Studies beginning in 1972; *Cultural Correspondence*, founded in 1975 with the subtitle "a strategic journal of popular culture"; and *Social Text*, founded in 1979. As Paul Buhle wrote of *Cultural Correspondence*, it was "the first political journal of culture to assume that its readers (and writers) watched television."[13]

The work of these intellectual tendencies was not a clever game of finding subversive moments in each piece of pop culture. Rather it attempted to change the way we thought about culture generally. All culture is mass culture under capitalism. There is no working-class culture that is not saturated with mass culture. The same historical transformations which produce a proletariat, labor power as a commodity, produce mass culture, culture as an "immense accumulation of commodities." There is now very little cultural production outside the commodity form.

Thus, the issue before us is twofold: first, how do we think the relations between commodity forms and class formations, between the omnipresent cultural commodities marketed by the cultural industries (and by the cultural apparatuses of the state) and the subcultures, class fractions, and social movements that produce and consume them; and second, how do we think the relations between the wide variety of cultural forms and media, how may we get beyond the dichotomy of high culture and low, canonic and noncanonic, the phrenologies of highbrow, middlebrow and lowbrow, the modernism/mass culture divide? It is not that these boundaries are not important, or without effects, but that we can no longer take them as starting points. We need a new conception of the spectrum of cultural forms.

Commodity Forms and Class Formations

How does the cultural critic or historian think about the relations between commodity forms and class formations? For the most part, they have seemed mutually exclusive, each the property of a distinctive kind of cultural studies. One powerful Marxist tradition of cultural studies depended on a notion of the relation between cultural products and social classes, enriching the foundational metaphors of base and superstructure with historical tropes that linked artistic genres and intellectual movements to the struggles between classes. It came to seem reductive, not only of the individual cultural products but of the cultural heterogeneity of class formations, and many of us cut our teeth on Sartre's celebrated complaint in *Search for a Method*: "Valéry is a petit bourgeois intellectual, no doubt about it. But not every petit bourgeois intellectual is Valéry."[14] But it remained the central aspect of what was to become the new labor history, with its attempt to reconstruct and delineate working-class cultures.

Paralleling the new labor history was a revival of a Marxist cultural criticism which largely abandoned class categories, stressing instead the effects of the commodity form on culture. The code mediating between social structure and individual text shifted from class to reification, and a powerful hermeneutic arose which could read the scars capitalist reification had left on the sentences, brush strokes, and rhythms of modern art as well as of mass culture. At times, however, this hermeneutic could seem less a revelation than an exegetical exercise, not unlike the fall from Empson's startling, even mystic, revelation of seven types of ambiguity to the all-too-predictable exercises in New Criticism. Interpretation is finally an act of metaphor, and suffers the same ritualization to cliché. But the reification hermeneutic also suffered from its lack of historical specificity; it often looked like a Marxist version of the ideologies of modernism and modernization, like them dependent on a too-simple dichotomy of before and after.

Perhaps the most disturbing aspect of the commodity form argument was its paralyzing of cultural practice. Do any cultural forms escape the logic of the commodity? Is there a political or oppositional art? In the class model, cultural practice was relatively clear; one aligned oneself – in a variety of complex ways – with the rising class, the popular classes. Was there a cultural practice in the face of reification? Fredric Jameson's work set the contradiction in plain view, at once arguing that there is "authentic cultural production" which draws "on the collective experience of marginal pockets of the social life of the world system," while recognizing that political art is a problem not a choice, that "you do not reinvent an access onto political art and authentic cultural production by studding your individual artistic discourse with class and political signals."[15] I do not mean to solve the problem of a political art here, but the success and failure of our popular culture criticism hinges on this issue: the sense that interpreting a mass culture is not the same as changing it, that the new criticism of mass culture has not contributed to the creation of a new popular culture.

There have been several attempts to reintegrate the interpretation of commodity forms with the history of class formations, to situate the interpretation of the products of the culture industry with an account of the communities that use them. This is not merely a reprise of an older Marxism, because it begins not from an assumption that cultures are somehow attached to already constituted classes, but that cultural conflicts are part of the process of class formation, the forging of alliances among class fractions, social groups, and ethnic and racial communities. The two most powerful and influential ways of rethinking class formations and commodity forms in cultural studies are the theory of the social construction of cultural value and the theory of hegemony.

The first of these, the investigation of the social construction of cultural values, grew out of the battles in literary studies over the canon, the resurrection of the almost moribund subdiscipline of sociology of culture, and the translation and appropriation of Pierre Bourdieu's *La Distinction*. In this work, one finds a turn away from judgments and interpretations of particular cultural works, and toward an exploration of the way cultural values, tastes, and hierarchies are established. What distinguishes this work from earlier sociologies of taste is its unwavering attention to the ideological consequences of taste, to the ways aesthetic distinctions are operations of domination and subordination. The relation between class formations and cultural commodities moves to the center, not because of some immanent or expressive class nature of particular cultural texts but because of the way they are mobilized as visible totems of class domination and as symbolic weapons in class conflict.

Consider the difference between the explanations of postmodernism offered by Fredric Jameson and Fred Pfeil. For Jameson, postmodernism is a stylistic dominant, a product of the "cultural logic of late capitalism," a new turn of the screw of reification. It is a new aesthetic, in the deepest sense: not only a new sense of rhythm and beauty and artistic value, but a new way of perception, of living the body, indeed a modification of the senses themselves in a world of simulacra and information, a society of cyborgs with amnesia, where human relations are not even relations between things but relations between the images of things. For Pfeil, on the other hand, postmodernism is the aesthetic, which is to say the cultural consumption habits, of a particular class generation, the youth of the US professional and managerial classes. Though he occasionally does look to Talking Heads and Laurie Anderson as the Pascal and Racine of a rising class fraction expressing their worldview, he more often elaborates their cultural consumption as a marking of distinctions, a creation of a habitus, a life style, as an example of the social construction of cultural value.[16]

Though in many ways complementary to Jameson's work (Jameson takes architecture, surely the form most amenable to a logic of capital argument, as representative of postmodernism; Pfeil looks to the cultural commodities an individual buys, such as recordings and paperbacks, for his argument), Pfeil's work points to a powerful trend in US cultural criticism which includes Lawrence Levine's *Highbrow Lowbrow*, Janice Radway's work on the Book-of-the-Month Club, Joan Shelley Rubin's study of middlebrow culture, and the discussions of cultural gatekeeping in the distribution of US fiction by Richard Ohmann, Jane Tompkins, Lawrence Schwartz, and Pfeil himself. In all of this work, the processes of establishing cultural hierarchies, taste communities, and canons becomes the focus of cultural criticism. There are, however, several curiosities about this emerging body of work.

First, unlike Bourdieu, whose book depends on a powerful, if debatable, articulation of a popular aesthetic, the elaboration of a working-class culture, the US writers on the social construction of cultural value focus on the tension between fractions of the middle classes, and particularly on the cultural power of the emerging professional and managerial classes. The early failure of an aristocratic or patrician culture financed by a corporate elite, combined with the apparent failure of a distinctive working-class culture have given the subsumed classes a disproportionately central role in the construction of American culture. Thus we see a history of the cultural distinctions created by a sometimes radically anti-commercial professional class, by the genteel tradition of a provincial middlebrow petit bourgeoisie, by the suburban culture that has been periodically chronicled in *The Lonely Crowd*, *The Feminine Mystique*, *The Culture of Narcissism*, and *Habits of the Heart*, and by postmodern yuppies. However, the US version of the social construction of cultural values needs to move beyond a debunking of the authorized standards and judgments of taste and value to a mapping of the popular aesthetic and the cultural values of the working classes.

It is not clear, however, whether this is possible, whether, that is to say, the investigation of the social construction of cultural tastes can ever break free of debunking. For the attraction of Bourdieu's work to US cultural critics owes something to his kinship with a classic American cultural critic, Thorstein Veblen. Like Veblen's attack on culture, Bourdieu's work cuts through the grease of most high cultural discourse. It is hard to take the rhetoric of the aesthetic disposition seriously when its uses as conspicuous consumption are so painstakingly unmasked. But like most powerful satires, it undermines the satirist as well. Whereas most of the attacks on the academic study of popular cultures are easily dismissed as the products of a populist or, more often, mandarin anti-intellectualism, it is more difficult to deny the power of Bourdieu's debunking:

> The struggles which aim . . . to transform or overturn the legitimate hierarchies through the legitimating of a still illegitimate art or genre, such as photography or the strip cartoon, or through the rehabilitation of "minor" or "neglected" authors etc., or to impose a new mode of appropriation, linked to another mode of acquisition, are precisely what creates legitimacy, by creating belief not in the value of this or that stake but in the value of the game in which the value of all the stakes is produced and reproduced. . . . "Middle-ground" arts such as cinema, jazz, and, even more, strip cartoons, science fiction or detective stories are predisposed to attract the investments either of those who have entirely succeeded in converting their cultural capital into educational capital or those who, not having acquired legitimate culture in the legitimate manner (i.e., through early familiarization), maintain an uneasy relationship with it, subjectively or objectively, or both. These arts, not yet fully legitimate, which are disdained or neglected by the big holders of educational capital, offer a refuge and a revenge to those who, by appropriating them, secure the best return on their cultural capital.[17]

By evacuating the content of cultural products and activities, by reading them as objects of consumption and markers in a symbolic class conflict, Bourdieu's work, far from providing a foundation for cultural studies or a reconstructive cultural practice, buries it. An investment theory of culture mimics the capitalist culture it critiques. If all cultural activity is a means of accumulating cultural capital, there is no place for a cultural politics. The consequences of cultural studies as a project are meager indeed.

The second major tendency that links class formations and cultural commodities offers a more persuasive account not only of the links between class and culture but between culture and politics: this is the theory of hegemony and historical blocs. This developed out of the remarkable revival of the work of Antonio Gramsci – it seemed at one point as if everyone was a Gramscian. However, the impact of Gramsci's work and the constellation of concepts he employed was uneven, emerging quite differently in various national, disciplinary, and political contexts. Unfortunately, the debates over the concept of hegemony among US historians did not do justice to the richness and originality of the theory.[18]

Two common misappropriations of Gramsci in the United States haunted these debates. First, the concept of hegemony was often understood as a functional equivalent of commodification and reification. Reducing the work of both Gramsci and the Frankfurt School to a general notion of consumer society, this tendency saw hegemony as domination through managed consumption and manipulated desire. Those persuaded by this view tended to be vehemently opposed to mass culture, and drew the fire of both socialist defenders of the utopian possibilities of the culture of abundance like Warren Susman and the defenders of consumer capitalism, like Walter Benn Michaels, the Daniel Boorstin of literary criticism. Second, the concept of hegemony all too often appeared as a synonym for consensus, leading to a revival of consensus historiography (though from a point of view that was critical of the consensus). One sees this in Sacvan Bercovitch's provocative theories of the rhetoric of the American consensus, and, despite explicit disclaimers, in Jackson Lears's elaboration of a theory of cultural hegemony. But as Eric Foner has noted of this "consensus/hegemony approach," "in adopting the notion of hegemony from Gramsci, American historians have often transformed it from a subtle mode of exploring the ways class struggle is muted and channeled in modern society, into a substitute for it. . . . Rather than being demonstrated, the 'hegemony' of mass culture and liberal values is inferred from the 'absence' of protest, and then this absence is attributed to the self-same 'hegemony'." It is this conception that Thomas Haskell satirized as "a feather pillow, perfect for catching falling Marxists."[19]

Jackson Lears's "The Concept of Cultural Hegemony" was the focus of much of the debate, and it is a symptomatic essay. Lears moved beyond the early American appropriations of hegemony by turning from issues of mass commodity culture to the history of class formations and subordinate groups:

> by clarifying the political functions of cultural symbols, the concept of cultural hegemony can aid intellectual historians trying to understand how ideas reinforce or undermine existing social structures and social historians seeking to reconcile the apparent contradiction between the power wielded by dominant groups and the relative cultural autonomy of subordinate groups whom they victimize.

Unfortunately, his concept (and this was characteristic of much of the US discussion that followed, whether defending or rejecting a concept of hegemony) continued to be framed by the opposition between accommodation and resistance, attempting to define how victims are complicit in their own victimization, caught in the murky realms of consciousness and false consciousness. For Lears, the fundamental question remained: to what degree are the working classes incorporated? As George Lipsitz put it well, "it is perhaps a measure of the inescapable irony of our time that Antonio Gramsci's ideas have gained popularity among scholars largely as a means of explaining the futility of efforts to change past and present capitalist societies."[20]

But Gramsci's concepts of hegemony and historical blocs do not begin with the functionalist premise of Lears ("how ideas reinforce or undermine existing social structures") which produces the characteristic deep freeze of contemporary accounts of hegemony. Rather they begin from the question of how social movements are organized among both the dominant and subordinate groups, of how social formations are led. Precisely because the theory of hegemony is a theory of action as well as of structure, because Gramsci and Hall are politicians, educators, intellectuals in the widest sense, they formulate the issue not in terms of true or false consciousness, but in terms of a popular thought and culture that is shaped, reshaped, and fought over. "Hegemonizing," as Stuart Hall put it, "is hard work." The building of hegemonic formations is not only a matter of ideas, and of winning hearts and minds, but also an issue of participation, in the sense of involving people both in cultural institutions – schools, churches, sporting events – and in long-term historic projects – waging wars, establishing colonies, gentrifying a city and developing a regional economy.

The power of this conception for the analysis of popular cultural artifacts is that it provides the necessary complement to the analysis of the social construction of cultural value. If that work establishes that there are no intrinsic values in cultural objects, and no natural or expressive relation between classes and cultural practices, a theory of hegemony provides the framework by which we may examine the historical articulations of class formations and commodity forms. No popular cultural practice is necessarily subversive or incorporated; it takes place in a situation, becomes articulated with a "party" in Gramsci's sense: an organized way of life, an alliance of class fractions, a conception of the universe, a historical bloc which creates the conditions for a political use or reading, the conditions for symbolizing class conflict.

The greatest difficulty in appropriating Gramsci's constellation of historical concepts for contemporary critiques of popular culture is that his work did not take full measure of mass culture, of broadcasting, film, recorded music, mass spectator sports, and the explosion of cheap mass-produced symbolic commodities – McDLTs, Levis, and the fantastic array of plastic objects that are sold as children's toys and adult novelties. It is this absence that can make Gramsci look old-fashioned; Adorno's screech against radio music may not be appealing but it is recognizable. For Gramsci, on the other hand, popular culture is figured by the Roman Catholic Church. Nevertheless, the advantages of Gramsci's framework may lie here as well: taking the Catholic Church rather than network television as the representative instance may avoid the brief historical scope of most thinking about popular culture and the temptation of concepts like manipulation, propaganda, and deception that haunt the apocalyptic imaginations of modernists and postmodernists alike. Whereas a characteristic US pragmatist socialist, Kenneth Burke, once suggested that socialists imitate advertisers, Gramsci would seem to argue that socialists imitate the clergy. Popular culture is more the product of long-term cultural organization and a symbolic community than a quick sale. Unfortunately, much of the recent revival of Gramsci's work for socialist cultural policies seems less Gramscian than Burkean.

Forms of Cultural Practice

We need a new way of thinking about the spectrum of cultural forms. If the theories of the social construction of cultural value give us a decoder of cultural hierarchies, boundaries, and canons, they remind us that no cultural form is fixed in the hierarchy: as Bourdieu argues, "the very meaning and value of a cultural object varies according to the system of objects in which it is placed."[21] It becomes less plausible to orchestrate cultural studies around those relational terms – high and low, mass and elite, popular and polite. Similarly, if the theories of hegemony and historical blocs offer ways of articulating cultural commodities and class formations, they also remind us that cultural forms have no necessary class allegiance; they can't be ranked as capitalist forms or proletarian forms.

One possible and commonly suggested solution is to avoid ranking cultural forms altogether, to see them either as somehow equal – ballet and break dancing, Shakespeare and soap opera – or as so unalike as to make comparisons unnecessary. In either case, as an aesthetic and historical precept, there is no disputing taste. This is unsatisfactory; the refusal of discrimination often becomes the tacit continuation of established discriminations. The difficulty that haunts the Jameson essay with which I began haunts all significant cultural studies: how does one map the relations between the polite forms of high culture, the products of a commercial or mass culture, and the marginal or oppositional forms that seem to demand some adjective like "authentic" or "organic?"

One attempt was Raymond Williams's oft-cited distinctions between dominant, residual, oppositional, and alternative cultures, terms which he himself noted were provisional. I would suggest that we develop some of the categories in his subsequent book, *Culture*, to think about cultural forms in a way which privileges the "popular" in a specific sense. In his chapter, "Means of Production," Williams discusses the development of cultural forms in terms of the "inherent resources" of the species (beginning his account not from literature or the novel, but from the social development of physical movement and voice in dance and song) and the degree of popular access to the form: "while anyone in the world, with normal physical resources, can watch dance or look at sculpture or listen to music, still some forty per cent of the world's present inhabitants can make no contact whatever with a piece of writing, and in earlier periods this percentage was much higher."[22] It is not surprising perhaps that the master art for Williams was the theater, the relatively simple development of the inherent resources of speech and movement for an audience that need have no special training in a notational system like writing. The great paradox of film and broadcasting has of course been that the genuine democratization of cultural audiences required such large capital investment and technical training as to have restricted greatly the production of films and broadcasts. Cultural studies should take up the challenge of Williams's cultural materialism by exploring the social investments required by different cultural forms at different times – the investments of time, training, and capital required for production and for consumption of cultural forms.

Thus any cultural studies worthy of the name should probably begin with those fundamental forms: song, dance, theater, and (the great absence in Williams's work) sport. Certainly any attention to working-class culture and aesthetics, which, as Bourdieu rightly argued, is a culture and aesthetic of necessity, would have to begin from these forms. And I would argue that such an exploration would radically challenge a number of our common assumptions about working-class culture and popular culture, taken as they are from an undifferentiated sense of the mass media and consumer society.

For example, much of Bourdieu's conception of the "popular aesthetic" depends on his assertion of "the hostility of the working class and of the middle-class fractions least rich in cultural capital towards every kind of formal experimentation."[23] However, his evidence is drawn from studies of cultural forms where people "least rich in cultural capital" have restricted access to the codes which make experiment and code breaking meaningful. If one looks to the forms where working people have elaborate bodies of knowledge, like popular sports, one finds an appreciation for experiment: think only of the way the formal innovations of such black artists as Rickey Henderson or Michael Jordan are elaborated on sandlots and playgrounds across the United States. The study of sports needs an entirely new perspective, which would break both from elaborations of the themes of

Critical Theory – "sport as a prison of measured time," in one formulation – and from the functionalist modernization framework that structures most mainstream sports sociology and history. One of the few examples of a hermeneutic of sport can be found in the writings of C.L.R. James on cricket, where he reads not sport or sports in general, but the ways of playing a sport – the moves – as symbolic actions. Sport remains a cultural form whose training, equipment and education is widely available, and whose preeminent artists are drawn predominantly from the working classes; and the enfranchisement of women as sports producers and consumers was arguably the most popular and significant *cultural* achievement of the American feminist movement.

Similarly, vernacular song has long been recognized as a sensitive barometer of working-class cultures, and it is not surprising that the finest discussions of contemporary working-class cultures in the United States and the United Kingdom have come from cultural critics writing on music: one thinks of Paul Gilroy's discussion of the musics of the black diaspora, or the essays of Dave Marsh, Nelson George, Hazel V. Carby, and George Lipsitz on the relations between postwar vernacular musics and the reshaping of the American working class. All these writers analyze not only the relations between popular audiences and industrial cultural production, but also the way cultural producers, in this case popular musicians, emerge from working-class communities, and serve as organic intellectuals in the formation of historical blocs.

If the study of popular culture is not to disintegrate into an antiquarian cataloging of fads and fashions or a postmodernist ransacking of retro styles, it must become part of a larger cultural studies. That cultural studies, I have argued, needs to be rooted in the exploration of the social construction of cultural value, the history of hegemonic formations, and the investigation of the material investments and constraints implied by various cultural forms. We have come to the end of mass culture; the debates and positions which named mass culture as an other have been superseded. There is no mass culture out there; it is the very element in which we all breath.

Afterword: The Ends of Ending Mass Culture

Since my title for this chapter, "The End of Mass Culture," seemed to confuse, and even to contradict, my argument, let me begin a reply to my critics by unraveling it.[24] An end is both a death and an outcome, and mass culture designates both the concept itself and the relatively new relations of cultural production it names. My argument, put simply, was that the outcome of these new relations of cultural production, the extraordinary success of the culture industries, has led to the decay – and imminent death – of the concept of mass culture that was used to name them. Since my essay could hardly hope to kill off the capitalist culture industries, my more modest goal was to kill off the concept that is no longer particularly useful for mapping and understanding them. Rather than continue to argue about mass culture, popular culture, and high culture, I suggested that we call them all "cultural commodities" – to reflect a leveling the culture industries have accomplished – and see what difference it makes for cultural studies, working-class history, and the politics of culture.

Luisa Passerini suggests that this will make no difference, that I confine the matter of mass culture to an academic debate among US and UK intellectuals.[25] To the absence of Continental thinkers, I plead guilty. My intent was to summarize US (and to a lesser extent UK) debates for an international gathering in Paris. And one of the striking features of the US debates has been the lack of reference to contemporary Continental work on mass culture. In part this is due to the continuing power of ideologies of American exceptionalism in US cultural studies. And, in part, it may reflect the rhythms of intellectual fashion: as the attractions of French post-structuralism waned in the United States, those of British cultural studies seem to have waxed. Intellectual work is itself a cultural commodity, and few of us are exempt from the forces of that market-place.

But Passerini's comment reminds us that the European debates have often fused mass culture and Americanization, deploring both for how they might treat European culture, misquoting Latin proverbs and reducing European thinkers to pale shadows. Though some European thinkers have welcomed mass culture for its apparent democracy and affront to established taste, much of the Continental intellectual tradition – from Adorno to Baudrillard (and including Passerini) – remains, as Adelheid von Saldern shows in her account of the German debates, hostile to mass-produced cultural commodities and their uses by working people.[26]

Thus, to my suggestion that a key cultural success of the US feminist movement was to enfranchise women as sports performers and audiences, Luisa Passerini retorts that this was promoted by Hitler and Mussolini. So what? Is this meant to suggest that the creation of a women's sports culture is politically meaningless or even fascist? This misses two points worth reiterating: first, cultural forms do not have a necessary political meaning, and may be appropriated and reappropriated by a variety of social movements seeking to lead a society; and second, cultural forms like sport have a central role in the cultural lives of working people, and thus should have a central place in a socialist cultural politics.

My essay was intended to be a map of intellectual arguments about mass culture, charting the relations between disparate bodies of work and situating that work as a reaction to the hegemony of Reaganism and to innovations in the culture industries. The call to dispense with mass culture as an organizing category will enable the kinds of cultural histories that William Taylor and Adelheid von Saldern sketch in their responses. The mass culture debates – the series of moral panics over cultural commodities – have rarely had a strong historical sense, either about the culture industries or the controversies surrounding them. In contrast, the new popular culture criticism and the recent discussions of working-class culture, including my own studies of US dime novels and British spy thrillers, have started by taking the history of popular entertainments and their audiences seriously. My polemic may demonstrate the "dangers of theory without history," but it was written to avoid the dangers of history without theory, to consider the situation, goals, and consequences of those critical and historical studies of popular entertainment.[27]

Janice Radway's illuminating response challenges the boundaries drawn in my essay, and the vision of cultural studies as a boundary-drawing, map-making enterprise. "How exactly are we to locate the boundaries between social groups?" she asks, and notes rightly that I "fall back on the older, materialist definition of class." The appeal to class as a central boundary has different consequences in different situations. I chose here to stress the relation of class and culture, in part because the conference and the journal found its common ground in the concern for working-class history. But more importantly, the criticism of mass/popular culture in the United States has underplayed the issue of class, and the history of class formations in the US has tended to speak little about culture. The most powerful parts of the new popular culture criticism (including Radway's *Reading the Romance*) have stressed boundaries of gender, particularly in film studies and in studies of popular fiction.[28]

That said, I would argue that one of the advantages of the vocabulary that British Gramscianism has created for English speakers has been its insistence that, in the analysis of specific historical blocs and specific struggles for hegemony, one should speak less of classes, ruling or ruled, than of dominant and subaltern formations. Dominant and subaltern formations are diverse, often temporary alliances among class fractions, gender fractions, and racial and ethnic fractions.

The questions Radway raises in discussing "how to identify, or better yet construct, social boundaries," how to grasp "the fluidity, flexibility, and frangibility of group formation" are vital ones, central to understanding the spectrum of the subaltern, or, to render Gramsci's military metaphor into more colloquial English, the underothers. But her questions do not fully address the key point of the third section of my essay, which is admittedly the shortest, least developed, and (on a number of occasions) the most controversial. Despite the difficulties Radway raises, the analytic categories of genders, classes, and peoples (the varieties of racial, ethnic, national, religious, and regional definitions which structure the political geography of the world-system) have given us powerful tools to analyze groups, communities, and social formations. However, the categories we have to analyze genres of cultural commodities – texts, artifacts, and performances – are much less powerful, more "recalcitrantly grounded in older sociologies and previous normative systems," to use Radway's words. Is it possible to discuss the relations of three distinct artists – say Toni Morrison, Tina Turner, and Florence Joyner – to US culture and to each other without either employing the invidious distinctions between the arts they practice or ignoring the differences between those arts?[29]

Raymond Williams's later work offered one historical and materialist way of thinking about the relations between cultural forms. To be frank, I share Radway's suspicion of Williams's appeal to human nature, to the "inherent resources" of the species (Williams's naturalism is argued more fully and powerfully in his essay on Timpanaro[30]). What I wish to emphasize in Williams's later work is the shift away from the problematic implicit in the title of his earlier theoretical summary, *Marxism and Literature*. Too often cultural studies – Marxist and non-Marxist – assume the centrality of cultural forms which require large and complex investments of time and training, notably literature. This is particularly true of one of the most influential contemporary versions of cultural studies in the US, the "new historicism." I am less interested in declaring which cultural forms are fundamental than in insisting that cultural studies must consider the social investments of time, training, and capital required by various cultural commodities.

Toward the end of her response, Radway poses a powerful and suggestive challenge to the development of cultural studies: "perhaps it is not only *mass* culture that has come to an end but 'the cultural' itself as a distinct, identifiable region separate from the rest of daily existence conceived as somehow more political and more real." This leads her to suggest the boundary-drawing, map-making model of cultural studies is fundamentally flawed, that "cultural studies should take as its governing metaphor not the map produced by the distant cartographer but the journey itself whereby concrete individuals wend their way from region to region, from experience to experience, trying not only to make sense of what they see and of their place within it but also trying to figure out what to do next." Here Radway raises key issues for cultural critics, but I am unpersuaded for three reasons.[31]

First, as long as culture depends on a social surplus, extracted through exploitative labor relations, the cultural as a distinct region will not disappear. As Terry Eagleton has put it, "men and women do not live by culture alone; the vast majority of them throughout history have been deprived of the chance of living by it at all, and those few who are fortunate enough to live by it now are able to do so because of the labour of those who do not. Any cultural or critical theory which does not begin from this single most important fact, and hold it steadily in mind in its activities, is . . . unlikely to be worth very much."[32] This is the lesson of Radway's own work on the reading of romance fiction; though the small surplus of time and money used to purchase and read romance novels was no less real than the work of daily life, it was seen as different, as a realm of imagination, desire, even freedom. Culture is not a given; one always begins with the question of the resources out of which a community builds a culture and the social relations involved in the appropriation and distribution of those resources.

This does imply a more limited definition of culture than is often used. Much of the debate at the conference on "Mass Culture and the Working Class" arose from conflicting definitions of culture. The frequently invoked dichotomy between workers' culture and mass culture appeared to oppose the adjectives: workers vs. mass. However, the opposition really lay in two different meanings of culture. Most of the invocations of workers' culture defined culture as a system of norms, values, and beliefs held by a particular group of people; most of the references to mass culture defined culture as a variety of texts, artifacts, and performances produced by artists or craftworkers and received by audiences. Neither of these definitions is wrong, nor is there much reason in holding out for one or the other. However, we must be aware of the distinction between the two meanings, and avoid any temptation to conflate them: cultural studies is both the study of systems of norms, values and beliefs, and the study of cultural texts, artifacts, and performances.

My own end in ending mass culture as a concept was to suggest first, that there is little evidence that the capitalist industrial production, reproduction, and mass distribution of cultural texts, artifacts, and performances has created a mass culture in the sense of a degraded, massified, and universal system of norms, values, and beliefs; and second, that mass culture is everywhere, in the sense that the cultural texts, artifacts, and performances – whether polite or popular, high or low – are almost entirely commodities. The question that we face in cultural studies – as teachers, critics, artists, and activists – is the relation between the great variety of cultural commodities and the norms, values, and beliefs of subaltern peoples. Why? Because norms, values, and beliefs are lived, communicated, and often shaped by the symbolic structures of cultural commodities, and because alliances between various underothers are often forged by shared cultural commodities, and, perhaps more frequently, through respect for cultural commodities that are not shared.

This is why I still choose maps over journeys, to cite Janice Radway's illuminating delineation of the possible "governing metaphors" for cultural studies. For me, cultural studies is not a collection of biographies or autobiographies: "the journey itself whereby concrete individuals wend their way from region to region."[33] Rather it is the drawing of maps by distant (unavoidable for those who study the past) and not so distant cartographers, maps which are always provisional, always abstractions. Anyone who uses maps knows they are not the same as the world, that the point of view of the cartographer is crucial, and that no single map tells us all we might want to know. Nonetheless, maps are ways of conceiving totalities, understanding the boundaries which join and separate, and imagining the terrains which are contested. The fact that our boundaries are not exact and our categories are always subject to revision should not lead us to give up the task.

7

THE ACADEMIC LEFT AND THE RISE OF CULTURAL STUDIES

When President George H.W. Bush entered the "political correctness" controversy with his 1991 University of Michigan commencement address, it marked the symbolic climax of the running battle over American universities. Having discovered "free speech under assault . . . on some college campuses," Bush warned that "political extremists roam the land, abusing the privilege of free speech, setting citizens against each other on the basis of their class or race." Throughout the Reagan years, conservative journalists and intellectuals had tried to bring the Reagan revolution to American higher education. Government and university administrators like William Bennett, Lynn Cheney, and John Silber, the neoconservative humanities intellectuals around the *New Criterion*, *Commentary*, and the National Association of Scholars (and their journal *Academic Questions*), and a host of right-wing journalists had regularly claimed that "tenured radicals" had taken over university teaching and scholarship in the humanities, launching an attack on the values of Western civilization. In the fall and winter of 1990–91, these charges became feature stories in the *New York Times* and *Newsweek*; and suddenly "political correctness," "multiculturalism," university speech codes, and the canon were hotly debated in newspapers and magazines across the country.[1]

Though the media storm subsided, and the ideological attack on the university gave way to a fiscal attack – and university budgets generated more controversy than university speech codes – the issues raised by the term "politically correct" and the existence of an academic left remain important. Not only does the right-wing offensive in American intellectual life continue, but the controversy over the cultural left in the university has divided liberal and left intellectuals. On the one hand, the cultural left, a broad, if contentious, alliance between left and liberal academics and administrators who have worked to reorganize higher education in the humanities under the banners of diversity, theory, affirmative action, the interdisciplinary, "reconstructing the canon," and cultural studies, began to respond to the conservative attacks in print, at professional conventions, and through the organization of Teachers for a Democratic Culture and the Union of Democratic Intellectuals. To these intellectuals, among whom I would number myself, there is a sense of embattlement; we feel we have been in an extended period of conservative attacks on any democratic and feminist conception of culture.

However, a number of liberal and left intellectuals have taken aim at this academic left, arguing that radicals in the academy – those whom David Bromwich has called "institutional radicals" – have betrayed the values, language, and calling of the critical intellectual. These writers lament the decline of a public culture in the United States and the complicity of the academic radicals in the professionalization of the humanities. For these writers – and they range from David Bromwich writing in *Dissent* to Barbara Epstein writing in *Socialist Review* – the controversy over political correctness is a symptom of serious political and intellectual shortcomings of the academic left. For them the academic left is made up of an unholy and unlikely marriage between identity politics and post-structuralist theory. Irving Howe called it "a strange mixture of American populist sentiment and French critical theorizing"; Barbara Epstein argued that "identity politics and the postmodern/poststructural sensibility do come together in the field of cultural studies, and, more broadly, in constituting the academic and intellectual arena that defines itself as radical". The result is a left which is only apparently radical. Howe called them "insurgents," refusing them the name left, and Epstein warned of "the danger . . . that a rising intellectual movement can appropriate the cachet of radicalism while remaining more interested in intellectual and cultural criticism than in social change." "If this is radicalism," wrote Louis Menand of "most *marxisant* critics," "it is about the most ineffectual radicalism imaginable."[2]

These charges are serious ones, but they are, I believe, mistaken. The moral panic over political correctness was indeed a symptom of the presence of a cultural left in the universities; but to understand the passions aroused on both the left and the right by "the most ineffectual radicalism imaginable," we need to understand the complexities and contradictions of those "institutional radicals" and the cultural studies they have forged.

Are You Now or Have You Ever Been Politically Correct?

Why politically correct? The decade-long storm over the humanities in the university had initially swirled around the threatened canon and obscurantist theory; meanwhile, in the arts communities, the vocabularies of obscenity, pornography, and even blasphemy structured the moral panics over rap and rock as well as the anxious attacks on the discourses of sexuality in the arts, and particularly on gay and lesbian expression. Political correctness arose (for all sides, I will suggest) as a principle of linkage, to use diplomatic jargon. The wide and often incompatible variety of academic radicalisms seemed to come together not under some party banner, but under a style of speech and behavior. Congressional committees will be hard pressed to ask this generation of academics, "Are you now or have you ever been a member of the Communist Party (or any other party)?" But perhaps "are you now or have you ever been politically correct?" will serve.

This is the heart of the right-wing critique: politically correct is the contemporary equivalent of the Stalinist party line, an emblem of the rigidity, intolerance, and humorlessness that the right has always projected onto leftists and feminists. When speaking to themselves rather than to the mass media, right-wing academics admit that the left does not control the university: "in the last analysis," Stephen Balch and Herbert London told the readers of *Commentary* in their article on "The Tenured Left," "it is less the academy's radical minority and more its liberal majority that is at the heart of the problem. . . . The future of higher education hinges on how the internal crisis in American liberalism is eventually resolved." In this battle over the "future of higher education," political correctness serves to bring together the threats to the canon and the theory explosion.[3]

For any who may have forgotten the Reagan years, let me recall that the slogan of the canon encompassed two different issues. On the one hand, within the professional disciplines, debates were joined over the place of teaching and scholarship which rejected the usual standards of appropriate subjects of study. Thus, in literature and the arts, one found a revaluation of women artists, black and ethnic artists, and the arts and cultures of non-Western societies, as well as of the popular or mass-produced arts. In historical scholarship, this meant a turn toward the various new social histories, studying peoples and aspects of daily life that had traditionally seemed outside history. On the other hand, the debate over the canon was also a debate over the forms of general education, a debate over whether a liberal arts education need have some core, some common ground, and a debate over what that common ground might be: the leading public controversies were over revisions to the various "great books" courses, which symbolized a common heritage.

The slogan of theory was even more diverse, including: a sympathy for the aesthetics and cultural styles associated with postmodernism; the varieties of antifoundational epistemologies associated with French post-structuralism and American neopragmatism; the various strains of symptomatic interpretation, most notably the symptomologies of psychoanalysis, the genealogies of the new historicism, and the ideologies of Marxism; and the somewhat arcane rhetorics and writing styles associated with these discourses.

One of the peculiarities of the controversy was the conflation of the "canonical criticism" (to use Paul Lauter's term) and theory. Far from inhabiting the same precincts, these two groups had eyed each other as much with suspicion and hostility as with respect and solidarity. It was precisely the incongruity of these different projects that made the satiric piece published in *Dissent*, "How Not to Write for *Dissent*," funny, uniting as it did the new studies of popular culture (which do not, for the most part, incorporate the discourses of theory) and the works of theory (which do not, for the most part, deal with *Gilligan's Island*). There are a few fools who have tried to bridge the two, myself included, but we'll come to them.[4]

The shift to a panic over political correctness was a sign that the right realized that they were losing the battles over the canon and theory: that is to say, that large numbers of non-left teachers and non-left students were persuaded of the intellectual value and pleasure involved both in revising the canons and in conducting vigorous theoretical controversies. As in the attack on New Deal liberals as "fellow travelers," "dupes" of the Communist "conspiracy," much of the right-wing argument suggested that seemingly innocuous tendencies like multiculturalism or the new historicism were part of, to use Kenneth Lynn's phrase, an "anti-American Studies." Much of the vehemence of the attack on political correctness was an unwillingness to concede the persuasiveness of certain leftist teaching and scholarship, and its success in the academic market-place.

Nevertheless, the right did not invent the phrase politically correct, and it bears examination. I have never been enamored of the phrase politically correct nor of the "p.c." and "p.i." shorthand, though I have long been interested in its genealogy.[5] For me, it always conjured up an image of a yardstick by which one might measure oneself. If anyone really were politically correct, we wouldn't be in the mess we're in. However, the media attention persuaded me that the undoubted currency of the phrase gave it a reality that needed consideration; if it was not part of my slang, that was probably because the fractions of the left through which I was socialized had different verbal tics. What does the phrase mean? How is it used? On the left, it is usually used with an ironic, self-mocking tone, to excuse personal tastes that are not part of the leftist, feminist, or gay subcultures, the inverse of a phrase like, "though I know it is very yuppie, preppie, I really like. . . ."

A more interesting, and more telling, usage does occur in university conversations: "I know this is not politically correct, but . . .," a phrase used by those – neither on the left nor right, perhaps unpolitical people – who worry about whether what they say is politically correct. This is a sign of two developments in the academy. On the one hand, the polarization of the university – whether over campus strikes, battles over curriculum, hiring and promotion, or in cases of disruption of university civility, like the *Dartmouth Review* case – makes a nonpolitical stand more difficult to maintain, and puts pressure on people to take sides. In this situation, the invocation of "I know this is not politically correct, but . . ." indicates not that the left has some grand power to punish the politically incorrect, but that leftist ideas have achieved enough persuasiveness to act as a bizarre kind of superego.

Clearly, the notion of the politically correct derives from the sense that there is a political meaning to personal style and behavior; thus an apparently nonpolitical action – the way a man relates to women in a group, the casual use of a racist or ethnic joke, and so on – can be interpreted politically. This is an idea with disparate roots: one source is surely the feminist notion of the personal being political; another, the Western Maoist notion of criticism-self-criticism which had some currency in the New Left. However, it is also deeply indebted to an intellectual ethic regarding the morality of style and taste that is associated with the New York Intellectuals, particularly Diana and Lionel Trilling. In this sense, political correctness is not at all a question of party line; here I think the right is quite mistaken. Rather it is more an issue of "correct" manners (and let us not forget that many of those who object are themselves usually great advocates of manners and decorum).[6] One finds a mirror image of this political correctness as critique of manners in the many diatribes against bad writing, which maintain that a certain style and ease of manner is required in order to be taken seriously.

One can see this better by exploring the curious double meaning of the term "self-consciousness": self-consciousness is a virtue when it means a genuinely reflective sense of one's own being, one's own situation in the world, and one's own impact on others; but this is dialectically related to self-consciousness in the other sense – awkwardness, embarrassment, the all-too-awful consciousness of one's own body and clothes and style in situations where one is out of place. But it is worth recalling that any genuine self-consciousness, the coming to consciousness, the "consciousness-raising" that marked the emergence of feminism, and indeed marks the emergence of any social movement of subaltern peoples, is in part the product of the realization that the negative form of self-consciousness, the embarrassment and awkwardness, the sense that one does not belong, has a political meaning.

Now this consciousness of the politics, even morality, of style is easily abused – as much in Leslie Fiedler's famous literary critique of the Rosenbergs' letters, or in Diana Trilling's attack on the bad taste of the Scarsdale diet doctor, as in the "policing" of political correctness in speech and behavior. Moreover, there are times for rudeness and giving offense, even in the university. But I find it difficult to think that civil discourse and respectful conversation are threatened because Robert Caserio finds he has to choose his words carefully in order not to offend his feminist colleagues or David Riesman has to go to great lengths to avoid the tag racist (both of them apparently made these statements to *Newsweek*[7]).

But the notion of the politically correct has a larger significance; it is, in a way, the principle of linkage that those on the right so fear. However, this is not because politically correct means that one holds certain views on capitalism, patriarchy, racism, imperialism, the decline of the West, and so on and so forth. Rather the notion of the politically correct is a consequence of the fact that the left has lost or given up its sense of a party line, a sense that an authoritative party or movement is in the vanguard. With the devolution, for better or worse, of the left into distinct social movements, political correctness becomes one mode of mediation between them.

Take an example from Faith Middleton, the host of public radio's "Open Air New England," a contemporary incarnation of the New England feminism of Catharine Beecher and Harriet Beecher Stowe. Her interview with activists for the rights of disabled people began with a discussion of which terms are, as she said somewhat ironically, "politically correct." While this discussion was only a short part of the interview, it raised the question of naming: the physically challenged, disabled people, people with disabilities, the handicapped, even a brief discussion of the use of the term "cripples" among the disabled. While recognizing that argument over the politically correct term should not replace the discussion of the rights and wrongs suffered by the disabled, she nonetheless sensed that the relations between different groups on the left required a certain decorum in language, that the struggle over names is not meaningless.

If this decorum is at times taken to absurd lengths – as when, for example, it implies that only insiders (of whatever sort) have the right to speak or criticize – it more often serves to enable genuine discussion, dialogue and criticism. Those who rightfully note that solidarity should never preclude criticism might recall the damage that criticism without solidarity can wreak. Anyone who has delved into the journals of the left, whether of Communists, Trotskyists, New Leftists, or feminists, knows that criticism is often a euphemism for name-calling and denunciation in which the notion of political correctness and incorrectness can easily degenerate. This is the "left moralism" that Barbara Epstein and Barbara Ehrenreich have both criticized. The rational kernel of political correctness, however, is what Richard Flacks calls an "ethic of collective responsibility." Flacks, in his brilliant meditation on the place of the left in the US, entitled *Making History*, suggested that one of the key contributions of the left has been articulating and fostering "an ethic of collective responsibility, a set of principles and rules for individual action that are morally binding on members, and that are capable of becoming obligatory for ever-widening circles of non-members as well." These range from norms against scabbing or crossing picket lines to rules about daily speech and interpersonal interaction between men and women, whites and blacks. He argues persuasively that this ethic is one of the major contributions of leftist movements to American culture.[8] If this be a defense of "politically correctness," so be it; but this is a minor skirmish. I am more interested in the larger question of the left in the academy: what our situation is, what our prospects are, and whether our agenda makes sense.

The Public and the Profession: The Tale of the "Tenured Radicals"

Has the turn to the left in the academy in fact occurred? Is the left now predominantly located in the universities? Should leftist intellectuals be in universities? Or have the successes of the left in the academy been Pyrrhic victories, as leftist ideals of general education and a public culture of dissent are displaced by a narrow professionalism and a cultivation of radical style? These are the significant questions raised by the political correctness controversy.

Has this turn to the left occurred in the university? I will be brief on this first question, but it seems to me one we need explore further. Much depends on the accuracy of our assessment of the current situation. In his critique of the "hard left" in the academy and its "oppositional style of criticism," Henry Louis Gates took for granted what he called "the celebrated turn to politics in literary studies in the past decade."[9] But has it happened? Has the left taken over?

In most ways, the answer is clearly no. In their *Commentary* essay, Balch and London (two leading figures in the National Association of Scholars) drew on a survey of faculty members conducted by the Carnegie Foundation for the Advancement of Teaching: given five labels to describe their political stance – left, liberal, middle of the road, moderately conservative, and strongly conservative – only 5.8 percent chose left. Proportions of left faculty were higher in sociology and political science (and in English, where 10.2 percent chose left), but overall the left was a relatively small minority. Even what Balch and London called "the liberal majority" was an illusion; only 33.8 of faculty called themselves liberal, so the combined forces of left and liberal professors were just under 40 percent of the profession. (A more recent Carnegie poll eliminated the categories left and strongly conservative for a more "balanced" if less informative spectrum: liberal, moderately liberal, middle of the road, moderately conservative, and conservative. To some, this poll might indicate a liberal majority – 57 percent are either liberal or moderately liberal; others might read this as a sign of overwhelming moderation – 69 percent are moderately liberal, middle of the road, or moderately conservative.) Moreover, these figures have been relatively constant since the late 1960s.[10]

Nevertheless, it is worth noting that since World War II, which is to say since the creation of the modern university system, faculty members have been somewhat more liberal, more likely to support Democratic candidates, than the general population. This, however, is apparently less a product of the university or of specific disciplines than a product of family background. Professors are more liberal than the general population not because they are professors but because they are more likely to come from liberal families.[11]

In another way, however, Gates's notion of a turn to politics in literary studies (and the humanities generally) rings true. Why? What is a turn to politics? What does politics mean in this context? In part, it means a turn to history. Various formalisms in the humanities, including deconstruction, are in disarray, and there are a number of new historicisms. Perhaps Roland Barthes's oft-cited maxim was true: "a little formalism turns one away from History, but . . . a lot brings one back to it."

In part, it means a turn to women. The one significant demographic change in faculty ranks in recent years has been the growing number of women in universities, particularly in the humanities. There is no question that this has changed daily life in the university, and has provided the rank and file for a variety of feminist studies.

And in part, it means a turn away from liberalism. Liberalism had a hard time in the Reagan years; it became the dreaded "L-word" both because of the attacks from the conservative right and because of a genuine loss of self-confidence. If the left has not taken over the university, it has begun to set the agenda for the liberal wing of the university. The call for reconstructing the canon moved from *Radical Teacher* and the Feminist Press to the mainstream of many departments. Theory moved from the Marxist literary groups and Lacanian theory circles that Harold Bloom satirized as "those academic covens akin to what Emerson . . . called 'philanthropic meetings and holy hurrahs'" to shift the intellectual frameworks of the humanities.[12]

For the right, this has corrupted the universities; for some on the left, it has corrupted the left. A number of critics – notably Russell Jacoby in his *The Last Intellectuals* – have argued that left intellectuals have abandoned the public for the profession. David Bromwich's essay, "The Future of Tradition," in *Dissent* epitomizes this critique. Its first half is a lament for the loss of a public culture – "what [professionalization] has most destroyed in America is our common sense of a public life"; the second half is an attack on the "institutional radicals" for their complicity in that destruction. The institutional radicals are, paradoxically, too political and not political enough. "The activist tone in scholarship," he wrote, "has been found compatible with a restriction of politics to the universities themselves. Indeed the standard defense of institutional radicalism in the humanities . . . is that scholars can have their deepest influence on public discourse simply by doing what they do anyway. . . . The adepts of institutional politics seldom encounter members of the general public which they have written off."[13]

It is not clear exactly what kinds of encounters with members of the general public Bromwich has in mind. I take it that he is not referring simply to circles of acquaintances nor to intimate encounters – like that between the businessman and the English professor in David Lodge's comic novel, *Nice Work*. Let us assume that he means face-to-face encounters with the general public in political activity, and encounters with the general public through the mediation of the written word (those members of the general public encountered during the work day, that is, students, don't seem to qualify for Bromwich, but I will return to them).

First, despite Bromwich's insinuations, there is little evidence to suggest that institutional radicals avoid face-to-face encounters with their fellow citizens; the scanty evidence available suggests that, because of their class and the relative freedom of their working conditions, professors in general are much more likely to be active as political citizens – in political campaigns and parties – than the general public. Moreover, as the most extensive study concludes, "it is the most liberal faculty who are the most active."[14] This picture of faculty citizen activism – so at odds with the image of the ivory tower – makes the opposition between the public and the profession far more complicated than it often appears. Bromwich is entirely mistaken to suggest that for the left in the academy, "what one does at a university will suffice as a complete account of what one does in society."

Let me suggest a picture slightly different from that of public and profession, of unattached intellectual and academic intellectual. In an underrated 1965 study of intellectuals, Lewis Coser noted that "one of the most important observations that can be made about unattached intellectuals in contemporary America is that there are so few of them." He suggests that the reasons for their decline are the rise of the postwar academy and the demise of avant-garde culture and radical ideology. If one follows his account, however, one finds that the "unattachment" of earlier intellectuals was largely an ideological identity, not a description of their means of livelihood. Like all other intellectuals, unattached ones had to eat, and most earned a living through some kind of intellectual occupation. They were not so much unattached intellectuals as market intellectuals; like Emerson, they abandoned the various forms of ministry and supported themselves by publishing for the market, lecturing to the market, and having a small legacy to smooth over the downturns in the market. By the early twentieth century, such market intellectuals were, by Coser's illuminating summary, doing putting-out work for publishers of books and magazines: writing reviews, assessing and editing manuscripts, serving on selection boards of book clubs. After the decline of the lyceums, the most successful market intellectuals were generally fiction writers, since fiction was the form of writing that sold the best.[15]

The decline of the market intellectual, the freelance intellectual entrepreneur, was the result of the vast expansion of the culture industries and the state cultural apparatuses, a complex which includes the postwar university. Thus the public sphere is not really the other side to the professions. Rather, one might more adequately imagine three spheres in elaborate orbits, each with their own professionals, part-timers, clerical proletariat, and public. These spheres include: first, the culture industries of film, broadcasting, recording, publishing, education, and journalism – those industries which serve to regulate and facilitate communication, as the financial industries regulate and facilitate the circulation of capital; second, the state cultural apparatuses, including a wide range of local, regional, and national agencies, libraries, museums, and schools; and third, the voluntary associations including unions, political associations, churches and religious congregations, foundations, high culture proper (privately supported orchestras, opera companies, universities and historical societies), the world of small alternative businesses (such as independent bookstores) and what remains of folk culture, groups of hobbyists and enthusiasts.

It is probably fair to say that most intellectuals work in these worlds; moreover, most people find them the sources of culture, intellectual life, and entertainment. Leftists can be found in almost all of these semi-public spheres, encountering a variety of "general publics." Though the university is sometimes painted as a left-wing island in a right-wing sea, much of contemporary left culture can be found among the voluntary associations, and many leftists work in the state cultural apparatuses. Indeed, I have always suspected that more than 5.8 percent of librarians would call themselves "left"; perhaps leftists are *under*-represented in the academy!

So, without saying that all politics should be restricted to the university or that the university is a microcosm of society (two beliefs that Bromwich attributes to "institutional radicals"), I will insist that the higher education industry is a crucial public sphere, a key part of American mass culture. Indeed, if, as he himself says, "it is an unhappy fact that most of the conversation about culture in America now is carried on in universities" (though I doubt it), it would be odd if leftists interested in culture avoided the universities.

Bromwich's nostalgia for unattached intellectuals and a lost general public embodies both the metropolitanism and the Leninism inherent in the traditions of the New York Intellectuals. On the one hand, the metropolitanism of the repeated call for a public culture barely conceals the dream that New York might yet be central to US culture. Russell Jacoby is most self-conscious on this issue, and his critique of the culture of provincial university towns is powerful. Nevertheless, the culture industries of image reproduction and distribution have rendered the metropolis culturally obsolete, and the seeds of any new left culture must lie within the forms and institutions of these de-centered and professionalized cultural industries.

On the other hand, a spilt Leninism lurks beneath the critique of the strategy of the institutional radicals. The notion of the intellectual as professional revolutionary, drawn from the vanguardist tradition where intellectuals are involved in real politics as party cadre, remains the main alternative to the New Left and democratic socialist notion of a long march through the institutions. And the memory of such an intellectual, a party intellectual creating a separate oppositional public sphere, haunts much of the critique of contemporary left academics. Even those who have rejected Leninist politics use it as the image of the "real" left intellectual (one sees it powerfully in Irving Howe's invocation of Trotsky and Lukács). For contemporary left academics, conversely, one of the attractions of Antonio Gramsci's work is precisely its break with and refashioning of the Leninist tradition.

If one wants to develop a body of socialist intellectuals, a culture of dissent, if one rejects a vanguard party of professional cadres as their locus, and if such intellectuals continue to be drawn predominately (though not exclusively) from the classes without capital, then of necessity they will be schizophrenic – half socialist intellectual and half professional intellectual of the legal, governmental, union, journalistic, or university type. No doubt strange mutants will appear, but neither Stanley Fish's celebrations of professionalism nor David Bromwich's laments for an imaginary public sphere offer much of a direction for those of us here.

The contradiction at the heart of this situation is not that of the intellectual – attached or unattached – and the general public, but the relation between this cultural fraction of the so-called "new class," and the other classes in American society. This professional and managerial class has always intrigued the Socialist (as opposed to the Communist) tradition in the United States, from Charles Steinmetz, William English Walling, and Lewis Corey, to Michael Harrington and Barbara Ehrenreich. As Ehrenreich has shown in her *Fear of Falling*, the specter of the new class is also close to the hearts of the neoconservatives. This is why it matters so little to Roger Kimball that his "tenured radicals" are not, for the most part, left-wing radicals; they are figures for the new class which is objectively anticapitalist, antitraditional, pro-left, a group of "elite liberals." This is the mirror image of left critiques of this same class as servants of power, ideological watchdogs, reproducing social relations through the media and the educational system, the infamous "ideological state apparatuses."

Both of these attacks are true, and that is one reason why the ideological debates about and within the professional-managerial class range from the sublime to the ridiculous. On the one hand, the very power of this class to shape the culture, combined with its historical ambivalence toward both capital and labor, makes the stakes very great indeed. It is worth recalling that the recent attack on the left in the universities is not unprecedented: the history of higher learning in the United States includes the 1890s purge of Populist social scientists, the attack on Socialist and antiwar professors during World War I, and the depression scare over Communists on campus, which grew into the postwar "McCarthyist" purge of the universities.[16] The anticommunist purge of the schools, and the blacklists in the film and broadcasting industries, did much to break a popular front between the intellectuals radicalized by the depression and the newly-organized workers of the CIO; similarly, the concerted effort by New Right corporations and foundations to build and fund a neoconservative culture was an important part of the Reagan revolution.

On the other hand, it is clear that many of the battles over theory, the canon, and the curriculum are merely skirmishes over the forms and ownership of cultural capital, a war of intraclass position. We are condemned to engage in arguments and struggles that combine elements of both – the genuine politics of culture in the United States and the pseudopolitics of distinction and careerism. Since individuals must make lives as well as history, to use Flacks's terms, we cannot avoid these entanglements.

In many ways, the cultural right has a better sense of what is at stake than the liberal and left critics of the "institutional radicals." Underneath the right's uproar over multiculturalism and Western civilization, one finds a persistent and insistent argument against affirmative action, an argument about who should have access to the resources and cultural capital controlled by the university. While Louis Menand laments "the most ineffectual radicalism imaginable," the National Association of Scholars accurately notes that the institutional radicals who have struggled over curriculum and theory are also the institutional radicals that have organized over university divestment from South Africa, over support for unions of university clerical and technical workers, and over affirmative action hirings and admissions.

The Emergence of Cultural Studies

But what of writing and teaching; surely one may accept the lineaments of this argument that higher education is a crucial public sphere, a "contested terrain" in the lingo of we academic radicals, and still insist that the academic left is marching through the institutions in the wrong direction.

In particular, the left academy, in its pursuit of cultural studies, has, according to its critics, given up clear writing, general education, even a commitment to social change. Barbara Epstein, who shares little of the *Dissent* nostalgia for the public intellectual, nevertheless criticized the "contempt for clear writing" she finds on the postmodern left, and sees the "shift from social analysis to cultural studies and the affiliation between radicalism and post-structuralism/postmodernism" as the unfortunate effect of the "defeat of the US left in the midseventies." "These [intellectual] currents," she argued, "were increasingly divorced from the aim of building a movement for social change."[17] Is cultural studies, which has emerged as the slogan of the academic left's intellectual project, a product of defeat, a fashionable substitute for a genuine left intellectual agenda? I think not, but Epstein's critique requires some account of what is meant by cultural studies.

There is no doubt that cultural studies has emerged over the last decade as a common slogan in the humanities. For the cynical, a look at a catalog of the University of California Press entitled Cultural Studies suggests that it is primarily an intellectual marketing strategy. Among the catalog's headings one finds not only the targets of the cultural right: new ethnography, gender studies, "the new historicism: studies in cultural poetics," theory, ethnic studies, urbanism, film, theatre and media, and popular culture, but the old humanities as well: the arts, literature, history, and classical studies. One is tempted to give up any attempt at definition.

But there is more coherence than might at first appear. After all, Roger Kimball claims that cultural studies is "the latest and most important academic effort to resuscitate Marxist analysis and liberate the humanities from an 'elitist' concern with high culture."[18] This is not inaccurate, but it does not capture the complexity of the moment. I will suggest that cultural studies, adopted from the British New Left, encompasses several trends in US culture: the emergence of the postmodern magazine; the reappearance of a left social-democratic conception of culture and cultural democracy; and an insurgent movement within the universities to reconceptualize the professional disciplines and the humanities themselves.

Cultural studies in the United States is an immigrant, a travelling theory, adopting its name from British cultural studies, which was itself something between an academic discipline and an intellectual movement of the New Left. There are now several accounts of and introductions to this tendency associated with the Birmingham Centre for Contemporary Cultural Studies, the social history pioneered by the historians around the journal *Past and Present* and the Communist Party Historians' Group, and the writings of Raymond Williams.[19] It was always an intervention in several publics, beginning in adult education, and moving into universities, polytechnics, the Open University, the magazines and journals of the Labour left, and the British Film Institute. For many of the institutional radicals, the figure of Raymond Williams – at once novelist, cultural journalist reviewing television, theatre and film, Marxist theorist, literary historian, political pamphleteer, and teacher in adult education and at Cambridge – is a more persuasive image of the socialist intellectual than the Edmund Wilsons and Lionel Trillings held out by the devotees of public discourse.

At times, the emergence of cultural studies in the United States looks like a second British invasion; just as American vernacular musics came back slightly estranged by the musicians of Liverpool, so American mass culture is made strange and wondrous by the critics of Birmingham. This is not to be scoffed at; from Tocqueville's America to Baudrillard's, it is arguable that the outsider's eye is a revealing one. Nevertheless, while acknowledging this heritage, I am reluctant to follow those who already see declension: what was critical and radical in Britain is flaccid and affirmative in America. For better or worse, cultural studies in the United States will be what we make of it.

Perhaps the most important aspect of US cultural studies may be seen in the emergence of a group of postmodern magazines and the imagined community of writers and readers surrounding them: *Social Text*, *October*, *Cultural Correspondence*, *Inscriptions*, *Discourse*, *Genders*, *differences*, *Representations*, *Telos*, *Semiotexte*, *South Atlantic Quarterly*, *Camera Obscura*, *Cultural Critique*, *Border/Lines*, *Cultural Studies*, *boundary 2*, *Tabloid*, *Polygraph*, *Public Culture*, *Third Text*, *Transition* and a number of others.

It is all too common to damn these magazines as full of jargon and bad writing, high theory and low culture; these are after all the precise examples of how the left in the academy has given in to professional standards and turned its back on the general reader. This is where they publish stuff written the way you shouldn't write for *Dissent*. This is very misleading. It is true that one does not look to this set of journals for literary and cultural journalism, the busywork of the fabled unattached intellectuals. Now I have nothing against such journalism, and there may well be declining outlets for it (though the success of the *Voice Literary Supplement* and the *Women's Review of Books* paralleled the rise in theory and cultural studies). But the demand that all left intellectuals be literary journalists, writing plain English for plain people, is no less objectionable than the old left demand that playwrights write agitprop and novelists stick to a comprehensible social realism.

At the same time as Bromwich and others lament the loss of the "little magazines," those "serious" journals neither academic nor popular, they miss the fact that these cultural studies or postmodern magazines are remarkably similar to *Partisan Review*, *Modern Quarterly*, *Politics* and the other legendary magazines that supported an oppositional public discourse for an earlier generation. Consider some similarities and differences. Like the earlier little magazines, these are not scholarly, professional journals. One would not mistake *October* for *PMLA* or the *American Historical Review*. They make no pretense to being refereed, objective forums for scholarship; they are magazines of a tendency, building a readership and a stable of writers. Like the little magazines, they tend to have small circulations, but are read seriously and thoroughly. Like the little magazines, they are seen from the outside as esoteric, specialized, and iconoclastic. Like the little magazines, some have institutional affiliations, a small grant, an office and so on. Like the little magazines, some are more concerned with politics and some with the arts; they shade off into overtly political journals like *Socialist Review* at one end and into basically academic journals like *Critical Inquiry* at the other.

There are differences; the one most remarked on is that the proportion of nonacademic contributors has decreased. An early study found that while only 9 percent of the contributors to the little magazines in the 1920s were teachers, 40 percent were teachers by the 1950s; the percentage in 1990s is no doubt much larger.[20] But this demonstrable shift from those working for advertisers, magazines, and publishing houses, to those working for universities masks a deeper continuity. Throughout the century, contributors thought of these magazines as a relatively free space, less subject to the popular market or the scholarly profession than one's occupation, whether that was writing for *Time* magazine or writing letters of recommendation.

Other differences are more striking; they make it possible for many people to overlook the similarities entirely. There is markedly less fiction and poetry in the postmodernist magazines than there was in the modernist little magazine. There is a much clearer separation between the fiction and poetry magazine world and the postmodern magazine which is almost all nonfictional prose. On the other hand, there is far more attention to popular culture, to photography, to the performance arts, and to popular musics than one ever found in the modernist little magazine.

I don't mean to flesh out a complete comparison between the modernist little magazine and the postmodern journal; I simply suggest that the contemporary journals do constitute an oppositional public sphere not unlike those remembered so fondly. If their prose style and layout are not those of *Dissent*, neither are they emblems of academic pedantry and professionalism; rather they embody the radical politics and avant-garde aesthetics one hopes for from any cultural left. One of the paradoxes of Russell Jacoby's own jeremiad – that his public voice should emerge out of one of the most esoteric and forbidding of these journals, *Telos* – is no paradox at all; public intellectuals are nurtured not in the mass media but in the little magazines. Barbara Ehrenreich's widely read *For Her Own Good* had its roots in her Feminist Press pamphlets; her *Fear of Falling* elaborates the essays on the professional-managerial class from *Radical America*.

If cultural studies is in one sense the space created by the postmodern magazine, it also marks the reappearance of the cultural politics of left social democracy, the cultural politics of the Popular Front. It is this legacy that marks the distance between contemporary cultural studies and the cultural politics of both the New York Intellectuals – living on in the work of Howe, Bromwich, Jacoby, and Berman (their ideal of cultural criticism has significantly different connotations than cultural studies) – and the radical counterculture of the 1960s. The roots of US cultural studies lie in the pioneering work in the 1930s and 1940s of such figures as Kenneth Burke, Constance Rourke, F.O. Matthiessen, Oliver Cromwell Cox, and

Carey McWilliams: though never a group of any sort (though they deeply influenced the development of postwar American studies), they shared a socialist or left social-democratic politics, an interest in the popular arts, a desire to rethink notions of race and ethnicity, nation and people, and a concern for cultural theory. The remarkable revival of interest in the work of Kenneth Burke may be taken as an emblem of this rediscovered genealogy.[21]

Two elements of this inheritance are particularly interesting. First, it sheds light on the most common critique of the new cultural studies: its apparently obsessive reduction of the world to race, class, and gender. Paul Berman argued that the "mélange" born of "68 philosophy" (his name for the French post-structuralisms) and American identity politics ought to be called "race/class/gender-ism." In his admitted caricature, "culture and language are themselves only reflections of various social groups, which are defined by race, gender, and sexual orientation. . . . Groups, not individuals, produce culture. Every group has its own culture, or would, if oppressors didn't get in the way." The problem with this critique of cultural studies is that it takes the starting point of cultural studies as its conclusion. Race, class, and gender are not the *answers* in cultural studies, the bottom-line explanation to which all life may be reduced; they are precisely the *problems* posed – their history, their formation, their "articulation" with particular historical events or artistic works. These are the issues to be explained and understood.[22]

The centrality of these concepts is not surprising, for the conceptual revolution embodied in cultural studies was precisely the shift from a notion of culture as individual cultivation toward a notion of culture as the set of traits, values, behaviors, and beliefs shared by groups: as Immanuel Wallerstein writes in an insightful critique of culturalist theories, "when we talk of traits which are neither universal nor idiosyncratic we often use the term 'culture'. . . . Culture is a way of summarizing the ways in which groups distinguish themselves from other groups."[23] The undoubted presence of race, class, and gender in cultural studies thus has three purposes: first, it stands as a critique of the dominant way of categorizing cultures, which remains national – American culture, English literature and so on; indeed the debate over the canon is not a debate about literature but one about national identity and national education. Second, it marks cultural studies' fundamental break with the humanities, with the assumption that the arts and letters are primarily reflections on the human, on those traits which are transhistorical and universal.

Third, the concepts of race, class, and gender are all attempts to solve the theoretical issues posed by the concept of culture itself. Here it is worth noting that part of the reason for the incantation of race-gender-class is that they are, in a deep sense, synonyms; Donna Haraway's wonderful exploration of the meaning of gender notes the etymological interferences between the words for kind, kin, stock, race, gender, and class.[24] Cultural studies is thus fundamentally about theorizing peoples. Moreover, since the historical formations of race, class, and gender are in many ways symbolic constructs, imagined communities and imagined boundaries, cultural analysis becomes central to understanding them. This is why we cannot simply return to "social analysis and political economy" as Epstein half-suggested.

Like any new conceptual framework, cultural studies presents its own conundrums and antinomies, perhaps none as crucial as that posed by Edward Said: "can one divide human reality, as indeed human reality seems to be genuinely divided, into clearly different cultures, histories, traditions, societies, even races, and survive the consequences humanly?"[25] Against the idealism of the older humanism, cultural studies will insist on the genuine divisions in human culture; indeed to speak of a "human" culture is to speak of something yet unseen and unimagined.

This understanding of culture does stand at a certain distance from any avant-garde conception with its cult of the individual artist (and here we may note the continuing tension between cultural studies as an intellectual project and those post-structuralisms which are indeed idiosyncratic and individual practices of experimental writing) and from the iconoclasm of the counterculture (an iconoclasm that persists in the arts community proper). Thus it is accurate to see cultural studies as embodying certain of the bureaucratic tendencies of social democracy. It does believe in an institutional radicalism which would transform from within the pedagogies and practices of the mass university.[26]

For this reason, cultural studies has become a new academic space, the name, as Roger Kimball rightly noted, for the academic left's intellectual agenda, the slogan of an alliance on the cultural left between the forces of theory and the forces of "radical teaching."[27] But this is more than a tactical political alliance; it grows out of the fact that the characteristic form of left academic work has been the critique of the liberal disciplines – one sees this in the emergence in the 1970s of radical caucuses in the disciplines of literature, history, sociology, and political science, among others. This characteristic form of academic radicalism – often piggybacked on the national conventions of the professional associations like the MLA, AHA, and ASA – was a sort of craft unionism. Cultural studies itself emerged out of this critique of the disciplines and, since there is little sign that the disciplinary structure will cease to organize teaching, scholarship, evaluation, and credentialing in the mass university, it remains an important project.[28]

Nevertheless, this engagement with the disciplines leaves the academic left vulnerable to those who rightly criticize the liberal disciplines, calling for general education. John Searle noted that "it is characteristic of American education that each stage is primarily designed to prepare the student for the next stage, so the best high schools prepare the student for college, and the best colleges prepare the student for graduate school. Since the professors think they know what they are doing in graduate education, it is not surprising that they also feel confident at designing undergraduate majors. . . . In general education the failure of nerve derives from the fact that we do not know what we are preparing the student for." For the left, we see too clearly what we are preparing students for. It is a truism to note that any radical pedagogy runs up against the visible ties between the university and the labor market and the fact that – as Evan Watkins argued in his excellent *Work Time* – neither teaching nor research, but *evaluation*, is the crucial labor process of the university.[29]

Nonetheless, recent decades have given new life to "general education" schemes; the liberally disciplined university is under a powerful and often populist attack. We on the academic left are now seen as the fellow travelers of the professional disciplines, the loyal opposition, replicating its professional structures and jargons (and thus provoking the ritual journalistic satire of the professional conventions). Thus it is necessary that we begin to imagine cultural studies not simply as the critique of the disciplines but as an alternative to the humanities themselves, a reformation of general education, for our encounter with the general public is usually our encounter with our students. They do try to see their education whole, and are often bored or amused by debates over disciplinary turf. We cannot cede the notion of a general education to those for whom it means a common curriculum of classics, an ahistorical conversation among great minds, transcending time and culture, and finally speaking of little of any importance.

We might begin such a new imagination of general education by turning to the history of general education itself; to date, our studies of mass culture have not paid sufficient attention to the history of the university as part of that mass culture. If the great books are a tradition, they are surely an invented one. From the start, general education (the great books in translation) combined middlebrow marketing with a conservative response to an immigrant and ethnic student body. The general education movement has been a key part of middlebrow culture, using the mass media and culture industries to distribute a packaged translation of the classical curriculum. The various core curriculum experiments of modern universities are the flip side of publishing ventures like the Five-Foot Shelf of Harvard Classics, the Chicago Great Books enterprise, and the Penguin Classics of the 1940s. All represented attempts by a genteel culture to maintain itself in the face of an ethnic working class and an exploding commercial culture.

At Columbia University, where I taught the fabled great books course and was driven to explore its history, one could see these pressures starkly. In 1916, Latin was dropped as an entrance requirement; by 1919, a core curriculum of classics in translation was established. Both of these changes were related to the changing student body; as a Columbia dean put it relatively frankly, "One of the commonest references that one hears with regard to Columbia is that its position at the gateway of European immigration makes it socially uninviting to students who come from homes of refinement. The form which the inquiry takes in these days of slowly dying race prejudice is, 'Isn't Columbia overrun with European Jews who are most unpleasant persons socially?'" The dean defended the admission of Jews, noting that "The Jews who have had the advantages of decent social surroundings for a generation or two are entirely satisfactory companions."[30] The great books course was instituted to bring in those imagined to be outside the common culture. This remains a central purpose of these courses, particularly in the face of the Asian and Latino immigration of the past three decades.

As many of us who have written on mass culture have argued, mass culture may well find critical readers; it is not all manipulation and deception. And there is no question that the piece of mass culture called general education exposed a generation of plebeian and working-class students to intellectual life. The stories of the conversions to the great books at Columbia, the University of Chicago, and elsewhere are no doubt true; and they lead to the passionate defenses of general education schemes and to the horror of the unconverted and the apostates. I myself am an apostate, having grown up with the Adler-Hutchins Great Books (my attempts to read them – with their lousy translations, monumental bulk and eyestraining double-column design – all failed after numerous starts through high school; I recall the silent battle with myself over whether I dared underline or write in such sacred books).

There was, indeed, a persistent debate among the advocates of general education between the Chicago and Columbia models, one which continues today. The Chicago model always imagined a philosophical and historical justification for such a course – the mythology of Western civilization was a crucial element, and this tradition continued in the work of Allan Bloom. The Columbia model chose a rhetorical modesty. One of the founders of Columbia's great books course, John Erskine, claimed that he had "no philosophy and no method for a total education; I hoped merely to teach how to read." One hears this echoed in the plain common sense of Irving Howe in *The New Republic* and David Bromwich in *Dissent*.

What is particularly interesting about this history is that general education was already a modernist revision of the canon. One of the fascinating aspects of Irving Howe's contradictory comments about the canon and general education is that he admits that he and his fellow students greatly resisted – indeed refused to deal with – the heritage of the West as it was then understood. He has written eloquently of his lack of any connection with Emerson and Thoreau – the Anglo-American canon. His connections were with those parts of the Western canon which had direct connections to his own ethnic culture – Shakespeare, as much a part of Yiddish culture as of Anglo-US culture, and the great novelists of the East – the Russians Tolstoy and Dostoyevsky, the Pole Conrad, and the Czech Kafka. What now seems so much a part of the tradition that the advocates of general education wish to pass on was as far from and as close to Western civilization as the Du Bois and Fanon that are now fought over. Howe denied this; he and his friends, he argued, saw Kafka and Joyce as "international" writers, not "ethnic" writers, to be set against American "parochialism."[31] But the same dialectic of ethnic culture and internationalist and cosmopolitan vision lies at the heart of contemporary critiques of the canon.

There is no doubt a need for general education, for a training that is not narrowly pre-professional and technical; but the energy for this new general education is not coming from the nostalgia for the past schemes. Rather it is emerging from the cultural left; even John Searle admitted that the course resulting from the Stanford civil war was a more powerful version of a liberal education than what preceded it. I am not suggesting a new core curriculum; I am suggesting that we resist thinking of cultural studies as another field, another program, and consider it as the place to think through an alternative to the humanities. It should be a global mapping of cultures, a way to explore not only the great books but the many arts that make up a culture, the relations between culture and society, the cultures of various classes, genders, and peoples. A sign that this shift is occurring is Roger Kimball's alarm that interdisciplinary humanities' centers across the country have found themselves drawn to cultural studies as a way of reconceiving the humanities.

The new intellectual space opened up in US culture by cultural studies is not a magic solution to the problems faced by left intellectuals nor even to leftists in the university. But we should not underestimate the openings and possibilities that are found there. The alternatives posed by the critics are less than persuasive: for Barbara Epstein, "the experience of being incorporated into academia has involved a profound defeat. . . . For those of us who hoped for something better, this situation produces various combinations of guilt and alienation." For Louis Menand, "talking about reforming the modern university is like talking about reforming a skyscraper. There's not much point in tinkering: you can knock the whole thing down, or you can go live somewhere else." "Perhaps if America were experiencing right now a significant movement for radical social reform," Paul Berman lectured us, "the temptation to embark on verbal campaigns and to invest these campaigns with outlandish hopes would be less, and the students and young professors would put their energy into real-life democratic movements instead, which might be a relief to their harassed colleagues."[32]

For those of us who inherited the "defeat," who inherited the universities and their "verbal campaigns," the "real-life democratic movements" of the 1980s and 1990s – including significant student activism – have not respected this imagined boundary between the university and the world: the struggles over university unionization, canons and curricula, affirmative action, divestment, and Central American intervention crossed this line. If we are incorporated in the university, it is because we are living in a corporation, not because conflicts and struggles have given way to "guilt and alienation." We do need a wider left agenda for higher education: a notion of the university as public resource like the public library; a national system of sabbaticals for working people; a more thorough-going affirmative action to open access to the resources of the university across lines of race and class; and the building of international links between university lefts around the world.

All culture, Kenneth Burke taught us, is symbolic action, and that phrase holds a significant ambiguity. As Fredric Jameson points out, "a symbolic act is on the one hand affirmed as a genuine *act*, albeit on the symbolic level, while on the other hand it is registered as an act that is merely 'symbolic.'" The term "academic left" holds a like ambiguity: leftists who are fighting within the academy, and leftists who are merely "academic." It is from that hesitation and contradiction, a hesitation at the heart of culture itself, that we must address the bad new times, not the good old days.

8

WHAT'S WRONG WITH CULTURAL STUDIES?

"What's wrong with cultural studies?" It's all in the inflection. The Marxist literary critic Michael Sprinker would have said it as a bill of indictment, without even the question mark: what's wrong with cultural studies. My own tendency is to say it with a shrug: what's wrong with cultural studies? But the suspicion of cultural studies is widely shared on the left these days. "In its original incarnation in the Birmingham School," a group of radical young critics of contemporary cultural studies wrote, "cultural studies was conceived as an interdisciplinary, historical materialist mode of inquiry which combated the Arnoldian notion of 'Culture' by focusing on forms of working-class and popular culture." But

> cultural studies' current privileging of discursive analysis tends to delink the ideological from a meaningful analysis of political economy, obscuring, for example, the relationship between cultural and economic globalization. [It] may not only obstruct analysis of agency and power but in fact increasingly reflect the complex ideology of late capitalism. . . . What is the relationship of cultural expression and resistance to organized, systematic revolution? Is cultural resistance sufficient to effect social transformation? In order to avoid idealizing local or popular culture as revolutionary, how can we understand what constitutes and contributes to emancipatory social change?[1]

Though these questions were posed in this form by the group of young scholars who organized and set the agenda for the "After Postcolonialism, Beyond Minority Discourse" conference at Cornell University in 1999, they resonate among many radical intellectuals in the wake of the unexpected academic success of cultural studies in the United States and around the world. Can one, should one, defend this cultural studies? What kind of politics is cultural politics? In this chapter, I want to briefly outline my way of understanding cultural studies, and offer a modest defense of it as a slogan, by considering its apparent retreat from class, its relation to the work of Antonio Gramsci, and the vexed question of cultural politics and cultural resistance.

First, a short disclaimer. I feel no need to defend all that is done in the name of cultural studies anymore than I need defend all that is done in the name of socialism, feminism, Marxism, or even democracy. Slogans after all are slogans; their purpose is to rally a formation. Like keywords, they are best seen as the sign of common questions, not common answers, a common *problématique* to invoke the Althusserian tradition with which many of us have affiliated ourselves at one time or another. And slogans are, as Kenneth Burke said, always being stolen back and forth; the stealing of slogans is one of the key means of ideological struggles. It is possible that we will lose the slogan of cultural studies to the right but we needn't cede it yet.

So what is cultural studies anyway? Let me suggest two ways of looking at cultural studies. First, cultural studies has become a new name for the humanities, or more accurately, the key slogan in the left's redefinition of the humanities. The right has not, for the most part, even tried to steal the slogan cultural studies, because they continue to take their stand on the ground of the humanities. Cultural studies stands as a fundamental break with the notion of the humanities, with the assumptions that the study of arts and letters is separate from the study of society, that the humanities are best represented by a canon of classics, and that the arts and letters are primarily reflections on the human. Cultural studies has become a powerful slogan in the places where the humanities reigned – the universities, museums, and other state cultural apparatuses – as an assertion that there is a connection between society and culture, labor and art, manual and mental labor. Moreover, the much satirized mantra of race, gender, and class remains not an answer but a question, an attempt to solve the theoretical issues raised by the concept of culture, the historical divisions in human culture that are the consequences of the long-term processes of proletarianization, racialization, and, to borrow from Maria Mies, "housewificization."

In this sense, cultural studies is best seen not as a new discipline, but as the critique of the disciplines. Following the example of Marx's critique of political economy, most of the early moves toward cultural studies began as the critique of disciplinary knowledges; if cultural studies continues to be the "critique of English," the "critique of history," the "critique of anthropology," the "critique of musicology," the "critique of art history," the critique of the concept of culture itself, it will remain a useful and important intellectual space.

As a new name for the humanities, and a space for the critique of the disciplines, cultural studies thus became the slogan of a tactical alliance of workers in the cultural industries and the state cultural apparatuses. Therefore, cultural studies always remains somewhat bureaucratic; it is the slogan of people whose work it is to teach classes, develop syllabi and programs, mount museum exhibitions, stage conferences, and compose scholarly books and articles: the cultural bureaucrats. Working artists on the left – characteristically torn between avant-gardism and populism – will remain rightly suspicious of cultural studies. Left journalists – part of a slightly different culture industry where the ideologies of the humanities have rarely had any influence, and where notions of plain prose for plain people led to a skepticism of any experimental form whether in art or scholarship – will also remain suspicious of cultural studies. So be it: I am not suggesting that all of left intellectual work be conducted under the slogan of cultural studies.

But cultural studies stands for more than the development of this quasi-discipline in the universities. The reason that cultural studies has emerged as a new name for the humanities is that it was a slogan for a wide range of New Left reflections on culture, the powerful rewriting of Marxism around the tropes of culture during the age of three worlds. Virtually all of the New Left Marxists – a generation of figures who came of age around the world in the two decades after World War II – took a cultural turn. Having recognized that one of the great failures of the Communist Marxisms had been their reductive understanding of the superstructures, the New Left intellectuals redefined culture neither as arts and letters nor as manners and customs, but as the new means of communication: the culture industries and the ideological state apparatuses, to use a couple of phrases that became central. Not all used the word "culture" – that was part of the vernacular of the British New Left – but any serious look at the variety of New Left Marxisms will find that each was reconsidering the relation of culture to society. These new analyses of the means of communication, of what came to be called "mass culture," were not simply added to an already established social or political theory. Rather, as is implied by the echo between means of communication and means of production, the mass media often appeared to be the central terrain, the dominant level, of a "postindustrial," "consumer" order. The new cultural materialisms were not simply a reassertion of the importance of the superstructure, but a rethinking of economy and politics in cultural terms. Cultural studies as a slogan is best understood as the name for this powerful turn in Marxist thought, a turn which has shaped many of us.

Now it may be that, after four decades, the reconsideration of the relationship between culture and society is *not* the most pressing issue facing Marxism. I agree. But cultural studies in this sense (the critical analysis of the cultural industries and the state ideological apparatuses, and the reflection on the intersection of these industries and apparatuses on the cultural formations of subaltern classes and peoples) is a permanent contribution to any serious twenty-first-century Marxism. The attempt to trivialize cultural studies by citing the worst examples of pop culture analysis is not dissimilar to the attempt to trivialize the liberation movements by citing ridiculous examples of so-called identity politics. Our moment is not the moment where liberation and culture are the key words. But we have much to learn from a left for whom they were the key words, and, as we try to build a newer left, a global left whose symbolic antagonists have been the IMF and the WTO, the new enclosures which are privatizing the commons established by the social movements of 1848 and 1968, we would do well to keep alive the promise and problems of a half-century of radical cultural analysis, for which our impoverished name remains, for the moment, cultural studies.

Does Cultural Studies Neglect Class?

"Does cultural studies neglect class?" is a question one hears regularly. In one sense, surely not. If cultural studies is best understood not as an intellectual formation or movement nor even as a new discipline or department, but rather as a slogan, a name for that wide expanse of formations and disciplines which used to be called the humanities, then part of its success is that it has brought a variety of group concepts, like class, into the humanities. The humanities took their vocation from a sense of the human, the transcultural and transhistorical, and saw the great accomplishments of Western civilization – Beethoven's Ninth Symphony, Shakespeare's *King Lear*, Cervantes' *Don Quixote* – as touchstones of what it meant to be human: the universals of freedom and necessity, birth and death and so on. Culture, on the other hand, is, as Immanuel Wallerstein put it, the word we use when speaking of traits that are neither universal nor idiosyncratic: "culture is a way of summarizing the ways in which groups distinguish themselves from other groups."[2] Thus it is not surprising that a key part of cultural studies, in its broadest sense, has been the discussion of the very terms by which we construct groups, terms like class, gender, race, and nation. American studies – the original identity discipline – was in this sense never really part of the humanities. If the humanities are about humans, the cultural studies are about peoples.

But does cultural studies neglect class, as opposed to other definitions of peoples? If it does, I'm not too worried, even as a Marxist. Class is *not* the defining category of Marxism, and I try not to forget that two of my key teachers neglected class in order to develop a Marxist cultural studies: Fred Jameson reinvented Marxist cultural studies in the United States around the concept of reification, and Stuart Hall's work was path breaking in its elaboration of the notion of the national-popular. The dual imperatives of Marxist dialectical thought are totality and contradiction – how does one think the totality? how does one think contradiction? – and they still seem to me more powerful than the other grand antinomies that are out there: identity and difference, self and other. The Marxist term that attempts to synthesize totality and contradiction is "mode of production," which has, historically, always been a mode of exploitation; and my first insistence will be that classes, like genders and peoples, are effects, not causes. The mode of production and exploitation – a way of making and remaking life, a way of extracting work – classes, races, genders, and nationalizes us. If it is hard to always use the terms as verbs rather than nouns, it helps to think that the issue is the process of racialization, the process of engendering, the process of proletarianization, etc. The result of these processes in a particular situation is a specific class formation, racial formation, gender formation. And the currency of that phrase "formation" is quite useful because it helps to break down the sense that we need decide whether the *real* cause, the most fundamental identity, is class, gender, or race.

Nevertheless, one influential argument sees the rise of cultural studies itself as part of a larger turn away from class in the age of three worlds: "the substitution of race for class as the great unsolved problem in American life," as Steve Fraser and Gary Gerstle put it in their influential collection, *The Rise and Fall of the New Deal Order.* In this account, our contemporary cultural studies is a descendent of the liberal cultural pluralism of the 1940s that had pushed aside the "labor question" of the 1930s, and of the New Left radicalism that had contemptuously dismissed the "labor metaphysic." However, curiously, this account of the decline of class is based on little class analysis. Whereas each of the earlier party systems they invoke were brought to an end by a crisis – the crisis over slavery which led to a civil war, the economic crisis of the 1890s, and the crash of 1929 and its aftermath – the New Deal order seems to evaporate because of a rhetorical shift, a curious forgetting about class. When this new preoccupation with cultural pluralism combined with the New Left's alleged contempt for white workers and its refusal of the New Deal languages of Americanism and populism, we are told, a classless cultural studies resulted.[3]

This is a misreading of the actual class transformations of the age of three worlds. First, there was a profound social crisis provoked by what Ernest Mandel called the second slump, figured in the oil crisis of 1974, and by the defeat of the United States in Vietnam. In a strange condensation of events – and crises are never simple – this crisis led to the resignation of both the vice president and the president, Agnew and Nixon. Second, the dramatic migration from the South to the North during and after World War II – the largest internal migration in US history – remade the class and racial formations of the New Deal years. The CIO working class was disorganized and reconstructed. Third, the new forms of class struggle in the 1960s and 1970s can be glimpsed in the remarkable organization of public employees, service employees, and white collar employees – three overlapping but distinct groups. If Franklin D. Roosevelt's National Industrial Recovery Act of 1933 kicked off a wave of industrial unionism in the 1930s, so John F. Kennedy's executive order allowing public employees to unionize kicked off an equally important wave of organizing over the next two decades, a social movement closely connected to the struggles for black liberation and women's liberation. Finally, the beginning of a new immigration from Asia and Latin America signaled by the Immigration Act of 1965 has led to the making of an as yet unorganized and largely uncharted post-Fordist working class. So the "turn to race" was not a rhetorical shift, a refusal of the languages of populism, Americanism, and industrial unionism (which is what is meant by class and the labor question in these accounts), but was the mark of a profound remaking of the working classes, in the United States and globally.

Thus it is not enough simply to assert the centrality of class or the labor question. Class analysis in the account of specific historical conjunctures requires not a static sense of the working class or the middle class, but an account of the making and remaking of specific historical blocs, and an attention to class generations and to what Pierre Bourdieu has usefully called "class trajectories."

If there is a neglect of class in cultural studies that should be noted, it is not the neglect of a certain class identity in favor of racial or gender identities; it is rather a neglect of class struggle. For example, in their otherwise excellent collection, *Rethinking Class*, Wai Chee Dimock and Michael Gilmore open by asking "how can we continue to use the word [class] with any sense of political efficacy, when its instrumental expression – 'class struggle' – has ceased to be a vital historical force?" One of their answers – in essays by Dimock and Mary Poovey – is that class needs to be seen as part of a wider modern tendency to classify, and that classification is a central technology of power – as Foucault put it, disciplines classify subjects. This is an important insight for cultural history, but it gives up too quickly on the continuing importance of class struggle as "a vital historical force." Even the work of classifying is an act of class struggle, as Pierre Bourdieu has argued. Bourdieu also sees class as the consequence of classifying; but Bourdieu sees all of us continually classifying and distinguishing. Class struggle is carried on in part by classing other people. In this instance, Bourdieu is more trenchant than Foucault, because he sees that what we might call vernacular classifying is a necessary and useful part of popular struggles, whereas Foucault leads one to think that classifying is simply a technique of power and surveillance, something to be avoided or resisted.[4]

Furthermore, this taxonomic version of class as an instance of classification misses the fact that class struggle is not a kind of drama with giant theatrical characters. Rather it is the continual battle over the social surplus: how it is produced, how it is appropriated, how it is distributed. Classes, both fundamental classes and subsumed classes, are constituted in part by those relations of exploitation, appropriation, and distribution. A key mechanism for distributing the surplus in contemporary societies is the state, which does indeed, as the right reminds us, tax and spend. Who it taxes and who it pays is a vital part of class struggle.

Finally, what we may neglect in cultural studies is not class, but work, something we are reminded of by C.L.R. James's *American Civilization.* The heart of James's account is the understanding of mass production: for James, as for many modern social thinkers, Americanism was Fordism. But for James, in Fordism lies the future in the present, and it is worth following his argument about Fordist mass production. First, Fordism signifies *both* the assembly line and the family car, the creation of a new labor process and a new form of mass-produced culture. And the two central chapters of James's study are the ones on the labor process and the popular arts. I stress this old story because it is in danger of being lost in much of contemporary cultural studies. Cultural studies as an intellectual and political formation was built in a variety of places around the creative tension between the analysis of the labor process – one needs to recall the extraordinary power of Harry Braverman's *Labor and Monopoly Capital*, with its analysis of the separation of conception and execution in mental and manual labor – and the analysis of mass culture. This was the dialectic around which Stanley Aronowitz's classic *False Promises* (1971) was built – "trivialized work, colonized leisure" was the title of one of his central chapters. In the Birmingham Centre for Contemporary Cultural Studies in the 1970s, the work of Stuart Hall and others on the media developed in a vital tension with the work of Paul Willis and others on the labor process. And the early works of socialist-feminist cultural critique, like those of Barbara Ehrenreich, tied the labor processes of housework, of feminized occupations, of birth itself to the mass culture addressed to women. The catch phrase of contemporary cultural studies, "contested terrain," originated in the studies of the labor process.

Too often, contemporary cultural studies reads the cultural commodities of postmodernism without interrogating the labor processes of post-Fordism, and James's notes on American civilization remind us of the necessity to yoke the two, even though he is writing about the very heartlands of Fordism. For James sought the utopian promise in both sides of mass production. Though he was aware that the logic of mass production was to colonize leisure and trivialize work, he also maintained that "*mass production* has created a vast populace, literate, technically trained, conscious of itself and of its inherent right to enjoy all the possibilities of the society."[5]

Thus, it is not class that is neglected in cultural studies, as critics of "identity politics" often assert. Cultural studies may rightly neglect class, if by that we mean an identity imagined to be prior to race, gender, ethnicity. But a critical understanding of class formations, class struggles, and the relation between work and culture, between the labor process and the popular arts, still seems to me the heart of an emancipatory cultural studies.

"A Study Might Be Made . . .": Gramsci and Cultural Studies

For me, cultural studies and the work of Antonio Gramsci have always been connected. When I arrived at the Birmingham Centre for Contemporary Cultural Studies from Boston in 1978, I was told by one of my fellow graduate students that I needed to read three books to get into the Centre's intellectual debates – Althusser's *Reading Capital*, Braverman's *Labor and Monopoly Capital* and Gramsci's *Prison Notebooks* – a kind of catch-up primitive accumulation. A wave of Gramscianism had swept across New Left Marxisms, and it became part of my vernacular. I am not a Gramsci scholar, but I have reread and taught the *Prison Notebooks* many times over the last twenty years, retailing what I got wholesale at the Centre, the now "old school" cultural studies interpretation of Gramsci associated with the powerful essays of Stuart Hall, and the Gramsci reader edited by David Forgacs.[6]

At the time Gramsci had little presence in the United States; the Frankfurt School dominated left cultural theory and I came to Birmingham full of Marcuse, Benjamin, and Adorno. Most of the American interpretations of Gramsci then available made him sound like an Italian Marcuse. Twenty years later, things have not shifted that much: the new translation of Benjamin's complete Arcades project has drawn much more attention and interest than Joseph Buttigieg's ongoing translation of the complete *Prison Notebooks*. Gramsci has had his American moments – the late 1980s controversy over hegemony among US historians (discussed above in chapter six); the reconsideration of Gramsci by Edward Said and other postcolonial critics; the 1990s interest of *boundary 2* in Gramscian writing; even the discovery of Gramsci by Rush Limbaugh and the right – but in general Gramsci is a minor presence. One might think that Gramsci's ideas have been absorbed but, aside from hegemony (a word that is fully American, emanating from international relations programs: one never needed Gramsci to speak a phrase like American hegemony), few of his keywords – historical bloc, national-popular, war of position, passive revolution – have become part of the intellectual vocabulary. An optimist of the will might say that we are in a trough, having long registered the impact of the classic *Selections*, while new interpretations await the completion of the translation of the critical edition.

I want not to offer a new interpretation of Gramsci nor to revive the debate over the British cultural studies interpretation of Gramsci, but to discuss Gramsci's work and the formation of research agendas in cultural studies. For the *Prison Notebooks* are full of research agendas; Gramsci is always saying: "A study might be made . . ."; "it must first be shown . . ."; "it is necessary to study . . ."[7] The notebooks are always beginning projects. I would suggest that the reason there are so many different Gramscis in circulation is not because his ideas are half-formed, elusive, and expressed in contradictory formulations but because he offers so many starting points. Gramsci's influence is often registered less by particular concepts or ideas than by starting points. One of the lasting influences of Quintin Hoare and Geoffrey Nowell Smith's edition, *Selections from the Prison Notebooks*, was their accenting of one particular Gramscian starting point: the plan to write a history of Italian intellectuals. Setting the passages on intellectuals and education at the beginning of their selection was not only an opening to the student New Left of 1971; it also contributed to the continuing focus on intellectuals and education in the English-language absorption of Gramsci – "organic intellectual" is probably the best-known Gramscian keyword in English.

A different Gramscian starting point oriented Ranajit Guha's famous preface to the first volume of *Subaltern Studies*: citing the passage from Notebook 25 where Gramsci outlines the way "it is necessary to study" the subaltern classes, Guha writes that "it will be idle of us, of course, to hope that the range of contributions to this series may even remotely match the six-point project envisaged by Antonio Gramsci in his 'Notes on Italian History'."[8]

For me, the impact of Gramsci has also been largely in starting points; reading Gramsci is often an exercise in clarifying how one should begin a study: what questions need be asked, what concepts reconsidered, what should be the, to use a favorite phrase of Gramsci, "methodological criteria." Three such Gramscian starting points have influenced me; I cite them not because they are necessarily the correct or best starting points, but because I have found them useful for thinking through the project of cultural studies.

The first was relatively direct: in the famous *für ewig* letter of 1927, where Gramsci outlined four ideas for "intense systematic study," he proposed "an essay on *feuilletons* [serial novels] and popular taste in literature." That unfinished project took hold among a group of us at Birmingham – one member even translated some of the key passages on popular literature that were later to appear in *Selections from Cultural Writings* – as we wrestled with the turn to popular literature studies within Marxist and feminist literary criticism. Gramsci's proposed project – an analysis of the "particular illusion that the serial novel provides, . . . its real way of day-dreaming," and an investigation of the place of popular fiction in working-class culture (he noted the "social obligation" to know the novel that the *Stampa* was publishing) – was almost unprecedented in the socialist tradition, breaking not only from the social-democratic conceptions of *Bildung* and *Kultur* which would appropriate the heritage of Beethoven, Goethe, and Schiller for workers, but also from the avant-gardism of the proletarian culture movement. One of the key notes was the critique of Paul Nizan's account of revolutionary literature:

> Nizan does not know how to deal with so-called "popular literature," that is with the success of serial literature . . . among the masses. . . . And yet, it is this question that represents the major part of the problem of a new literature as the expression of moral and intellectual renewal, for only from the readers of serial literature can one select a sufficient and necessary public for creating the cultural base of a new literature.

"The most common prejudice," Gramsci continues, "is this: that the new literature has to identify itself with an artistic school of intellectual origins, as was the case with Futurism." However, "the premiss of the new literature cannot but be historical, political and popular"; it must "sink its roots into the humus of popular culture as it is, with its tastes and tendencies and with its moral and intellectual world." This project of Gramsci's reverberated with those of us on the rebound from a variety of New Left avant-gardisms and experimentalisms, and lay behind the work of the CCCS English Studies group and my own study of American dime novels and working-class culture.[9]

An explicit Gramscian starting point also guided my study of the culture of the Popular Front social movement of mid-century United States, *The Cultural Front*, a title I borrowed in part from Gramsci's draft essay on Croce. The US 1930s – the period of the New Deal and the old left – are a kind of American Risorgimento, a passive revolution from above, an incomplete and failed popular struggle that has haunted later generations just as the Italian Risorgimento of the 1850s and 1860s haunted Gramsci: most of his lists of projects included a study of "the Age of Risorgimento." In both cases, one begins from a crisis: "a crisis occurs, sometimes lasting for decades." In the famous note, "Analysis of Situations. Relations of Force," from Notebook 13, Gramsci explores several "principles of historical methodology." "It is the problem of the relations between structure and superstructure which must be accurately posed and resolved," Gramsci writes, "if the forces which are active in the history of a particular period are to be correctly analysed." Moreover, "when a historical period comes to be studied, the great importance of [the] distinction" between organic movements and conjunctural ones "becomes clear." This double articulation – on the one hand, imagining the social whole, on the other, characterizing historical moments or periods – remain at the heart of any serious cultural studies, and Gramsci's great trope of the "historical bloc" is one of the most imaginative attempts to bring them together. "Historical bloc," like many useful theoretical terms, has two distinct meanings: it connotes both an alliance of social forces and a specific social formation. It serves, in its limited sense, as the name for a conjunctural assembly of forces – like the historical blocs represented by the names of Tony Blair or George W. Bush – and, in its expanded sense, as the name for the entire social formation, the totality made up of base and superstructure. The conceptual slippage or sleight of hand is brought off by the concept of hegemony, for a moment of hegemony is when a historical bloc in the first sense – a particular alliance of class fractions and social forces – is able to lead a society for a period of time, winning consent through a form of representation, and thereby establishing an historical bloc in the second sense – a specific social formation. In such moments, one often finds the historical period taking its name from the social alliance, as in the case of the New Deal, at once Roosevelt's successful political alliance and the common term for the United States in the 1930s and 1940s.[10]

However, if Gramsci's methodological criteria helped formulate a way of thinking about the organic and conjunctural, the structure and superstructure of the New Deal "passive revolution," the plan of *The Modern Prince* outlined in "Brief Notes on Machiavelli's Politics" is, for me, the heart of Gramsci's cultural studies, and the place I begin when teaching the

Prison Notebooks. "Two basic points," he writes, "should structure the entire work": the formation of a national-popular collective will – "when can the conditions for awakening and developing a national-popular collective will be said to exist?" – and the "question of intellectual and moral reform." The first point opens up Gramsci as a socialist theorist of classes, parties, social movements and subaltern groups: the five-point project for analyzing a social movement at the end of "Some Theoretical and Practical Aspects of 'Economism'," in Notebook 13, is a brilliant counterpart to the six-point project for analyzing the subaltern classes that Guha noted. The second point opens up Gramsci's understanding of "conceptions of the world" and the "cultural movements" that seek "to replace common sense and old conceptions of the world." It is in the context of these cultural movements that the specific analyses of intellectuals and education make sense. Moreover, Gramsci's conception of Marxism, the philosophy of praxis, as such a movement of intellectual and moral renewal, remains the most vital way of understanding any contemporary Marxism.[11]

My own attempt to unravel the moment of "a national-popular collective will" that took shape in the Popular Front social movement of the 1930s and 1940s, and to understand the "intellectual and moral renewal" attempted by its cultural front, was profoundly shaped by this Gramscian starting point, this research agenda. But in doing so, I was also struck by the fact that Gramsci was not alone in turning to the cultural front. Gramsci's prison writings of the 1930s were paralleled by the work of a number of socialist intellectuals trying to forge a theory of culture. In fact, it is arguable that before mid-century, there was no specifically Marxist theory of culture, the way there was, from Mehring and Plekhanov to Christopher Caudwell and Ernst Fischer, a Marxist aesthetics. Culture as a term belonged to two great modernist traditions – the literary and humanistic notion of culture as *sweetness and light* and the anthropological notion of culture as *customs and morals*. The postmodern concept of culture – distant from *arts and letters* and *customs and morals* – comes out of reflection on the cultural industries and the state cultural apparatuses, what Gramsci and others called the cultural front. This inaugurates cultural studies, not as an academic discipline, but as the critical reflection on the culture industries and the cultural apparatuses. This is why the pioneering works of that epoch – Benjamin's "Work of Art in the Age of Mechanical Reproduction," Adorno and Horkheimer's *Dialectic of Enlightenment*, James's *American Civilization*, and Gramsci's *Prison Notebooks* – remain closer to us than Eliot's *Notes toward a Definition of Culture* or Kroeber and Kluckholn's *Culture*. As long as we are faced with this culture, Gramsci remains a starting point not only methodologically, but historically, part of the infinity of traces that the historical process has deposited in us.

What Kind of Politics is Cultural Politics?

What kind of politics is cultural politics? No politics, many would say. The idea of a cultural politics is not popular these days. In the United States, we regularly hear fellow activists and militants complaining that the turn to culture and the popularity of cultural studies has distracted people from real political organizing and issues of political economy. "If the 30s left had undersold culture," Terry Eagleton has quipped, "the postmodern left overvalued it." And one can be excused from wondering how culture could be a political practice in a world where the global cultural market is dominated by a handful of world-spanning corporations – Disney, Sony, News Corp, AOL-Time Warner, and the like (Viacom, Vivendi, Bertelsmann); where styles of subcultural resistance seem to be immediately appropriated and marketed by the entertainment industry; and where even a radical cultural politics often takes the form of celebrity endorsement.[12]

Of course, the notion of cultural politics has always had an unavoidable ambiguity: is it a cultural *politics* or a politics that is *merely* cultural? What is the relationship of cultural expression and resistance to organized radical or revolutionary politics? Can cultural resistance effect social transformation? In order to avoid idealizing local or popular culture as revolutionary, how can we understand what constitutes and contributes to emancipatory social change?[13]

Cultural studies, or Marxist cultural critique in the age of three worlds, began from the understanding of cultural politics from above: how cultural industries and state cultural apparatuses fought the class war, so to speak, through cultural interventions. It focused its attention on policing and disciplining of subjects through the mass media, the educational system, and the prisons. The formative generation of New Left intellectuals whose work lay the ground of cultural studies looked at processes of reproduction (Bourdieu), hegemony (Hall), ideology and ideological state apparatuses (Althusser), discipline (Foucault), subject formation, and cultural imperialism (Dorfman and Mattelart). The major New Left alternative to this version of the politics of culture lay in the pioneering accounts of the role of culture in revolutionary and postrevolutionary struggles for national liberation: one thinks of the influential essays of Fanon and Amilcar Cabral, the work of C.L.R. James (relatively unknown at the time), and the potent metaphor of cultural revolution coming from Maoist China. But the imaginative divide between First and Third World, between the space of incorporation and that of revolution, meant that these tricontinental concepts of cultural politics had little impact on North Atlantic cultural analysis. Indeed, the emblem of the postcolonial turning point in North Atlantic cultural studies, Edward Said's *Orientalism*, was more Foucaultian than Cabralist in its sense of cultural politics, stressing the cultural processes by which political – imperial – power was secured.

In the 1980s, a number of figures tried to theorize cultural resistance, often in Gramscian terms. But the rise of a neoliberal "market populism" or consumer populism and a fairly indiscriminate use of the term "resistance" made these Gramscian invocations of the popular ring hollow. Much of the contemporary skepticism about cultural politics derives from this "crisis of the popular": if shopping or watching television can be understood as forms of cultural resistance, haven't we lost any sense of an effective politics?

Thus, for the most part our understanding of cultural politics remains crudely dichotomous, stuck in binaries of social control and resistance, incorporation and subversion, and we often get lost in what Priya Gopal called "a general stew of inchoate resistance-talk."[14] Haunting these binaries were the old and inadequate habits of separating false consciousness from enlightened class consciousness, and reactionary from progressive art. Raymond Williams's fourfold scheme of alternative, oppositional, residual, and emergent cultures was often cited, since it seemed to offer a step beyond the simple binaries, but it was rarely used systematically because it was too like a simple genre classification. To label a culture or subculture – rave, ethnic studies, or surfing – as alternative, oppositional, residual, or emergent was more subtle than praising or denouncing it as progressive or reactionary, but the logic was not dissimilar.

We need, I think, an account of what we might call, following Ranajit Guha, the elementary forms of cultural politics, the fundamental moves on the cultural front, the equivalent of Foucault's analysis of the simple forms of discipline. As a contribution to such an analysis, I would suggest that there are three moments, or levels, of cultural politics: cultural resistance, the struggle for cultural justice, and cultural revolution. Each has its own forms, importance, and political meaning; however, to confuse or conflate them leads us to mistake the point of cultural politics.

The first moment, or level, of cultural politics is the moment of resistance. If domination is, as James Scott suggests in his study of the arts of domination and the arts of resistance, "the use of power to extract work, production, services, taxes against the will of the dominated" and resistance is thus the effort at "minimizing the exactions, labor and humiliations to which [subordinates] are subject," perhaps cultural resistance should be kept, as a concept, to precisely those acts of ideological insubordination which, openly or secretly, minimize symbolic humiliations and refuse to pay what Scott calls "symbolic taxes," the assent and respect claimed by both a high culture consisting largely of the valuable objects the wealthy have collected and display in museums, universities, and concert halls, and a popular culture consisting largely of the latest speculative investments of culture industry producers in digitized sound and picture.[15]

Thus cultural resistance ranges from cutting school and defacing billboards with graffiti to violations of public taste by forms of clothing, hair style, manners of speech, and high-volume boomboxes. At times, these forms of cultural resistance may cement small communities of resistance, what cultural studies came to call subcultures, a term which connotes not the culture of a part – a minority, regional, or occupational culture – but a culture underneath the main culture, somewhere between the underground and the mainstream. Widespread forms of cultural resistance may serve to unite countercultures, those moments – historically associated with the

1920s and 1960s – when a wide range of subcultures adopted by young people merge into a generational structure of feeling. Nevertheless, even in these moments, cultural resistance remains akin to classic forms of material resistance – pilfering, sabotage, slowdowns, monkey wrenching – and it has an analogous complex relation to organized political struggles.

For the most part, cultural bureaucrats like ourselves – teachers, artists, activists – do not practice cultural resistance (in fact, we too often practice the arts of cultural domination). But an emancipatory cultural studies should always pay close attention to these practices, not to congratulate ourselves on our taste for resistance, but to understand what is taking place in the culture.

The second moment, or level, of cultural politics – and much of what we think of when we use the term "cultural politics" – is more properly called the struggle for cultural justice, a term I borrow from Andrew Ross. It is a more accurate name for what state bureaucrats call affirmative action; it is closely related to the so-called identity politics of the liberation movements; and it is named by contemporary political philosophy as the politics of recognition. It is here we find the struggles to reassert the dignity of despised cultural identifications: the assertion that black is beautiful, that gay and lesbian romance and sexuality are as central to our collective narratives (novels, movies, pop songs) as are heterosexual marriage and adultery, that art forms practiced by women are not "minor" forms, that speakers of minority languages have rights to cultural autonomy and representation. This battle for cultural justice has a long tradition, and it includes the proletarian cultural movements and folk culture revivals that flourished around the world in the early twentieth century, stressing the dignity of working people and their cultural practices.[16]

At this level of cultural politics, we see the characteristic forms of self-organization by artists, intellectuals, and cultural workers: writers' unions, theater groups, and so forth. Here again there are several distinct aspects that might be identified. First, there are the avant-gardes, those experimental, intentionally nonpopular cultural innovations, many of which prove idiosyncratic, flukes, passing fads, but some of which open the doors of perception. Second, there are movement cultures, when alliances are built between particular social movements and particular cultural formations, when particular songs become anthems, and when movement cultural institutions – night schools, bookstores, little theaters – are created. Third, there are the struggles within the institutions of mass culture: the culture industries and the state cultural apparatuses. These include not only struggles to reshape the content of popular culture, but the struggles for the rights of cultural workers, for free expression, and for culture industry unions. It also includes the struggles for equal access to the institutions of cultural production and cultural distribution: schools, museums, film and recording studios. The historic breaking of color, gender, and class bars are fundamental parts of this kind of cultural politics, and the battles for affirmative action and diversity in admissions to cultural institutions remain crucial, if only a scratching of the surface of what is needed. Imagine sabbaticals for working people at our universities, so as to support forms of adult and continuing education; indeed, as Raymond Williams often reminded us, cultural studies itself was invented *not* in the university, but in the labor movement's own institutions of further education.

The struggle for cultural justice is also a struggle to reshape the selective traditions that determine which works of art and culture will be preserved, kept in print, taught to young people, and displayed in museums, and which cans of film will be housed, whose manuscripts and letters will be archived and indexed. These struggles for cultural justice have been the center of the most visible "culture wars" and they are the place where cultural bureaucrats like us – artists, writers, teachers, and activists – are most directly involved. This is the realm of the battle over the relations of representation.

Out of these organized forms of struggle for cultural justice and the sometimes unorganized forms of popular cultural resistance may come a third moment, or level, of cultural politics: the formation of a new culture, a new "conception of the world," as Gramsci put it, a cultural revolution. This is the least predictable form of cultural politics and a reminder of why cultural activists like ourselves must have a certain humility; the history of the left is littered with examples of left-wing cultural bureaucrats unable to recognize and support new forms of art, new cultures, even in revolutionary moments.

Indeed, the Marxist understanding of revolution has always been marked by a hesitation, and ambiguity, between two notions of revolution: political revolution and the revolutionizing of modes of production. And cultural revolution also holds these two senses. It is at once the term for those epochal and world historical moments usually associated with political revolutions, when the world is turned upside down, new calendars are invented, old statues torn down and new ones erected. These volcanic cultural revolutions are relatively rare, and are always difficult to assess and understand. But it is also the term for that massive transformation of human lives and activities that accompanies changes in modes of production. This may take generations to come to fruition, as new forms and media are invented, new ways of living and clothing the body develop: this is what Raymond Williams meant by the "long revolution." However, this form of cultural revolution has also been lived and experienced over the last two centuries by migrants whose journeys have taken them from one end of the capitalist world-system to the other.

The point of this brief elaboration of the elementary forms of cultural politics is to get us beyond the simple dichotomies of incorporation and subversion, the ritual invocation of resistance. We should not, in our justifiable anger at the trivialization of cultural studies and cultural politics, give up the sense that there are forms of cultural politics that are irreducible to the politics of the workplace, the state, or the household. Understanding and distinguishing these three moments of cultural politics – cultural resistance, the struggle for cultural justice, and cultural revolution – may help us avoid an unwarranted triumphalism and a paralyzing despair.

PART THREE

THE AMERICAN IDEOLOGY: THE AGE OF THREE WORLDS AS THE AMERICAN CENTURY

9

"THE SPECIAL AMERICAN CONDITIONS": MARXISM AND AMERICAN STUDIES

. . . and then there are the special American conditions . . .

Friedrich Engels, 1851

But there is also another reason for the poverty of theory in American Studies, and that is the reluctance to utilize one of the most extensive literatures of cultural theory in modern scholarship, coming out of the Marxist intellectual tradition.

Robert Sklar, "The Problem of an American Studies 'Philosophy,'" 1975

In a limited sense, this is a "Marxist" book; in many senses, it is unrecognizably Marxist. For American intellectuals, pro and contra Marx, this is probably as it should be. While it may come close to impossible to think about progressive change without engaging Marxist categories, one of the lessons to be drawn from Kenneth Burke's career is that an American ("self-reliant") Marxism is fundamentally an absurd proposition. The "active" critical soul in America, from Emerson to Burke, joins parties of one, because it is there, in America, that critical power flourishes.

Frank Lentricchia, 1983

In his survey of developments in New Left Marxism in the 1970s, Perry Anderson argued that "the sheer density of ongoing economic, political, sociological and cultural research on the Marxist Left in Britain or North America, with its undergrowth of journals and discussions, eclipses any equivalent in the older lands of the Western Marxist tradition proper. . . . Today the *predominant* centres of intellectual production seem to lie in the English-speaking world." This New Left intellectual renaissance had a powerful impact on the universities in the United States, as graduate students and young faculty members created "radical caucuses" and alternative journals in the disciplines and professional associations that structured the "multiversity," the mass universities created during the age of three worlds. In the face of this, the place of Marxism in the study of American culture, in American studies, was somewhat anomalous. For here, there had been little engagement with Marxism by American studies scholars, and few Marxists interpreting American culture: American cultural history had not seen the revisionist historiography that marked American diplomatic, labor, and social history in the work, for example, of William Appleman Williams, David Montgomery, and Eugene Genovese. American studies, which had taken shape in the early years of the Cold War, had become – despite the intentions of some of its intellectual founders – a part of what might be called "the American ideology" of the age of three worlds: the deep sense of the exceptionalism of this "people of plenty," the unquestioned virtue of democracy and the "American way of life," and the sense that the world was entering an American century.[1]

Thus, the intellectual history of American studies – and its curious relation to the New Left renaissance in Marxist thought – offers a telling glimpse into the self-consciousness and contradictions of the American ideology. In this chapter, I will offer an interpretative history of American studies, outlining its founding break with the Marxism of the 1930s, and suggesting that American studies has served as a substitute for Marxism in a variety of ways, leading to the curious sense, held by Marxists and non-Marxists alike, that "American Marxism" is "an absurd proposition," at once an oxymoron and a pleonasm.

American Studies as a Substitute for Marxism

> When we examine the meaning of Americanism, we discover that Americanism is to the American not a tradition or a territory, . . . but a doctrine – what socialism is to a socialist. Like socialism, Americanism is looked upon not patriotically, as a personal attachment, but rather as a highly attenuated, conceptualized, platonic, impersonal attraction toward a system of ideas, a solemn assent to a handful of final notions – democracy, liberty, opportunity, to all of which the American adheres rationalistically much as a socialist adheres to his socialism – because it does him good, because it gives him work, because, so he thinks, it guarantees his happiness. Americanism has thus served as a substitute for socialism.
>
> Leon Samson, 1934

There are two principal reasons why there were not substantial Marxist cultural studies dealing with the United States. The first had to do with the way Marxist cultural thought reentered American intellectual activity between 1960 and 1985. It came through the rediscovery, translation, and interpretation of continental "Western Marxists:" Lukács, Gramsci, Adorno, Benjamin, Marcuse, Korsch, Sartre, Althusser, Lefebvre. Fredric Jameson's 1971 book *Marxism and Form* may stand as the epitome of this work, and it is significant that his professional affiliation was French language and literature. The most interesting work of American Marxist cultural critics remained centered on European theory, texts, and culture, and was found in journals like *Telos*, *New German Critique*, and *Semiotexte*. Unlike the powerful impact of the British Marxist historians (E. P. Thompson, Eric Hobsbawm, and Christopher Hill, among others) on American history writing, European Marxist cultural theory left little imprint on American cultural studies.[2]

The second reason lay in the peculiar formation of American studies itself, which had served as a substitute for a developed Marxist culture.

American studies emerged as both a continuation of and response to the popular discovery and invention of "American culture" in the 1930s, a discovery marked in such contrary slogans as "the American way of life" and "Communism is twentieth-century Americanism." Though Warren Susman, the finest analyst of the culture of the thirties, saw this concept of culture as finally conservative – nationalist, nostalgic, and sentimentally populist – I would argue that its wide ideological range allowed the American studies it spawned to function as a substitute Marxism in two quite different ways. First, American studies served as the quintessential alternative to Marxist explanations, the embodiment and explicator of the American way, the "genius of American politics": its interdisciplinary and totalizing (perhaps pluralizing) ambitions rivaled those of Marxism, which was understood simply as Soviet ideology. American studies in its imperial guise was based on the uniqueness of the American experience, and, as Gene Wise pointed out, this Cold War vision of the American tradition attracted corporate funding and moved overseas as an intellectual arm of American foreign policy. One might take the work of Daniel Boorstin as the epitome of this side of American studies: both his testimony before the House Un-American Activities Committee, naming names, affirming that "a member of the Communist Party should not be employed by a university," and placing his own work in the context of the anti-Communist crusade; and his three-volume *The Americans* (1958, 1965, 1974), the finest cultural history of the United States from the point of view of capitalism. For this American studies, American Marxism was surely an oxymoron: Americanism substituted for Marxism as an antidote.[3]

Yet there was another strain in American studies which had a more complex relation to the Marxist tradition: the practice of American cultural history as a form of radical culture critique. The "myth/symbol" school, Alan Trachtenberg argued, had its origins in "a strain within American cultural history itself, its own 'usable past' so to speak, in a line which runs at least from Emerson through Whitman and Van Wyck Brooks and Lewis Mumford, . . . a cultural-political current brought to a particular focus in the work and career of F.O. Matthiessen, whose importance in the launching of a 'myth and symbol' enterprise can hardly be stressed enough." This tradition, he maintains, saw "cultural criticism as a form of cultural reconstruction" and attempted a "comprehensive view of American life, a view in which the distinctions as well as the relations between culture and society were clear and definitive." Its politics began from "an embattled posture against what it defined as 'commercialism,' a cultural reflex . . . of corporate consumer capitalism." The myth and symbol group shared "a critical vision of Cold War America and . . . a critical view of American historical experience." Out of this tradition of radical cultural criticism have come the most significant early works in American studies, and this tradition continued to draw the fire of the academic right, as when Kenneth Lynn, in a review of Jackson Lears' *No Place of Grace*, dubbed it "anti-American Studies."[4]

Ironically, this critical American studies also served as a "substitute Marxism." For its direct ancestry is less Emerson than the peculiar union of the "usable past" cultural criticism – that of Brooks, Mumford, and Waldo Frank – and the cultural politics of Popular Front Communism, which recovered and celebrated American folk culture in the late 1930s and 1940s. The figure of F.O. Matthiessen was indeed central to this union and to its later influence in American studies.

This ancestry had several consequences for the relation between Marxism and American cultural studies. On the one hand, this moment established the left politics and critical stance of an important element of American studies; and, in a sort of intellectual popular front, the work of these cultural critics, like the progressive history writing of Beard and Parrington which influenced it, was occasionally mistaken for an American Marxism.[5] Moreover, by combining the search for a usable past with Popular Front "Americanism," this group of intellectuals entered a more serious engagement with American culture than did the other major left cultural formation of the thirties, the group of anti-Stalinist modernists around *Partisan Review*. A sign of the difference is their respective treatments of Melville. For the "Americanist" cultural critics, Melville became a key figure of the usable past in the work of Mumford, Matthiessen, Newton Arvin, and Leo Marx. The avowedly cosmopolitan New York Intellectuals kept their distance from Melville, finding the sources of a critical culture in European modernism.[6]

However, the possibility of an American Marxist cultural studies was also blocked by this formation. The political alliance with the Popular Front prevented an engagement with the more sophisticated Marxism of the anti-Stalinist left; thus no Americanists were associated with the short-lived *Marxist Quarterly* which attracted the US equivalents of Western Marxism: Sidney Hook, Lewis Corey, and Meyer Shapiro, among others. But the Stalinized Marxism of the Communist Party could not support a serious cultural criticism, and F.O. Matthiessen's critical reviews of the Marxist literary histories by Granville Hicks and V.F. Calverton are a sign of this tradition's formative break with that "vulgar Marxism."[7]

As a result, this critical tradition of American studies often combined radical dissent with an ambivalence toward Marxist theory, a disposition it shared with the emerging New Left.[8] Leo Marx accurately noted in 1983:

> In retrospect, Matthiessen's rejection of what he took to be Marxism is . . . ironic. . . . Some of today's practicing Marxist critics, Raymond Williams for example, would consider Matthiessen's literary theory . . . to be more acceptable – closer to their own theories – than the rigid economistic version of Marxism that Matthiessen found repugnant. . . . The overall tendency of Marxist thought during the last twenty years has been to allow much greater historical efficacy to ideas and non-material culture than was allowed by the mainstream Marxism of the Stalin era. It is this development which now makes Matthiessen's thought seem less distant from Marxism than he himself believed it to be.

However, this ambivalence toward Marxism led to a common, if curious, rhetoric in American cultural studies, which finds an exaggerated, but not unusual, example in Jackson Lears' oft-cited essay on cultural hegemony. After repeatedly condemning the "rigidities of orthodox Marxism," "Marxist teleology," and "Marx's epigones" (without citing them by name), he builds his argument around the contributions of Gramsci, Genovese, Jameson, Bakhtin, Williams, Thompson, Stuart Hall, and Henri Lefebvre – all Marxists. Marx, like any other important thinker, has his epigones – second-rate imitators and followers – and worse. But the straw man of orthodox Marxism obscures the fact that the figures Lears cites positively are central to the Marxist tradition. Thus, the continuing specter of a Second International or Stalinist Marxism often prevented a serious engagement with contemporary Marxism, and led to the random borrowing of terms from a Gramsci, a Williams, a Benjamin – borrowings that too often ignored the context and role of the concepts in a larger conceptual system and tradition.[9]

So this critical American studies became a "substitute Marxism" in the pleonastic sense, from the Popular Front claim that Communism was simply twentieth-century Americanism, to the New Left sense that there was an indigenous radical tradition that preempted Marxism, and then to the covert, pragmatic appropriation and Americanization of Marxist concepts without the baggage of the Marxist tradition. Behind this dance of Marxism and Americanism lies, however, not merely the circumstances of the arrival and Americanization of the immigrant Marxism but the larger question of American exceptionalism.

The notion of American exceptionalism is in many ways the foundation of the discipline of American studies; whether the answers are cast in terms of the American mind, the national character, American myths and symbols, or American culture, the founding question of the discipline was "What is American?" Consider the difference if the discipline had been constituted as cultural studies, as was the case with the analogous formation that grew out of the work of Richard Hoggart, Raymond Williams, and Stuart Hall in Britain during the same period. Like American studies, British cultural studies grew out of a dissatisfaction with an ahistorical and technical literary criticism and with a Stalinist Marxism in the 1950s. Both disciplines practiced cultural criticism to recover a usable past for cultural reconstruction: F.O. Matthiessen's *American Renaissance* (1941) and Leo Marx's *The Machine in the Garden* (1964) on one side of the Atlantic were paralleled by Richard Hoggart's *The Uses of Literacy* (1957) and Raymond Williams's *Culture and Society* (1958) on the other.[10] But in cultural studies, the central questions – "What is culture?", "What are its forms and how is it related to material production?" – formed a more productive theoretical agenda, and allowed a more serious engagement with Marxism than did the question "What is American?" As a result, the work of Raymond Williams proved richer and more prolific than any of the founding generation of American studies, and the underfunded and understaffed Birmingham University Centre for Contemporary Cultural Studies produced a body of work with greater political and intellectual influence than that of any American studies program.[11] In American studies, the focus on American uniqueness often prevented the emergence of a more general cultural studies, and tended to ignore non-American theoretical paradigms.

The issue of American exceptionalism may be cast in many ways, but for socialists, and for those implicitly or explicitly debating them, it is summed up in the question the German sociologist Werner Sombart posed in 1905: "Why no socialism in America?" Despite perennial attempts to dismiss it as one of those fruitless "negative" historical questions, it has been continually returned to since Sombart. In the question lie two different issues which have not been sufficiently distinguished. The first is an historical question: why has there been no (or so little) socialist consciousness among American workers, or, as it is usually put, why has there not developed a major labor, social-democratic, or Communist party in the United States? There are a number of excellent reviews of this question, and I will not recapitulate them.[12] The second, theoretical, question is, however, central to the relation between Marxism and American studies: do the categories of Marxism apply to the United States? Is the historical experience of the US so unique, so exceptional, as to require an entirely new theoretical framework?

The sense that America has "disproved" Marx pervades much of the exceptionalist debate. In part this is because most exceptionalists continue to take the evolutionary Marxism of the Second International which forecast an inevitable transition to socialism as Marxism; thus to disprove the "inevitability of socialism" is to disprove the entire theory. However, the historical defeats of the socialist and workers' movements in the aftermath of World War I and the complex history of the Soviet Union have purged from contemporary Marxism any simple (or even complex) inevitabilism. The Western Marxism that American studies confronts is a tradition of more than half a century which begins from the defeat of inevitabilist hopes and assumptions, a tradition which has chastened the prophetic mode without forgoing engagement.[13]

Nevertheless, other exceptionalists see American development as disproving not only the prediction of a socialist opposition or future, but also the methods and categories of Marxist analysis, historical materialism. This often remains implicit or cast in ambiguous formulations. Take this formula of Louis Hartz: "Marx fades because of the fading of Laud." Does this simply mean that there will not be a Marxist opposition because there is not a Laudian establishment (Hartz's plausible historical argument of no feudalism, no socialism), or does it mean, as its rhetorical structure suggests, that Marx's analysis becomes wrong, or at least irrelevant, in the liberal fragment society? There are several reasons why the latter claim remains rhetorically implied rather than explicitly argued. First, most treatments of American exceptionalism have recognized that European Marxists, from Marx and Engels to Lenin, Trotsky, and Gramsci, themselves suggested the factors that have made the United States exceptional – the absence of feudalism, the "free" land of the frontier, the appearance of greater prosperity and mobility, the centrality of race and ethnicity, and the ideological power of Americanism – and debated their effects on the development of a workers' movement in the United States. So Marxism as a theoretical framework does not necessarily blind one to the peculiarities of the Americans.[14]

Second, the relation between history and theory posited by the anti-Marxist American exceptionalists is a crude pragmatism – if it doesn't work, it's not true – or a simple historicism – in another time, in another place, Marx was right. The first is tricky because it provokes the question of whether the United States' uniquely un-Marxist character means that, in nonexceptional countries, Marxism is true; the latter – often calling itself post-Marxism – responds by characterizing Marx and his progeny as old-fashioned. In the end, neither of these work. To establish that American development is in many senses unique is not to demonstrate the irrelevance of Marxist theory. American studies must mount a theoretical argument that could persuade us that its methods, its categories, and its discipline are more adequate to cultural studies than is Marxism. Though such an argument might be constructed on a number of grounds, the most common theme has been to stress Marxism's undervaluing of the power of ideological factors. So Louis Hartz early wrote that "the instinctive tendency of all Marxists to discredit the ideological factors as such blinded them to many of the consequences, purely psychological in nature, flowing from the nonfeudal issue. Was not the whole complex of 'Americanism' an ideological question?"[15] In the next section of this chapter, I will consider four major cultural and ideological grounds for American exceptionalism, all of which, it could be argued, have founded the distinctive work of American studies, and have seemed beyond Marxist abilities: the distinctive American literary tradition of the romance, the role of the frontier in American imagination, the ideological power of the Puritan covenant, and the consumer culture of the "people of plenty." A Marxist revision of American cultural history would have to revise persuasively our understanding of these aspects of American culture; I hope to show that New Left Marxists began that revision.[16]

The New Left's Revisionist History of American Culture

Since American studies grew out of literary criticism, it is not surprising that one of its earliest cultural revisions lay in literary history: a powerful argument that the uniqueness of American fiction lay in its repeated flight from history and society, its myth of Adamic innocence, and its reconstitution of romance within the novel form. Though somewhat shopworn and battered, this interpretive paradigm – founded by R.W.B. Lewis, Richard Chase, and Leslie Fiedler – continues to inform studies of American literature, and, perhaps more importantly, forms a part of the common sense of American literary history. Further, this understanding of American fiction would seem to disable the social and historical concerns that characterize Marxist critics of the European novel from Lukács to Jameson. If Balzac is the classic instance for a Marxist criticism, Melville would seem to lie beyond its boundaries. However, several New Left critics turned to the work of Georg Lukács to contest or revise our understanding of the American romance. The pioneering efforts were Harry Henderson's use of Lukács's treatment of the historical novel in his *Versions of the Past* (1974), a discussion of the historical fiction written by "classic" American writers, and Myra Jehlen's use of Lukács's distinction between epic and novel, in her "New World Epics: The Novel and the Middle-Class in America" (1977), to recast the romance as a failed flight from an exceptionally pervasive ideological hegemony of the middle class. Yet the most powerful Lukácsian readings of American literature derived from his analysis of the cultural effects of the commodity form, his theory of reification: Michael T. Gilmore's *American Romanticism and the Marketplace* (1985) which analyzes the response of the romantics to the commodification of literature, and Carolyn Porter's *Seeing and Being* (1981), which combines theoretical reflection with close readings to show that the antinomies of participant and observer in American texts are a response to reification. Thus, she argues, we can "no longer either luxuriate or despair in a belief that American literature's classic tradition was defined primarily by a flight from society and the constraints of civilized life, but must at least entertain the possibility that, as a result of the relatively unimpeded development of capitalism in America, its literary history harbors a set of texts in which is inscribed, in its own terms, as deep and as penetrating a response to history and social reality as any to be found in the work of a Balzac or a George Eliot."[17]

The other response by Marxist critics to the exceptionalism of the American romance has been to uncover and recover other literary traditions. A long overdue Marxist reevaluation of the naturalist tradition appeared in June Howard's *Form and History in American Literary Naturalism* (1985) and Rachel Bowlby's *Just Looking* (1985). The work of leftist writers of the 1930s was reexamined by Alan Wald and Robert Rosen, and H. Bruce Franklin's recovery and interpretation of working-class and minority writing founds a thorough revision of American literary history in *The Victim as Criminal and Artist* (1978).[18]

Though Marxist-feminist scholarship focused more on women's work and the politics and economics of gender than on women's writing, the making of a Marxist-feminist literary criticism can be seen in Lillian Robinson's influential collection, *Sex, Class, and Culture* (1978), and Rachel Blau DuPlessis' *Writing Beyond the Ending* (1985), which focuses on the relation between narrative and ideology in women's writing. The important discussion of the politics and ideologies of women's romantic fiction in the work of Ann Snitow, Tania Modleski, and Janice Radway was informed by Marxist-feminist theories of gender and sexuality as well as by Marxist debates over popular literary forms.[19] And a similar concern for popular fiction produced significant Marxist work on science fiction.[20] In these works, Marxist literary criticism moved beyond offering "Marxist readings" of particular texts, and began to reshape the contours of American literary history.

Behind the romance interpretation of American literary history lay perhaps the most durable explanatory framework for American history and culture, the frontier thesis. American studies in many ways restored the centrality of the frontier by shifting the debate from the economic and the political – the frontier as safety valve for class antagonisms, or as the source of democratic institutions – to the ideological – the frontier as a key to the American imagination. From Henry Nash Smith's classic *Virgin Land* (1950) to Richard Slotkin's *Regeneration through Violence* (a 1973 revision provoked by the question "why are we in Vietnam?"), and Annette Kolodny's *The Land Before Her*, a 1984 feminist revision, the study of the myths of the frontier lies close to the heart of the method, content, and politics of American studies. So it is perhaps not surprising that the frontier provoked something very close to a Marxist revision of American culture in the work of Richard Slotkin, Michael Rogin, and Ronald Takaki. Slotkin's *The Fatal Environment* (1985) offers, first, an engagement between the methods and categories of American studies and those of contemporary Marxist cultural criticism, between, in short, "myth" and "ideology;" and second, an argument that, in the frontier myth, "the simple fable of the discovery of new land and the dispossession of the Indians substitutes for the complexities of capital formation, class and interest-group competition, and the subordination of society to the imperatives of capitalist development." Michael Rogin combined historical materialism and a historical psychoanalysis in *Fathers and Children* (1975) and *Subversive Genealogy* (1983) to show how slavery and Indian war in American "primitive accumulation" gave a distinctive racial cast to American class conflict: the "American 1848," he argues, was the struggle over slavery. Ronald Takaki analyzes the domination of various peoples of color within the context of the development of capitalism and class divisions in his *Iron Cages* (1979), a work that draws on both the critical American studies tradition and Marxist theory. Focusing on white "culture-makers and policy makers," he explores the "cultural hegemony" of the republican, corporate, and imperial "iron cages."[21]

What Slotkin, Rogin, and Takaki did was to recast the "special American conditions" of culture in an historical materialist way, suggesting that the uniqueness of the United States lay in the contradictions of a specifically "settler colonial" capitalism. Perhaps the solution to the endless debates about American exceptionalism is to suspend the analogies with the development of capitalism in Western Europe and look to the settler colonial cultures in South Africa, Australia, and North and South America. For when Marx wrote that the account of the development outlined in *Capital* was "*expressly* limited to the *countries of western Europe*," he referred specifically to its path of primitive accumulation. The absence of feudalism in settler colonial societies does not imply the absence of precapitalist modes of production. Capitalism in the settler colonial societies was built not primarily on the expropriation and proletarianization of a peasantry nor on the "gift" of free land, but on the dispossession of the native peoples, imported slave and free labor, and racialized class structures.[22]

From Marx's statement that "labor in a white skin cannot emancipate itself where it is branded in a black skin" to the political controversies between black and white Marxists, and between Marxists and non-Marxists in black liberation movements, the history of slavery and the subsequent entangling of race and class has always been seen by Marxists, in the US and abroad, as fundamental to understanding American history and society.[23] In African-American cultural studies from a Marxist perspective, there has been particular attention to what Cornel West called the "two *organic* intellectual traditions in Afro-American life: *The Black Christian Tradition of Preaching* and *The Black Musical Tradition of Performance*." The interpretation of black religion forms the heart of Eugene Genovese's cultural history, *Roll, Jordan, Roll* (1974), and is central both to Cornel West's treatment of black intellectual traditions in his *Prophecy Deliverance!* (1982) and to V.P. Franklin's elaboration of "mass testimonies" in his *Black Self-Determination* (1984). Black music found interpreters in a number of Marxist traditions, including Popular Front Communism (Sidney Finkelstein), the Frankfurt School (Theodor Adorno), American Trotskyism (Frank Kofsky), and New Left Marxist surrealism (Paul Garon).[24]

A critique of the Black Arts Movement and the "Black Aesthetic" of the 1960s was the starting point for two very different contemporary

Marxist literary theories: Amiri Baraka's Marxist-Leninist essays collected in *Daggers and Javelins* (1984), and the post-structuralist Marxism of Houston Baker's *Blues, Ideology, and Afro-American Literature* (1984). Though one finds its poetry in the political slogan and the other in the tropics of discourse, they both attempt to base literary analysis in a vernacular culture and the material conditions of black life. A cultural materialism grounds the essays of John Brown Childs on Afro-American intellectuals of the early twentieth century, and Hazel Carby's *Reconstructing Womanhood* (1987), a study of the ways nineteenth-century black women writers reconstructed dominant sexual and racial ideologies.[25] These historical materialist analyses of Afro-American culture join the Marxist revisions of the meaning of the myths of the frontier to establish racial formation and conflict rather than wilderness and virgin land as the center of American cultural studies.

Few controversies over the nature of American culture have failed to contest the image of the Puritans. "Perhaps no other historical image, except that of the frontier," Warren Susman noted, "has been so crucial during the development of our culture. Almost unchallenged has been the contention that Puritanism and the Puritan past somehow determined much that has become characteristic of the nation." For American studies, the reassessments of the errand of the "peculiar people" have not only figured the peculiarities of the Americans, but have provided exemplars of the "interdiscipline." For the distance, even marginality, of the Puritans from the canons of orthodox literary criticism, historiography, political science, sociology, and religious studies, combined with their presumed centrality to American culture, has allowed a richness of interdisciplinary work that is unparalleled in other fields of American studies. In the face of this, it is striking that, though the study of English Puritanism is dominated by the prolific Marxist historian Christopher Hill, there was no significant Marxist revision of the New England Puritan past. In part, this may be an implicit challenge to the assumption that the Puritan legacy did determine the characteristics of the United States; and in part, it may be a result of the debate among Marxists as to how to characterize the mode of production of the North American colonies.[26]

Nevertheless, the issue of Puritanism confronted New Left Marxist cultural critics for, in the work of Sacvan Bercovitch, it grounded an influential and powerful version of American exceptionalism. In the rhetoric of the Puritans, particularly in the form of the jeremiad, Bercovitch found the source of "an increasingly pervasive middle-class hegemony": "The ritual of the jeremiad bespeaks an ideological consensus – in moral, religious, economic, social, and intellectual matters – unmatched in any other modern culture." In one sense, Bercovitch's argument adds a formal and rhetorical aspect to what might be called the "Americanism" thesis, the principal ideological answer to the question "why no socialism in America?" This argument is succinctly stated by Leon Samson, a little-known American socialist thinker: "Every concept in socialism has its substitutive counter-concept in Americanism, and that is why the socialist argument falls so fruitlessly on the American ear." Thus, for Bercovitch, no appeal to an American revolution can escape the proleptic force of the tradition of the jeremiad, "the official ritual form of continuing revolution"; the form of the jeremiad has contained and paralyzed American radical dissent. However, Bercovitch himself, in a minor but not insignificant moment, substitutes a Marxist category – hegemony – for his more usual "Americanist" category – consensus.[27] These two issues – the ideology of "Americanism" and the use of hegemony as a substitute for consensus in American studies – have had their widest influence not in Puritan studies but in the debates over American consumer or mass culture.

The discussion of American mass culture involves American exceptionalism in two different ways. First, mass culture, whether celebrated as a culture of affluence, the culture of a people of plenty, or denounced as mass deception, was usually seen not as uniquely American, but as coming from the United States. Unlike the Puritan past or the frontier, mass consumer culture was part of the "American way of life" that could be exported. Second, mass culture has been increasingly invoked as an explanation of the failure of socialism. Whether formulated as the "embourgeoisment" of workers through mass consumerism or as the channeling of desire by the instruments of the mass media, mass culture is often seen as a central aspect of middle-class hegemony in twentieth-century America.

Perhaps because of the international repercussions of "Americanism and

Fordism,"[28] the interpretation and critique of American mass culture is the only area of American studies that engaged the Western Marxists: though Gramsci's prison notes on "Americanism and Fordism" were not translated into English until 1971, the work of the Frankfurt School on mass culture began appearing in English in the journal *Studies in Philosophy and Social Science* in 1939, and essays by Theodor Adorno and Leo Lowenthal were included in the pioneering 1957 anthology, *Mass Culture*.[29] The Frankfurt School's particular analyses of film, television, radio, jazz, magazine serials, and horoscopes found their theoretical base in Adorno and Horkheimer's conception of the "culture industry" and Herbert Marcuse's later account of "one-dimensional man." Elaborating the theory of reification, they explored the distortions and mystifications inherent in the penetration of culture by the commodity form. The experience of fascist culture in Germany combined with the shock of American mass culture led the émigré Frankfurt Marxists on Morningside Heights to an overwhelmingly negative response to the products of the culture industry. The dominance of the commodity form reduced all culture, high and low, to varieties of advertisements. The products of the culture industry were a degeneration of earlier folk and art forms, and numbed and anesthetized the senses.

The Frankfurt School analysis has been criticized as a mirror image of conservative cultural elitism, and as an undialectical picture of a logic of the commodity that permits neither contradiction nor resistance; indeed, it became common for Marxist and non-Marxist discussions of mass culture to open with ritual exorcisms of the Frankfurt School. However, within Frankfurt critical theory, an alternative view of the "age of mechanical reproduction" could be found in the essays of Walter Benjamin and the later work of Herbert Marcuse. The controversies within and over the Frankfurt critique of mass culture reinvigorated discussions of mass, consumer, or popular culture.[30] Perhaps the most important and influential theoretical reformulation was Fredric Jameson's "Reification and Utopia in Mass Culture" (1979). After arguing that we must "read high and mass culture as objectively related and dialectically interdependent phenomena, as twin and inseparable forms of the fission of aesthetic production under late capitalism," Jameson suggested that "works of mass culture cannot be ideological without at one and the same time being implicitly or explicitly Utopian as well"; his interpretations attempt to avoid both denunciation and celebration by showing that works of mass culture cannot "manage anxieties about the social order unless they have first revived them and given them some rudimentary expression."[31]

Among the New Left works that analyzed the institutions and products of the culture industry, Stuart Ewen's pioneering study of advertising, *Captains of Consciousness* (1976), was perhaps the most directly inspired by the Frankfurt School, and was criticized for its depiction of the overwhelming power of advertising to shape desire and paralyze dissent; a more dialectical understanding of mass culture emerged in the subsequent book by Elizabeth and Stuart Ewen, *Channels of Desire* (1982). The work of Herbert Schiller focused on the economic organization of the culture industry, with particular attention to its international power. The related work of the Chilean Ariel Dorfman focused on the impact of American mass culture in Latin America, in the classic *How to Read Donald Duck* (1975) and *The Empire's Old Clothes* (1983). Todd Gitlin drew on the Marxist cultural theory of Stuart Hall in a detailed analysis of the effects of news coverage on oppositional movements, *The Whole World is Watching* (1980), and in one of the first significant studies of entertainment television, *Inside Prime Time* (1983).[32]

Film studies, which developed somewhat separately, has had a vital Marxist strain, particularly in Europe: American films were the subject of such classic essays as "John Ford's *Young Mr. Lincoln*" by the editors of *Cahiers du Cinéma* and Laura Mulvey's "Visual pleasure and narrative cinema" in the British journal *Screen*. American Marxist film studies developed in such journals as *Jump Cut* and *Cineaste*, and in the work of Bill Nichols, E. Ann Kaplan, Peter Biskind, and Robert Ray.[33]

A dissatisfaction with an exclusive focus on the institutions and products of mass culture, and with assumptions of a passive and undifferentiated audience, provoked a number of works that focused on the intersection of mass culture and class cultures. One line of work, following key essays by Martin Sklar on the cultural consequences of capitalism's transition from accumulation to "disaccumulation," and by Barbara and John Ehrenreich on the "professional-managerial class," explored the relations between mass culture, the new middle classes, and an emerging culture of abundance, consumption, and personality.[34]

Stanley Aronowitz's *False Promises* (1973), on the other hand, remains the most ambitious attempt to interpret working-class history through the analysis of the effects of the commodity form on the labor process and culture, "trivialized work, colonized leisure." Further, it stands as one of the few works that places the experience of American workers at the center of a thorough revision of American cultural history. For, though the "new" labor history of the 1960s and 1970s reconstructed the picture of American workers and their lives, it did not fundamentally revise American cultural history.[35] "The story of American culture," according to socialist cultural historian Warren Susman, "remains largely the story of . . . the enormous American middle class." However, by the 1980s, work building on the "new" labor history began to interpret American culture as the product of conflicts between classes and class fractions: Dan Schiller's *Objectivity and the News* (1981) reinterprets the rise of the penny press through an attention to its artisan readers; my own *Mechanic Accents* (1987) interprets cheap sensational fiction by reconstructing its place within working-class culture; and Roy Rosenzweig's *Eight Hours for What We Will* (1983) examines the class conflicts over institutions of culture and leisure – the saloon, the nickelodeon, parks, and holiday celebrations. Sarah Eisenstein's path breaking essays on working women's consciousness were followed by Elizabeth Ewen's *Immigrant Women in the Land of Dollars* (1985), which examines the contradictory impact of American mass culture on Italian and Jewish immigrant women, and Kathy Peiss' *Cheap Amusements* (1986), which analyzes the rituals and styles of working women's leisure activities. George Lipsitz offered a provocative view of the class origins of the popular culture of the 1940s and 1950s in *Class and Culture in the Cold War* (1982). Perhaps the major revisionist synthesis was Alan Trachtenberg's *The Incorporation of America* (1982), which explores the effects of the corporate system on culture, and interprets the literal and figurative struggles between "incorporation" and "union" in the late nineteenth century.[36]

Finally, there were a few major contributions to Marxist cultural theory by North American Marxists. Clearly the most influential figure was Fredric Jameson. *Marxism and Form* in many ways inaugurated the revival of

Marxist cultural theory, and *The Political Unconscious* (1981), which included both a model for Marxist interpretation and a rewriting of the history of the novel, was probably the most debated Marxist cultural text of the period.[37] Stanley Aronowitz's *The Crisis of Historical Materialism* engaged tendencies in European Marxism from the standpoint of American developments in politics and theory, and offered an important rethinking of Marxism through cultural categories. Bertell Ollman's *Alienation* (1976) was a major contribution to the elaboration of Marx's theory. Richard Ohmann's *English in America* (1976) stands as a major critique of a central discipline of cultural studies, and the engagement of Marxism with other critical theories was the focus of Michael Ryan's *Marxism and Deconstruction* (1982), John Fekete's *The Critical Twilight* (1977), and Frank Lentricchia's *Criticism and Social Change*. Cornel West charted the relationship between Marxism and several strands of American thought: Afro-American critical thought, pragmatism, and Christianity. And though Edward Said's *The World, the Text, and the Critic* (1983) stands self-consciously apart from Marxism, the "oppositional criticism" and "cultural materialism" it develops both draw on and offer much to contemporary Marxists.[38]

Why Marxism?

A reader may follow me thus far, and still step back and echo Edward Said who, in discussing his relation to Marxism, noted that he had "been more influenced by Marxists than by Marxism or by any other ism." Indeed, some of the writers I have cited do take Said's position and are reluctant to call themselves Marxists. Why call oneself a Marxist? Why not be pragmatic, American, and take from Marxists what works and leave the rest, including that foreign, "un-American" name? Let me conclude by suggesting some answers.[39]

First, there is a political reason. Though by no means the only tradition of socialist thought, Marxism remains the dominant and most developed body of theory and practice in socialist movements. As a result it is an international discourse with an international vocabulary. Spoken in a variety of national and continental accents, it remains, for socialists, a way of avoiding the provincialities of an American tradition – "Emersonianism," Irving Howe dubs it – without ignoring the peculiarities of the United States.

Second, Marxism provides a tradition, a paradigm, a "problematic:" a discourse united not by a dogma nor by a set of fixed assumptions, but by a set of questions. In the case of Marxism, these are neither eternal philosophical questions nor pragmatic technical questions of efficiency, but they are questions raised in the last instance by the politics of emancipation, by the need for a critical understanding of the world. Such a problematic is necessary in part to avoid the tyranny of fashion in contemporary theory – who will be the theorist to know and cite next year? – but also because, as the theoretical and historical work of Said and Lentricchia themselves demonstrates, cultural power, even in America, does not lie with parties of one, but in the "affiliations," to use Said's term, an intellectual makes. Despite American antinomianism, just as there is no fully "authored" discourse of one, there are no "parties of one." We are condemned to affiliation. Said argues:

> It is the case, with cultural or aesthetic activity that the possibilities and circumstances of its production get their authority by virtue of what I have called affiliation, that implicit network of peculiarly cultural associations between forms, statements, and other aesthetic elaborations on the one hand, and, on the other, institutions, agencies, classes, and amorphous social forces.

By affiliation, then, I mean more than simply political party affiliation, though that was the focus of the purge of the academy in the 1950s. The New Left revision of American cultural history depended not only on the social movements of 1968 but on the networks established among socialist scholars: the Socialist Scholars Conferences of 1965–70, revived annually after 1983; and the journals, both those, like *Science and Society, Dissent*, and *Monthly Review*, which survived from the old left, and those, like *Socialist Revolution* (later *Socialist Review*) and *Radical America*, that were products of the New Left. The journals of the new Marxist cultural studies flourished in the 1970s and 1980s: *Social Text*, *Cultural Correspondence*, *Tabloid: A Review of*

Mass Culture and Everyday Life, *Praxis*, *Radical History Review*, *Radical Teacher*, *Minnesota Review*, *Cultural Critique*, and the short-lived *Marxist Perspectives*.[40]

Third, Marxism does offer one of the few coherent alternatives to the search for an "interdisciplinary method" that has long haunted American studies. The dream of semiotics as a master science of signs and the structuralist promise of uniting the disciplines around a common linguistic model both faded in the face of post-structuralist critiques and the skepticism of historians. "Modernization theory" made a comeback in American studies when its life in sociology seemed over, but it remains, with its traditional/modern dichotomy, more reductive than even Second International Marxism. Indeed, precisely because of the economistic reductionism of early versions of the base/superstructure model, Marxists are more aware of the dangers of reductionism and essentialism than most other scholars: it is among non-Marxists that one finds reductive and essentialist accounts like Marvin Harris's "cultural materialism," the appeal to the last instance of demography, and accounts of the "essence" of a nation, race, gender, or period.[41]

Indeed, Marxism now has a number of ways of considering the relationship between culture and society, of showing how "social being determines social consciousness," of dealing with the issues raised by the metaphor of base and superstructure.[42] We can characterize the four main modes of Marxist cultural studies at present by their central concepts: commodity/reification; ideology; class/hegemony; and cultural materialism.

The first is based on Marx's account of the fetishism of commodities and Lukács's subsequent elaboration of the theory of reification. The effects of the commodity form on culture: this lens dominates much of the work of the Frankfurt School and of Fredric Jameson, and finds its particular strengths both in illuminating the inscription of the social on apparently apolitical modernist and postmodernist texts, and in the analysis of the mass-produced formulas of the culture industry.

The second line of work draws on the concept of ideology. As Slotkin recognizes, this is close to the "myth/symbol" approach to American studies. It analyzes the lineaments and functions of ideologies, as a crucial mediation between texts and institutions. This work has been enriched by the displacement of notions of ideology as a systematic world view or as a false consciousness by recent Marxist redefinitions: Louis Althusser's sense of ideology as a social process of addressing and constituting subjects; Fredric Jameson's notion of ideology as narrative in form; and Terry Eagleton's examination of "aesthetic ideologies."[43]

The third mode begins from Marxist theories of class, and attempts to specify the relations between class and culture. If this had led to occasional reductiveness when applied to individual artists, it has proved indispensable in analyses of working-class cultures, youth subcultures, slave cultures, the impact and uses of mass culture, traditional and invented cultural institutions, and the uses of leisure time. Gramsci's theoretical framework – hegemony, "historical bloc," "common sense/good sense," the national-popular – have allowed this work to escape both the class reductiveness where, as Nicos Poulantzas joked, classes wear their cultures like license plates, and the liberal appropriation of hegemony as a more sophisticated and more fashionable synonym for consensus.[44]

The fourth direction of Marxist cultural studies focuses on the material production and consumption of culture. It is exemplified by Raymond Williams's project of "cultural materialism: a theory of the specificities of material cultural and literary production within historical materialism." Williams's attention to the processes of the "selective traditions," to cultural institutions, formations, means of production, and conventions, and to the relationships of dominant, residual, alternative, oppositional, and emergent cultures provides the conceptual frame for such work.[45]

None of these paradigms exist in isolation from the others; nevertheless, they do indicate tendencies and emphases in contemporary work. The first two tend to be more text-oriented, more "literary-critical;" the latter two tend to engage more in historical or sociological work. Together they offer a rich and complex approach to cultural studies. This new American Marxism has its weaknesses, deriving, as Edward Said notes, from "the comparative absence of a continuous native Marxist theoretical tradition or culture to back it up and its relative isolation from any concrete political struggle."[46] But to dismiss it as "academic Marxism" is to ignore the relative autonomy of cultural work, and to mistake the nature of the academy in American society. The post-World War II university is a part of mass culture, of the culture industry, a central economic and ideological apparatus of American capitalism. Though right-wing nightmares of a Marxist takeover of the humanities were particularly absurd in the reign of Reagan and Bennett, it is worth recalling that, in the development of Marxism, it has been in times of political defeat and downturn that theoretical and cultural works have ripened, often at an unavoidable distance from working-class struggles. To these labors of reconstructing a critical and emancipatory understanding of American culture, one might eventually say, "well worked, old mole."

10

THE PECULIARITIES OF THE AMERICANS: RECONSIDERING *DEMOCRACY IN AMERICA*

The attempt in the previous chapter to juxtapose, articulate, interrogate, perhaps even reconcile the renaissance in the Marxist tradition, particularly in cultural studies, with the history and interpretation of American culture, particularly as it is organized by American studies, led me to some old questions, the questions of American exceptionalism, of why is there no socialism in the United States, of, to amend one of E.P. Thompson's titles, the "peculiarities of the Americans."

One possible, and all too tempting, response to these boring old questions is to dismiss them as meaningless questions. To speak of American exceptionalism is to presume a norm from which it deviates, and the proliferation of peculiar national developments – there are even peculiarities of the English, whose development Marx takes as the classic form – throws the existence of any such norm into doubt. Similarly, we may dismiss the 1905 question posed by the German sociologist Werner Sombart – "why is there no socialism in the United States?" – as one of those fruitless negative historical questions; as Aileen Kraditor puts it, the Sombartian approach is "counterfactual . . . tautological . . . teleological . . . antihistorical . . . and reductionist." The trouble with dismissing one or another form of the question is that the underlying theoretical, historical, and political issues remain unresolved. Is there something distinctive about American development, culture, national character, and social history? And, if so, does this limit the relevance of European – and particularly Marxist – social theories? For that is the issue: not only the historical question of why American workers have demonstrated so little class consciousness and why no major social-democratic, labor, or Communist party emerged, but the theoretical question of whether the categories of historical materialism can illuminate United States culture and society, or whether, as the critic Frank Lentricchia put it, "while it may come close to impossible to think about progressive change without engaging Marxist categories, . . . an American ('self-reliant') Marxism is fundamentally an absurd proposition."[1]

In this chapter, I want to think about the meaning of American exceptionalism in the age of three worlds, by returning to the work that served as the founding text for the American ideology, Tocqueville's *Democracy in America.* "Ignoring Tocqueville, the first theorist of 'American exceptionalism'," the historian John Diggins wrote, "New Left scholars drew on Marx and Engels, Gramsci, and Hegel for their analytical tools."[2] This was a mistake, Diggins maintains. Since Diggins's description is correct in the case of this "New Left scholar," I come to Tocqueville neither as a Tocqueville scholar nor as a disinterested reader of a classic; rather, accepting Diggins's challenge, I come first in search of the theoretical and analytical tools that would lead me to place *Democracy in America* next to *Capital* and the *Prison Notebooks* on my bookshelf. But I also come to Tocqueville because of his canonic status, the authority of his text in American culture.

In 1956, Clinton Rossiter wrote that "No book on an American subject is thought complete these days without a few insightful words from Alexis de Tocqueville." This had not always been the case. The several accounts of the history of the reception of *Democracy in America* tell basically the same story: written after a nine-month visit to the United States in 1831 and 1832, it was published as two books: the first in 1835, the second in 1840, and it met with extraordinarily wide acclaim in France, Britain, and the United States. After the Civil War, however, it was eclipsed. Robert Nisbet notes that "from the late 1860s to the late 1930s only an occasional monograph or article on Tocqueville appeared – nothing, really, that lifted him from the ranks of literally dozens of other French writers of the early nineteenth century." The historians Marshall and Drescher point out that the major American historians of the period, Frederick Jackson Turner and Charles Beard, "found no use for Tocqueville in their creative periods." The revival of Tocqueville may be dated to George Pierson's 1938 history, *Tocqueville and Beaumont in America* or to Knopf's 1945 edition of *Democracy in America*; in either case, as Warren Susman put it in 1965, "those who quoted (or misquoted) Marx in the 1930s now without fail quote Tocqueville." Susman's juxtaposition of Tocqueville and Marx is not accidental; for the post-World War II revival set Tocqueville against Marx, a point agreed upon by the conservative Nisbet, the liberal Diggins, and the socialist Susman. I will continue to set Tocqueville beside Marx, though I hope to avoid the temptations of either a Cold War polarization – Tocqueville versus Marx – or an easy appropriation, making Tocqueville a Marxist before Marx.[3]

What is most remarkable about Tocqueville's canonic status is not so much the development of a Tocquevillian social or political theory: only a few sociologists have attempted to set him alongside Comte, Durkheim, and Weber or to elaborate systematically the principles of a Tocquevillian sociology. Rather his status comes from the quotation. Tocqueville's place in American culture is that of the epigraph, whether literally placed at the head of the book or chapter, or inscribed in an introduction or conclusion. I will come back to the epigrammatic nature of Tocqueville's prose; for now I want to suggest that Tocqueville's canonic status depends on observations, both in the sense of something seen and in the sense of an idle remark, rather than in a theoretical framework. This leads to the curious structure of a key work in the revival of Tocqueville, Louis Hartz's brilliant *The Liberal Tradition in America* of 1955. Hartz builds his classic account of the peculiarities of the Americans – based on the ways the absence of feudalism has allowed an unchallenged liberal tradition, an "irrational Lockianism," to dominate American political thought – on an epigraph taken from Tocqueville: "The great advantage of the Americans is, that they arrived at a state of democracy without having to endure a democratic revolution; and that they are born equal, instead of becoming so." However, Hartz – who is scathingly scornful of American Marxists: "the American Marxist learns nothing and forgets nothing" – elaborates Tocqueville's observation about the Americans through a consistent and explicit use of Trotsky's "law of combined and uneven development," producing a curious anti-Marxist Tocquevillian Marxism.[4]

More often, however, the use of the authoritative Tocqueville epigraph allows the writer to assert something which is a fundamental presupposition of the work, but whose proof is absent or perhaps even excluded from the text. These presuppositions include, in various writers, the assumptions that American culture is democratic, egalitarian, homogeneous, middle-class, traceable to the Puritans, individualistic, and white. These may be obvious, or obviously wrong, depending on your perspective, but with an introduction like this it is not surprising that New Left scholars rarely turned to Tocqueville. Let us turn to *Democracy in America* to see whether he has been well-served by his canonizers.

I want to begin with two preliminary considerations: the question of Tocqueville's situation as an interpreter of the United States, and the question of the degree to which *Democracy in America* is about the United States. Tocqueville was a young French aristocrat (only twenty-five when he arrived in the United States) with a training in the law and a position as a kind of apprentice magistrate who, along with his friend Beaumont, arranged to visit the United States in 1831 under the avowed purpose of studying the innovative prison systems of Jacksonian America, but also to avoid the political turmoil that followed the July revolution of 1830. To anyone in the Marxist tradition, *Democracy in America* has an eerie familiarity; it is less in the genres of travel writing or social theory than in the genre Hans Enzensberger called "tourism of the revolution." Though Tocqueville denies writing a panegyric, the effect, certainly of the 1835 volume, is not far from Lincoln Steffens's famous response to Soviet Russia: "I have been over into the future, and it works." "I did not study America just to satisfy curiosity," Tocqueville writes in his introduction, "I sought there lessons from which we might profit." I remark on this because Tocqueville shared this with other European liberals, radicals, and socialists who came to the United States; and to see Tocqueville, Harriet Martineau, Frances Wright, Thomas Hamilton, the Owenite John Finch, the Chartist Lawrence Pitkeithley as simply "foreign travelers," observers of the United States, is to miss the rich ideological motives that produced these reports of a new world. As Lewis Feuer persuasively argued some years ago, a crucial element in the emerging communism of young Marx and Engels was their reading of travelers' accounts of North America, particularly the numerous reports of the utopian communist communities, and Thomas Hamilton's description, in his 1833 *Men and Manners in America*, of the Workingman's Party in New York, both of which, by the way, are missing from Tocqueville's *Democracy in America*.[5]

Moreover, Tocqueville's point of view, and as George Pierson points out, the enthusiastic reception of Tocqueville and Beaumont in the United States, was influenced by the project to study American penal practice and reform. One could read Tocqueville's America through the categories of penal discipline and punishment with which he was engaged: the debates over solitary confinement and over the delicate balancing of consent and coercion. When Tocqueville writes of the innovative Sing Sing that "although the discipline is perfect, one feels that it rests on fragile foundations: it is due to a *tour de force* which is reborn unceasingly and which has to be reproduced each day," one hears an echo of his account of the fragile foundations of the American Union.[6]

On a more general level, however, Tocqueville's privilege as an interpreter of the United States derives from the privilege Tocqueville accords to "the position of lawyers as interpreters." Tocqueville's fascinating discussion of lawyers constitutes his theory of the intellectual. In a social state where all are equal, lawyers are the tricksters:

> By birth and interest a lawyer is one of the people, but he is an aristocrat in his habits and tastes. . . . Lawyers, forming the only enlightened class not distrusted by the people, are naturally called on to fill most public functions. The legislatures are full of them, and they head administrations. . . . In the United States the lawyers constitute a power which is little dreaded and hardly noticed . . . it enwraps the whole of society, penetrating each component class and constantly working in secret upon its unconscious patient, till in the end it has molded it to its desire. . . . the whole people have contracted some of the ways and tastes of a magistrate.

If, for Veblen, the Soviet Union was a "soviet of technicians," for Tocqueville, one might say, America was a democracy of lawyers.[7]

The second preliminary question is to what extent is *Democracy in America* about the United States. Tocqueville's desire to *extract* lessons from the American experience leads him to *abstract* democracy from America. As a result, *Democracy in America* is not simply a book about America; it is also a book about democracy. Early in the second volume, that of 1840, Tocqueville criticizes the tendency of "some Europeans" to "unintentionally . . . confuse what is democratic with what is only American;" it is a tendency, however, that runs throughout his work, but which any interpreter must come to terms with. In the beginning he saw the work as about America: "We are leaving," he wrote in 1831, "with the intention of examining, in detail and as scientifically as possible, all the mechanism of that vast American society which every one talks of and no one knows. And if events leave us the time, we are counting on bringing back the elements of a fine work or, at the very least, of a new work; for there is nothing on this subject." By 1838, as he finished the second volume, he wrote in a letter:

> Now that I can see nearly the whole book, I perceive that it is much more a question of the general effects of equality on mores than of the particular effects that it produces in America. Is that bad? Is my former reader so tied to what I already said of the United States that he will follow me only regretfully onto another terrain? In short, does he like America better than me?[8]

In practice, interpreters make a choice. Sociologists and political theorists attempting to elaborate a Tocquevillian theory of mass society or democratic institutions tend to treat the American material as illustrative, finding common themes in his later writings on the French Revolution, on England and Ireland, and on slavery in Algeria. Students of American culture elaborate his accounts of the peculiarities of the Americans, and use his observations as a primary – even original – source. I will try to consider both his theory and his history in making three arguments about *Democracy in America*: the first has to do with his master concept, "equality of conditions"; the second with his "theory of association"; and the third with the relation between theory and narrative in his account of the peculiarities of the Americans.

"Equality of conditions" is Tocqueville's master concept, and it unites "democracy" and "America." *Democracy in America* opens by stating:

> No novelty in the United States struck me more vividly during my stay there than the equality of conditions. It was easy to see the immense influence of this basic fact on the whole course of society. . . . I soon realized that the influence of this fact extends far beyond political mores and laws, exercising dominion over civil society as much as over the government; it creates opinions, gives birth to feelings, suggests customs, and modifies whatever it does not create.

Indeed in the preface to volume two, Tocqueville feels it necessary to warn the reader that "Noticing how many effects I hold due to equality, he might suppose that I consider equality the sole cause of everything that is happening now. That would be a very narrow view to attribute to me." Nevertheless, after quickly suggesting some other factors, he does admit that he wishes to demonstrate how equality has modified our inclinations and our ideas.[9]

Though Tocqueville is often accused of neglecting economic and material circumstances in his detailed accounts of political institutions and the realm of ideology, what he calls mores, this seems to me unjust. For he is, in many ways, a historical materialist. It is true that he rejects what he calls materialist explanations – those based on geography, climate, and race – but these are what Marxists characterize as vulgar materialisms. For Tocqueville, as for Marx, social being determines social consciousness, the base conditions the superstructure.

> The social state is commonly the result of circumstances, sometimes of laws, but most often of a combination of the two. But once it has come into being, it may itself be considered as the prime cause of most of the laws, customs, and ideas which control the nation's behavior; it modifies even those things which it does not cause. . . . I have no doubt that the social and political structure of a nation predisposes people in favor of certain tastes and beliefs which then flourish carefree; and the same reason, without deliberate striving and indeed almost unconsciously, keeps other opinions and inclinations out of mind.[10]

No: the trouble with Tocqueville's account is not that it ignores material conditions, "the social state," but that his account of those conditions is simply wrong. "Equality of conditions" as Tocqueville defines them – equality of rights, of mental endowments (through equality of education), and equality of fortune – did not exist even among white men in the Jacksonian America Tocqueville visited. The key point is "equality of fortunes." I am not holding Tocqueville and Jacksonian America to an absolute equality of wealth and income that he never intended to imply. But as the historian Edward Pessen has carefully and persuasively shown, none of the key features of Tocqueville's egalitarian premise – that "fortunes are scanty" by contemporary European standards, that "most of the rich men were formerly poor," (only two percent of the Jacksonian economic elite were born poor, and only six percent started in "middling" circumstances), that fortunes were "insecure," with wealth circulating with "inconceivable rapidity," that there was an increasing distribution, that is equalization, of wealth, and that "the more affluent classes of society are . . . directly removed from the direction of political affairs in the United States" – none of these stand up to historical examination.[11] Since Pessen is a historian rather than a theorist, concerned with revising understanding of Jacksonian America rather than challenging Tocqueville's theoretical framework, he does not really ask the question that I, with his help, will ask. What remains of Tocqueville's theory if we reject the central premise of equality of conditions? Many of his specific observations of mores may stand, but they cannot be considered effects of equality unless one wants to redefine equality as simply political equality, something Tocqueville rightly does not do.

One response is simply to find another theory that offers a more adequate account of the American social state than does Tocqueville. I will return to this possibility, but first I want suggest that this serious limitation does not vitiate the interest of the book. Nonetheless, it demands a different reading. Liberals – those whose problematic is defined by the central antinomies of freedom and equality, individual and society, the useful and the aesthetic, minority culture and mass civilization, and so on – have read Tocqueville by accepting and assuming the egalitarian premise, and thus emphasizing the Tocqueville who writes that "men's taste for freedom and their taste for equality are in fact distinct . . . and among democracies they are two unequal elements."[12] This is the Tocqueville who writes on the dangers equality holds for freedom: the tyranny of the majority, the tyranny of public opinion, and so forth.

If, on the other hand, we do not assume equality of conditions, we may see what Tocqueville thought necessary for an egalitarian democracy. The key section is his theory of association. For freedom in Tocqueville does not mean protecting individualism; individualism is a clear danger. Freedom is quintessentially the freedom of association. A free press, for example, is discussed not so much in terms of freedom of speech but in terms of associations: "there is a necessary connection between associations and newspapers. . . . hardly any democratic association can carry on without a newspaper. . . . the newspaper represents the association." Let us look closer at the consequences of the fact that "Americans of all ages, all stations in life, and all types of disposition are forever forming associations." For in Tocqueville's account of associations lie the energies and contradictions of his larger theory.[13]

There are two principal types of associations, political and civil. Political associations are "great free schools to which all citizens come to be taught the general theory of association. . . . Thus . . . the technique of association becomes the mother of every other technique; everyone studies and applies it." This technique he elsewhere calls the "knowledge of how to combine." "If men are to remain civilized or to become civilized," he continues, "the art of association must develop and improve among them at the same speed as equality of conditions spreads." Clearly political parties are a central form of political association; but the energy of Tocqueville's concept comes not from particular parties but from a "permanent association," the New England township. The New England township with its equality of conditions, town meeting government, administration by selectmen, and local autonomy is to Tocqueville what the commodity is to Marx, the simple, if paradoxical, starting point. It is, he says, "to liberty what primary schools are to science . . . they teach people to appreciate its peaceful enjoyment and accustom them to make use of it." The township is the fundamental structure in Tocqueville's account of the way federation solves the classic dilemma of extended republics by combining governmental centralization with administrative decentralization. And indeed the centrality of the township is negatively demonstrated in the famous and ominous footnote about the growth of cities: "I regard the size of some American cities and especially the nature of their inhabitants ["a rabble, . . . freed Negroes condemned by law and opinion to a hereditary state of degradation" and "a crowd of Europeans driven by misfortune or misbehavior to the shores of the New World"] as a real danger threatening the future of the democratic republics of the New World, and I should not hesitate to predict that it is through them that they will perish, unless their government succeeds in creating an armed force which, while remaining subject to the wishes of the national majority, is independent of the peoples of the towns and capable of suppressing their excesses."[14]

The other form of association is civil, private association. This takes two forms: what he calls "intellectual and moral associations" and "manufacturing and trading companies." This is a fateful conflation. Usually in Tocqueville and certainly in his revivalists, the capitalist enterprise becomes one of many civil associations, whose free activity is necessary to the preservation of equality and freedom; here then is one source of theories of "democratic capitalism." It is an ironic conflation for two reasons. First, in the 1830s, the term association was commonly used to refer to the cooperative communities based on religious or socialist principles that were springing up across North America. They were of intense interest to European visitors and to the journeymen of the American cities. At the risk of overstatement, but in the interests of defamiliarization, let me suggest that, to the contemporary eye, the communist experiments at Brook Farm and New Harmony may not have seemed any more or less utopian than the capitalist experiments at Lowell. Second, though Tocqueville may have appropriated the democratic term, association, to baptize "manufacturing and trading companies," he did at times recognize the resulting tension. For in the chapter, "How An Aristocracy May Be Created By Industry," where he says that "the manufacturing aristocracy which we see rising before our eyes is one of the hardest that have appeared on earth" and may bring back "permanent inequality of conditions," he also notes the limits of the theory of association: "Between workman and master there are frequent relations but no true association."[15]

I want to turn now to my third argument which has to do with Tocqueville's rhetorical strategy, particularly the meaning of the gap between theory, or what he calls "generalization," and narrative in *Democracy in America.* F.O. Matthiessen said that "the quality that makes Tocqueville's book the most penetrating study of our society ever written by a European . . . is his rare ability to ground philosophic generalizations on trenchantly observed and representative facts."[16] This is simply not true unless "a trenchantly observed and representative fact" is really already a high level of generalization. Tocqueville is himself more accurate when he asserts that "starting from a theoretical approach, I came to the same conclusions that they [educated Englishmen observing the Americans] had reached empirically." I haven't yet worked out the appropriate rhetorical labels, but let me list briefly the rhetorical structures that dominate this book, particularly the ones that give the effect of "a trenchantly observed and representative fact." First, there is the epigram, the real reason Tocqueville seems so wise and so quotable. He is a master of this concise, polished, and often antithetical genre. Opening the book at random, my eye catches the telltale single sentence paragraph: "No American public official has a uniform, but all receive salaries."[17]

Second, he constructs facts by balanced oppositions, the main ones being "in aristocracies, it is this, in democracies, it is that," "In France, we do thus, in America, they do otherwise." I quote this in epigrammatic form – "Aristocracies produce a few great pictures, democracies a multitude of little ones" – but the principle is extended through sentences, paragraphs, and chapters.[18]

Third, there is the representative narrative:

> An American navigator leaves Boston to go and buy tea in China. He arrives at Canton, stays a few days there, and comes back. In less than two years he has gone around the whole globe, and only once has he seen land. Throughout a voyage of eight or ten months he has drunk brackish water and eaten salted meat; he has striven continually against

> the sea, disease, and boredom; but on his return he can sell tea a farthing cheaper than an English merchant can: he has attained his aim.
>
> I cannot express my thoughts better than by saying that the Americans put something heroic into their way of trading.[19]

This and many other miniature narratives of "the American" are, one might say, the "socialist realism" of the young American republic, against which we might place *Moby Dick* itself.

Finally, there is the deductive narrative, in which an opening generalization informs an omniscient narration: take this excerpt from his history of American political parties:

> America is the land of democracy.
>
> Consequently, the Federalists were always in a minority, but they included almost all the great men thrown up by the War of Independence, and their moral authority was very far-reaching. . . . The ruin of the first Confederation made the people afraid of falling into anarchy, and the Federalists profited from this passing tendency. For ten or twelve years they directed affairs . . .
>
> In 1801, the Republicans finally got control of the government. Thomas Jefferson was elected President; he brought them the support of a famous name, great talents, and immense popularity . . .
>
> The Federalists, feeling themselves defeated, without resources, and isolated within the nation, divided up. . . . For many years now they have entirely ceased to exist as a party.
>
> The period of Federalist power was, in my view, one of the luckiest circumstances attending the birth of the great American Union.[20]

This canonizing history gains its authority because the reader doesn't know that, as Lewis Feuer put it, "Tocqueville's discussions and interviews were largely with disillusioned Federalists; as a sociological interviewer, his sample was distinctly unrepresentative."[21] Feuer's debunking aside, Tocqueville's characteristic elision of his own authorities points, however, to a remarkable absence in his book: the paucity of anecdote, observation, and reported dialogue that one expects and finds in the other travel narratives of foreign visitors to the United States. There are only eighteen such travel anecdotes in the first volume, and only six in the second. What is interesting, however, is not only the absence of this common rhetorical framework – Americans are like this because I saw this in Chicago, or someone told me this in St. Louis – but the striking nature of its presence. None of the six in the second volume is particularly significant; they total only ten paragraphs in three hundred pages. But fully half of them in the first volume concern American Indians and American blacks; indeed a third of the anecdotes appear in the long chapter on the "present state and probable future of the three races that inhabit the territory of the United States," a chapter which begins "I have now finished the main task. . . . I could stop here."[22]

The dispossession of Indians and the enslavement of Africans disrupt the rhetorical and theoretical structures of *Democracy in America*. He writes that "with my own eyes I have seen some of the miseries just described; I have witnessed afflictions beyond my powers to portray." Paradoxically, this means that he is unable to write a representative or deductive narrative, and turns instead to the traveler's anecdote. It is not that he doesn't try to incorporate the other two races into his theory; he makes them figures of the extremes of freedom: "The Negro has reached the ultimate limits of slavery, whereas the Indian lives on the extreme end of freedom. The effect of slavery on the former is not more fatal than that of independence on the latter." But the narrative digressions – his witnessing of the Iroquois reduced to begging and of the removal of the Choctaws, his encounter with the slave owner delirious at his death over the fate of his slave sons – take over the chapter, and the moment when he meets, at a forest spring in Alabama, a Negro woman, an Indian woman, and a white child, presents his most striking tableau of the peculiarities of the Americans.[23]

It is not enough to overturn the structure of his book; and references to either Indians or blacks are rare in *Democracy in America* outside of that appended chapter. Even when he gets to the conclusion that immediately follows the chapter on the three races of North America, he is able to write, "In truth . . . there are only two rival races sharing the New World today: the Spaniards and the English." The contradiction occasionally surfaces. In a chapter entitled "Why Great Revolutions Will Become Rare," a canonic chapter in most interpretations of Tocqueville – "as there is no longer a race of poor men, so there is not a race of rich men;" "in no other country in the world is the love of property keener . . . and nowhere else does the majority display less inclination toward doctrines which in any way threaten the way property is owned" – it is in this chapter that, as an aside, Tocqueville notes: "If there ever are great revolutions there, they will be caused by the presence of the blacks on American soil."[24]

Racial division, the presence of three peoples with radically distinct relationships to the social state, is the exception on which Tocqueville as the first theorist of American exceptionalism founders. It is a tribute to his intellectual range that he did write that final extra chapter of the first volume; though it may also be a tribute to his lesser-known collaborator Beaumont who returned to France to write his American book, not *Democracy in America* but *Marie, or Slavery in the United States*. It is not that Tocqueville does not identify many of the factors that make the North American republic different; but he shares this with a number of nineteenth-century observers, including Engels in several of his letters to Americans. Rather, an adequate theory of American exceptionalism must be able to unite "democracy in America" with "slavery in America" and "Indian dispossession in America" in a persuasive way. Thus to conclude I want to briefly mention two contemporary works, one from a Tocquevillian tradition and one from a Marxist perspective, which offer directions for a theory of American exceptionalism.

The most interesting of the latter-day Americanist Tocquevillians, Louis Hartz, seems to have repeated Tocqueville's own antinomy. *The Liberal Tradition in America*, based on the epigram about Americans being "born equal," spoke little of slavery and Indian removal and less of blacks and Indians. But Hartz's consistent demand for comparative history, for avoiding the provincialities of a nationalist history, his firm if ironic belief in the law of combined and uneven development, and, one imagines, the development of the movement for civil rights and black liberation, led him in the early 1960s to a creative approach to American exceptionalism which has not been greatly developed since. In *The Founding of New Societies*, he began a comparative history of a number of settler societies, using the comparison as a tool for generating new questions about American (and other) histories. Not that he implied that the settler societies were identical;

rather their family resemblances allowed him to highlight individual peculiarities. His theoretical model was idealist, quasi-Hegelian, seeing the settler societies as fragments of European ideologies incorporated in new settings. Obviously this drew on his account of Locke planted in North America, but I would suggest that the essential trope of his theory lies in the traditional account of the French language in Quebec. Brought to Quebec at a particular moment and subsequently preserved from European developments, the French of Quebec became a curiously archaic language. Interestingly, Tocqueville fades in this work; there are no direct references to *Democracy in America*. And though there are difficulties with his theory of the "fragment society," it clearly allows Hartz to see the constitutive nature of race in a way not present in *The Liberal Tradition*. For example, he reconsiders the significance of the exclusion of the American Indian from American history: if a significant Indian or mestizo population had been incorporated into the American settler society as it was elsewhere, "Jackson," he writes, "instead of rationalizing the extinction of the Indian from the White House, might well not have been there: or he might not have been a 'democrat'." In that brief counterfactual speculation lies the germ of the revisionist history of Jackson by a "New Left Hartzian," Michael Rogin.[25]

Since Hartz's *The Founding of New Societies*, there has been some comparative work along the lines he suggests, particularly in the fields of frontier history, and the history of slavery and race relations. But the full challenge of that work has not yet been met, though Donald Denoon has turned to a similar kind of comparative history in his extremely suggestive *Settler Capitalism*, which looks at six settler societies in the southern hemisphere – Australia, New Zealand, South Africa, Chile, Argentina, and Uruguay. Denoon's work comes out of a concern for Third World history, and the particular dilemmas posed by theories of dependency and underdevelopment: how can one explain the gap between dependent settler colonies and other dependent colonies, "the pattern of settler prosperity and peasant misery?" He begins to offer a historical and materialist account of the settler road to capitalism, of a "settler capitalist mode of production." In what were often the least prized colonies, garrisoned for strategic purposes, Europeans encountered not established civilizations but nomadic societies practicing hunting, gathering, and herding. The history of that encounter is, first, the history of the destruction, to varying degrees, of the nomadic societies, as "frontiers" of capitalist agriculture, commercial pastoralism, and mining are opened, and second, of an enduring crisis of labor supply, which is met by various forms of coerced labor – slavery, indentured servitude, and convict labor – and eventually by large numbers of immigrants from the European semiperiphery and parts of Asia. Denoon's work is primarily comparative economic and political history, and it only occasionally suggests parallels to the European settlement of North America and Siberia; but he does mention ideological elements in the historiography of the settler societies, elements that parallel accounts of American exceptionalism. The native peoples were not part of national history, but became subjects for anthropology; class analyses of the society were commonly deemed irrelevant, classes having been left in Europe. "It is not at all remarkable," Denoon writes, "to find a society's rulers insisting that society is homogeneous, but it is striking to find so many radical opposition leaders sharing that point of view." "The literature of our societies," he concludes, "is replete with exceptionalist arguments deriving from the self-image of the settlers themselves."[26]

The notion of a "settler exceptionalism" – both the recognition by cultural historians that "exceptionalist" ideologies were common to settler regimes, and the development of a comparative history of the settler colonial road to capitalism – offers a way of avoiding the endless arguments about American exceptionalism and their inextricable relation to the American ideology itself, while recognizing the distinctiveness of, and perhaps family resemblances between, the regional and national histories shaped by settler colonialism. It is not a happy view, for their histories are tragic and seemingly intractable; from Ireland to the United States, from South Africa to Israel, the fusion of race and class has left a legacy of nations which are, in Dos Passos's words, two nations. In such an exploration, I will turn not only to Tocqueville's contradictory legacy but to his canonic adversary, the Marx who concludes the first volume of *Capital* with a chapter entitled "The Modern Theory of Colonization," which is not about what would later come to be known as imperialism, the British in India, for example, but about settler colonialism. In a few brief pages, Marx brings together in a single framework the apparent equality of conditions in the United States and Australia – the development of independent, noncapitalist producers – and the slavery and dispossession of native peoples that accompany it, "so-called primitive accumulation." Marx concludes by noting that "we are not concerned here with the condition of the colonies," and turns back to the political economy of the Old World. The task of American Marxists is to return to the unfinished "modern theory of [settler] colonialism."

11

NEITHER CAPITALIST NOR AMERICAN: THE DEMOCRACY AS SOCIAL MOVEMENT

Democracy is a difficult subject, in part because it has become a universal value: we are all democrats now. In a sense, this has been true for half a century: in 1951, a UNESCO report noted that "for the first time in the history of the world, no doctrines are advanced as antidemocratic. . . . practical politicians and political theorists agree in stressing the democratic element in the institutions they defend and the theories they advocate." And for Americans, this is hard to resist: the United States, we are regularly told, was the first democratic state. "The Revolution created American democracy," the historian Gordon Wood writes, and "made Americans . . . the first people in the modern world to possess a truly democratic government and society." As a result Americans often think of democracy as they think of Coke: invented in the United States and exported to a grateful world. It is a fundamental part of the American ideology. One might be forgiven for thinking that the title of Tocqueville's famous book was "democracy *is* America," even though Tocqueville himself warned against confusing "what is democratic with what is only American": "we should therefore give up looking at all democratic peoples through American spectacles and try at last to see them as they actually are." It is worth recalling that for Tocqueville, with all his limitations, democracy was not simply about elections: it was about the equality of conditions. The US was a democracy, he argued, because it had no proletarians and no tenant farmers; and he explicitly said that his account of democracy only pertained to "the parts of the country where there is no slavery."[1]

Tocqueville himself stands in a long tradition of antidemocrats defining democracy, a tradition that goes back to the early American federalists like Madison and Hamilton and continues in the twentieth century with figures like Joseph Schumpeter and Samuel Huntington. What does it mean when antidemocrats like Huntington, who twenty-five years ago was warning against the excesses of democracy, is now seen as the champion of a "third wave" of world democratization in the last quarter of the twentieth century? What do we make of the fact that the rise of political democracy around the world – celebrated in an enormous scholarly literature on the "transition to democracy" – has been accompanied by a global collapse of social democracy: the savaging of social safety nets, welfare systems and price subsidies, and the global privatization of public lands, public industries, and public services – a new round of enclosures?

Our latter-day democrats have dropped equality of condition from their definitions. The theoretical accomplishment of Schumpeter was simply to redefine democracy as the free market in votes: democracies are states not where the people rule, nor where there is equality of condition, but simply where ruling elites compete for votes in the market-place of elections. It is not surprising that democracy and capitalism emerge as virtual synonyms, and democratic capitalism appears to be the global consensus.

American and capitalist: it's almost enough to make you give up the term. But is that democracy? What do we mean by democracy? Is it the name of a type of political regime? Much of what counts as the debate over democracy pits "utopian" theorists, who tell us what democracy should look like, against "tough-minded" realists who use minimal definitions of democracy to describe what we might call "actually existing democracy." In this chapter, I would like to cut across this debate by reflecting on the history of democracy, arguing that democracy is neither American nor capitalist, but is the social movement that fought for and created the democratic institutions of the state and civil society that we have. Indeed one of the earliest names for that social movement was "the Democracy." Moreover, since every democratic victory is threatened by powerful forces opposed to democracy, the democracy remains the social movements that fight to preserve and extend those democratic institutions. We are *not* all democrats.

The Democracy

In the years between the 1820s and the 1850s when the modern social movements were invented, a new use of the word democracy appeared, one that seems strange to our ears: "the democracy." "The portion of the people whose injury is the most manifest, have got or taken the title of the 'democracy,'" Thomas Perronet Thompson, one of the philosophical radicals who edited the *Westminster Review*, wrote in 1842. Tocqueville himself, writing in the 1830s, occasionally uses the term in this way: "Is it credible that the democracy which has annihilated the feudal system, and vanquished kings, will respect the citizen and the capitalist?" And John Stuart Mill, in his 1840 review of Tocqueville, writes that "the middle class in this country [England], is as little in danger of being outstripped by the democracy below, as being kept down by the aristocracy above." The *Oxford English Dictionary* places the first use of this meaning of the democracy in 1828, and there are clear analogues in French and German. By the time of the Paris Commune, the *Times* of London was capitalizing the phrase, denouncing the "dangerous sentiment of the Democracy, this conspiracy against civilisation in its so-called capital."[2]

How do we understand this meaning of the democracy? In the eighteenth century, the term democracy was rarely used in a positive sense: educated philosophers and political thinkers including the American constitutionalists disparaged it. An extensive study of the rhetoric of democracy in North America concludes that, in the eighteenth century, democracy was a term of derogation: "there were very few men willing to call themselves democrats." Even Gordon Wood admits that "democracy was commonly used vituperatively"; to find a celebration of democracy, he leaps more than a generation to quote "a renegade Baptist" in 1809.[3]

At the same time, among the sailors, slaves, indentured servants, and dispossessed peasants who lived through the enclosures, impressments, slave trades, and witch hunts of Atlantic capitalism's primitive accumulation, democracy was not a slogan. The "many-headed hydra" of food rioters, slave rebels, pirates, and heretics (whose history has been recovered in the book of that name by Peter Linebaugh and Marcus Rediker) appealed to vernacular hopes and ideals: they spoke of levelling, of the commons, of jubilee, not democracy. Though the struggles for independence in the North American colonies in the 1770s were a key moment in the development of democratic ideas and institutions, they were not unique: as Linebaugh and Rediker argue, they were themselves part of two centuries of insurrection by that "motley crew," ranging from Masaniello's revolt in Naples and the struggles of the Levellers, Diggers, and Ranters in the English Revolution in the 1640s to the wave of eighteenth-century slave rebellions inaugurated by Tacky's Revolt in Jamaica in 1760.[4]

It is into these struggles that democracy – one of those Greek and Latin words, like proletarian, that Renaissance and Enlightenment political theorists with classical education reclaimed from antiquity – begins to filter in the 1790s, as a few Jacobin radicals in France, England, and the United States invoked democracy positively. But after two decades of world war between Napoleon's revolutionary empire and Britain's counterrevolutionary empire, little of democracy – as theory, practice, or even as word – remained in the North Atlantic world. Modern democracy – "the democracy" – emerged in two extraordinary decades (the 1830s and 1840s) when the modern social movements – the labor movement, the women's movement, the abolitionist movement, the anti-imperial national movements and the new ideologies of socialism and communism – were all born. The most comprehensive historian of the word democracy notes that "broad application" of the word does not occur until the 1830s, and that 1848 "represents the zenith in the application of 'democracy'." In England, it was in these years that the Chartists, the first mass working-class movement in the world, and perhaps the largest mass political activity in any European country during the nineteenth century, came to speak of the Democracy as the movement of the people, often capitalizing the word in their press.[5]

In the early 1840s, the young Germans Friedrich Engels and Karl Marx adopted this usage from the Chartists, as they joined "democrats of all nations" in founding the Society of Fraternal Democrats. In the midst of the German revolution of 1848, they subtitled their newspaper "Organ of the Democracy:" "Through their personal connections with the heads of the Democratic party in England, France, Italy, Belgium and North America, the editors," they write, "are in a position to reflect the politico-social movement abroad. . . . In this respect, the *Neue Rheinische Zeitung* is the organ not simply of the German but of the European Democracy."[6] The democracy becomes a synonym for the "social movement," a phrase that also appears first in the 1830s and 1840s, uniting new forms of popular mobilization – marches, rallies, demonstrations, petitions, cheap pamphlets, and newspapers – with new ideologies of emancipation.

In the United States, there are many uses of "the democracy" in this sense in the 1830s and 1840s, though individual instances are tricky to interpret because Andrew Jackson's political alliance successfully appropriated the phrase for its party: what we call in retrospect the Democratic Party was usually referred to as the Democracy. So an address to the democracy, a common subtitle of speeches of the era, sometimes means an address to the followers of Jackson, and sometimes means simply an address to the people, to the social movement. Abolitionist critics of Jackson's Democracy called themselves the "True Democracy," and the working-class opposition to New York's Tammany Hall called itself the "shirtless" Democracy. Transatlantic connections between "the democrats of all nations" abounded: among women's rights activists, among abolitionists – Frederick Douglass, like Friedrich Engels, met with Chartists when he was in England in the 1840s – and among radical artisans.

The revolutionary upheavals that broke out throughout the capitalist world-system in 1848 were seen as an act of "the democracy:" Thomas Carlyle spoke of "this universal revolt of the European populations, which calls itself Democracy" and François Guizot noted that "the chaos today hides itself under a word, Democracy . . . it is the sovereign, universal word." If the democracy was the name of the movement, emancipation was its aim. Emancipation was the great aspiration of the period: with its origins in the abolitionist movement's struggle for the emancipation of the enslaved and in the early nineteenth-century battles for the political emancipation of Jews in Europe and for Catholic emancipation in Ireland, emancipation also became the keyword among early women's rights activists and labor activists: "the emancipation of the working classes must be conquered by the working classes themselves," Marx writes at the formation of the International Working Men's Association.[7]

But within a year or two, the revolutionary republics were defeated, the Chartist leaders were imprisoned, the Fugitive Slave Law had been passed, and the democracy was in tatters. In the wake of the defeats, the democracy began to fragment. As a few elite political figures attempted to claim the banner of the democracy, one sees democrats of the social movement beginning to make a separation between political and social democracy, between bourgeois and popular democracy. As early as 1845, Mike Walsh, the tribune of New York's working-class "subterranean" or "shirtless" Democracy, wrote that "No man can be a good political democrat without he's a good social democrat." In 1851, Marx, now in exile in England, satirized prime minister Lord Russell's claim that "the Democracy of the country . . . has as fair a right to the enjoyment of its rights as monarchy or nobility," because Lord Russell had redefined the Democracy as "the Bourgeoisie, the industrious and commercial middle class," a "king-loving, lords-respecting, bishop-conserving 'Democracy'."[8]

If the "democrats of all nations" of 1848 were the founders of the modern democracy, none of them knew the universal-suffrage parliamentary state that we associate with democracy. The democratic state did not exist anywhere by the middle of the nineteenth century. Where did it come from? What is the relation between the democracy and the democratic state?

The Democratic State

Democratic states are youthful institutions, but most claim more ancient lineages. 1688, 1776, 1789: it is not only in the United States that we imagine that democracy sprang forth from the rhetoric of a founding bourgeois revolution. In reality, the democratic state – the universal-suffrage parliamentary state, with the freedoms of political opposition – is, as Robert Dahl notes at the beginning of his *On Democracy*, "a product of the twentieth century."[9] Though historians and political scientists argue over the history of particular countries and the criteria of the democratic state – the extent of the franchise, of freedom of opposition, of peaceful alternation of regimes – there is general agreement that the universal suffrage state first emerges in the late nineteenth and early twentieth century, and was well established only after World War II.

Nevertheless, democratic states are often called capitalist or bourgeois, as if they were created, fostered, and supported by capitalists. "No bourgeoisie, no democracy," Barrington Moore wrote in 1966, and few on the left or the right would have disagreed.[10] It was precisely this analysis that had led one tradition of Marxism – that of Lenin – to reject what it called "bourgeois democracy" completely. But a quarter-century of scholarship – going back to a pioneering essay by Göran Therborn – has fundamentally transformed our understanding of the roots of the democratic state. The democratic state may have emerged in capitalist societies, but not because capitalists created it. Rather capitalism creates and strengthens large working classes, and, to quote the major comparative history of democratic states in Europe, North America, and South America, "the working class, not the middle class, was the driving force behind democracy."[11]

This interpretation of the relation between working-class movements – the "democracy" – and the rise of the democratic state illuminates several key aspects of the history of democracy. First, this argument that working-class self-organization was central to democracy makes sense of the timing of the universal-suffrage parliamentary states: they were first decisively, though not irrevocably, won not in the age of Capital, the great boom years of the 1850s and 1860s, but a half-century later, as a result of the organization of workers in the labor movements and socialist parties of the Second International, and the revival of the women's movement in the militant new feminism of the suffrage campaigns. Bourgeois democracy, Therborn rightly notes, was the "principal historical accomplishment" of the Second International. Schumpeter himself recognizes this; his *Capitalism, Socialism and Democracy* concludes with a historical sketch of the socialist parties.

Second, though the success of democratic reforms depended on the strength of working-class organizations – the weakness of Latin American democracy was in part due to its comparatively small working classes – it is clear that workers were not strong enough to win democratic states on their own in Europe, North America, or South America. Democratic victories depended on alliances with middle classes, either urban or rural, and the middle classes were always an ambivalent ally. They also depended on the weakness or defeat of the most consistent opponents of democracy, the large landlords who depended on cheap agricultural labor. Democracy failed where large landlords were strong enough to control the state. Capitalist development and democracy are therefore correlated because "capitalist development weakens the landed upper class and strengthens the working class."[12]

The bourgeoisie, far from being a driving force behind democracy, was rarely even a positive force. Even the contemporary political scientists most impressed with capitalist democracy admit that capitalist elites are not supporters of democracy. Several even suggest that capitalists are so strongly opposed to democracy that political democracy can only exist and thrive if there is a strong party of the right to protect the interest of elites, and if large parts of social and economic life are not subject to political control, if, in other words, issues of social justice are not on the agenda. Without those restrictions, corporate elites support authoritarian attacks on democracy. As Perry Anderson once noted, though we have yet to see a parliamentary transition to socialism, we have seen parliamentary transitions to fascism.[13]

Third, the argument about the relation between working-class mobilization and democracy is not only an historical one; there is strong evidence that the working classes continue to be the driving force in the democratizations of the late twentieth century. Though little of the "transition to democracy" literature has seriously studied late twentieth-century workers, the role of Poland's Solidarity, of the black unions of South Africa's COSATU, of Brazil's Workers' Party, and of the South Korean strikes of the mid-1990s would indicate that the organization and mobilization of working people continues to be fundamental to the establishment of universal-suffrage parliamentary states.[14]

This account also helps us make some sense of the contradictory assessments of US democracy: Samuel Huntington claims that the US was the first democratic country, placing the date at 1828 with suffrage for a bare majority of white men; Therborn, among others, places the US as the last of the core capitalist democracies, dating it from 1970 with the enfranchisement of black Southerners. How do we make sense of this simultaneous originality and belatedness? The extension of the franchise in the early nineteenth-century North did create a kind of democracy of small-holders, that historians have likened to those of Norway and Switzerland at the same time. But the continental United States was hardly akin to Norway and Switzerland, and what looks from one angle like remarkably early democratic institutions looks from another like a brief and regional exception. In most of Europe, after all, opposition to the extension of the franchise came from two sources: labor-repressive landlords who opposed political rights for the peasantry and capitalists who opposed voting rights for workers. "The American peasantry, however, was," as Alexander Keyssar points out in his history of *The Right to Vote*, "peculiar: it was enslaved" and thus not "part of the calculus . . . of suffrage reform."[15] The South was not a democracy but an authoritarian landlord regime. Similarly, as long as industrial workers remained far outnumbered by farmers in the North and West, they were a small part of the calculus of suffrage. In the only state where manufacturing workers outnumbered farmers in the 1840s – Rhode Island – those workers were excluded from political rights. The struggle of Rhode Island workers for the right to vote in 1841–42 resulted in the formation of a People's Convention and a separate, parallel constitution and government that challenged the legitimacy of the state government – a Providence Commune, if you like. An armed confrontation over control of the state arsenal led to the defeat and imprisonment of the suffrage advocates, a history that parallels the struggles of the Chartists across the Atlantic. The spokesman of the Dorr Rebellion, the carpenter Seth Luther, author of *Address on the Right of Free Suffrage*, stands as one of the great plebeian theorists of democracy.[16]

With the end of slavery and the growth of an immigrant working class, the United States witnessed a half-century of disenfranchisement, "a sustained nationwide contraction of suffrage rights."[17] By the early twentieth century, the United States was not a democratic state; the present democratic state in the US was the consequence of the self-organization of industrial workers in the CIO during the 1930s and 1940s and the self-organization of black Americans in the Civil Rights Movement of the 1950s and 1960s. From Seth Luther fighting for suffrage in Providence to Robert Moses and Fannie Lou Hamer fighting for voting rights in Mississippi: that has been the line of the Democracy, not the antidemocratic meditations of Hamilton and Madison.

If we understand the close historical tie between the Democracy in the nineteenth-century sense – the social movements of working people – and democratic institutions of universal suffrage and freedom of assembly and speech, we see as well the mistake made by many contemporary scholars of democracy who would artificially separate political democracy from social democracy. For just as there is a close correlation between the strength of democratic politics and that of working-class organization, so there is a close correlation between the strength of welfare states and that of working-class mobilization. As Alexander Hicks notes in his recent study of social democracy and welfare capitalism, "even though democracy did not open the floodgate to demands for mass redistribution, it did function . . . as a sluice gate that permitted an ample flow of income security reforms." This is the case even outside the North Atlantic states: Patrick Heller's recent study of the Indian state of Kerala notes that

> under the impetus of a broad-based working-class movement organized by the Communist Party, successive governments in Kerala have pursued what is arguably the most successful strategy of redistributive development outside the socialist world. Direct redistributive measures have included the most far-reaching land reforms on the subcontinent and labor market interventions, that, combined with extensive unionization, have pushed both rural and informal sector wages well above regional levels. . . . On all indicators of the physical quality of life Kerala far surpasses any Indian state and compares favorably with the more developed nations of Asia.

If the universal suffrage state was the historical accomplishment of the turn of the century social democracy, the welfare state with its social rights to income security in the face of unemployment, injury, sickness, retirement, and parenting, as well as its rights to universal public education, was the democratic work of social democracy in the age of three worlds. And the role of the social movement in the struggle for feminist democracy is equally clear: if women's suffrage was the historical accomplishment of the first wave of feminist movements, the reproductive rights of divorce, contraception, and abortion have been the democratic victories of the second wave. Democracy depends on "the democracy."[18]

How then can the savaging of social democracy – the enclosure of the commons, the attack on social rights, and the privatization of public goods – that has taken place over the last two decades be seen as a "wave of democratization"? Why do democratic theorists wax lyrical about civil society, that most undemocratic sphere?

The Democratic Society

The irony of the democratic state has been that the extension of citizenship has been accomplished with a devaluation of the political and a restriction of the powers of the public. The political theorist Ellen Meiksins Wood has argued that this was the theoretical accomplishment of the American Federalists: "it was the anti-democratic victors in the USA who gave the modern world their definition of democracy, a definition in which the dilution of popular power is an essential ingredient." The "freeing" of the market from the political realm – particularly the market in those two commodities that had rarely been considered alienable commodities, labor and land – made victories in the political realm often hollow. As labor historian David Montgomery wrote of nineteenth-century America: "the more that active participation in government was opened to the propertyless strata of society, the less capacity elected officials seemed to have to shape the basic contours of social life . . . both the contraction of the domain of governmental activity and the strengthening of government's coercive power contributed to the hegemony of business and professional men."[19]

This is now a fundamental part of the theories of democracy promoted by the "Washington consensus," which insist that economic or social democracy has nothing to do with political democracy. In fact, they argue that economic decision making must be carefully insulated from political power and from popular pressures for a more thoroughgoing democratization of society. As a result, over the last two decades, many of the victories of new democratic states have been undermined by capitalist forces of privatization. Privatization, or what the Midnight Notes group have called the new enclosures, is the devolution of public lands, public industries, public schools and public services from a realm which is potentially democratic to a realm where democracy rarely exists, a realm euphemistically called "civil society."[20]

"Civil society," we are told by a chorus of its admirers, is the realm of freedom and democracy, the realm of voluntary associations and civic participation, outside the bureaucracies of the state. For Tocqueville, a fundamental part of democracy was freedom of association, and he argued that "Americans of all ages, all stations in life, and all types of disposition are forever forming associations." "If men are to remain civilized or to become civilized," he wrote, "the art of association must develop and improve among them." This was the closest Tocqueville came to the new socialisms of his era, for association was a common synonym for socialism in the 1830s and 1840s. Unfortunately, it was at this point that Tocqueville made a fateful conflation of what he called "intellectual and moral associations" and "manufacturing and trading companies." In Tocqueville and especially in his revivalists, capitalist enterprises are seen as simply one form of "civil association," whose free activity is necessary to the preservation of equality and liberty: this is one source of theories of democratic capitalism. The same slippage can be seen in the German tradition that gave us the concept of civil society: the German word, *bürgerliche Gesellschaft*, means both civil society and bourgeois society.[21]

However, if democracy has its limits even inside the universal-suffrage parliamentary state, rarely penetrating beyond the legislative branch through to the high courts, the bureaucratic apparatuses of the civil services, not to mention the national security state, it hardly exists outside the state. As the Italian political theorist Norberto Bobbio put it, "the present problem of democracy no longer concerns 'who' votes but 'where' we vote." "Today, if you want an indication of the development of democracy in a country, you must consider not just the number of people with the right to vote, but also the number of different places besides the traditional area of politics in which the right to vote is exercised."[22] By this measure, we continue to live in very restricted democracies. One finds little or no democracy in the institutions of civil society, and particularly in manufacturing and trading companies.

There have been struggles to democratize civil society, particularly in the realm of work and economic activity. An important tradition of liberal and socialist thought, going back to John Stuart Mill and including figures like Bertrand Russell, John Dewey, and Robert Dahl, developed notions of "economic democracy" or "industrial democracy," which would extend the procedures of representative democracy into the workplace. But unlike extensions of the franchise, there has been little advance in these rights that the Europeans called "co-determination." It was on the agenda of the European social democratic-parties, particularly in Sweden, in the late 1970s, only to fall victim to the counterrevolution against social democracy mounted by Reagan and Thatcher. A quarter-century later, these issues – the possibilities for democratic control of the workplace and the labor process, for democratic control of a firm's capital and investment, and for democratic elections of corporate and university boards, in short, for the democratization of civil society – are hardly visible, though they will be on the agenda of the democracy of the twenty-first century.

Rather, at the present, the counterdemocracy has set the agenda: the privatization of public spheres and the expanding place of the market and civil society in people's lives has had profoundly undemocratic effects. Paradoxically, it is in Tocqueville's realm of association – the civil society of the corporation – that the very right of free association is under threat. In the words of a Human Rights Watch report of 2000, "workers' freedom of association is under sustained attack in the United States, and the government is often failing its responsibility under international human rights standards to deter such attacks and protect workers' rights." The report continues:

> Millions of workers are expressly barred from the law's protection of the right to organize. US legal doctrine allowing employers to permanently replace workers who exercise the right to strike effectively nullifies the right. Mutual support among workers and unions recognized in most of

> the world as legitimate expressions of solidarity is harshly proscribed under US law as illegal secondary boycotts. . . . [There are] millions of part-time, temporary, subcontracted, and otherwise "atypical" or "contingent" workers whose exercise of the right to freedom of association is frustrated by the law's inadequacy.[23]

At the very moment that workers' movements were driving the "third wave" of democratization around the world, the United States experienced two dramatic reversals in workers' rights. First, the 1981 crushing of the air traffic controllers' union by the Reagan administration and the 1980 "Yeshiva" ruling by the Supreme Court which curbed faculty unionism ended two decades of dramatic labor movement victories in organizing public-sector and white-collar workers. Second, US workers effectively lost the right to strike with the 1983 *Belknap v. Hale* Supreme Court decision that enabled Phelps Dodge to replace striking workers permanently in the midst of the Arizona miners' strike. Over the next decade, striking workers were permanently replaced in several major transport (Greyhound, Continental Airlines, Eastern Airlines) and newspaper (*Chicago Tribune*, *New York Daily News*) strikes; by the end of the century, strikes had essentially vanished from the United States.[24]

The "United States is almost alone in the world in allowing permanent replacement of workers who exercise the right to strike," the 2000 Human Rights Watch report notes, and it tells the story of the destruction of unions and lives with the permanent replacement of strikers in towns ranging from Pueblo, Colorado, to Jay, Maine. It also finds examples of workers whose right to organize is under attack in all sectors of the economy: from black workers in hog-processing plants in North Carolina to "perma-temps" working for Microsoft in the Northwest, from Mexican-American and Mexican agricultural workers in the orchards of Washington and the fruit and vegetable fields of North Carolina to Asian and Latina immigrant women working in garment sweatshops in New York, from Haitian-American nursing home workers in Florida to shipyard workers in New Orleans.[25]

This attack on the right to organize has also characterized apparently "nonprofit" institutions of civil society over the last decade. At Yale

University, a battleground for university unionism over more than three decades, graduate teachers and hospital workers attempting to form unions have met vigorous opposition and formal and informal intimidation. As Rebecca Ruquist, a graduate teacher in the French Department and an organizer for the Graduate Employees and Students Organization (GESO), told a Yale audience:

> I have taught two semesters of French 115, two semesters of French 130, both of which met five days a week, where I did the teaching, the grading, and all of the work for the course except for syllabus design. When I told the Director of Graduate Studies in my department a year ago that I was going to become GESO's next Chair, he fought with me for an hour about how I was wasting my time, and how ungrateful graduate students were to want a union. When in a meeting I suggested to the current DGS that she advocate for her graduate students with the administration, she pulled me into her office alone to lecture me about keeping graduate school issues out of department meetings. She promised me that she would include a mention of my GESO organizing in a future letter of recommendation. Both professors have refused to declare their neutrality towards GESO organizing in the department to the French Ph.D. students. This is wrong: it is our right to organize a union here, and faculty need to respect that. The Yale administration should not ask professors to bust their own teaching assistants' union. Yale needs more than to live up to the letter of the law, it needs to live up to the spirit of the law.[26]

Similarly, Peg Tamulevich, a secretary in Medical Records who has worked at the Yale-New Haven Hospital for twenty-three years, said:

> I have joined with many of my co-workers at the Hospital to organize a union. We want better patient care, wages and benefits, but more importantly, we want respect. When I was handing out union leaflets outside the hospital, police officers with guns, who are employed by Yale-New Haven, told me that I would be arrested and forced me to stop. This is just one example of intimidation tactics used by the hospital. I care deeply about our democracy in America. At Yale-New Haven Hospital, the fight for democracy is an everyday battle.[27]

Incidents like these are echoed throughout the case studies in the Human Rights Watch report: the one-on-one "meetings" with workers as well as the use of police and security services to harass organizers. Employers regularly walk just inside the law, and just as regularly break it, since there is no punishment for law-breakers. Under US labor law, employers found guilty of violating a worker's rights only have to post a notice saying they will not do it again.

The celebrants of civil society's voluntary associations and democratic deliberations rarely consider civil society's fundamental institution, the workplace. Similarly, economists rarely grapple with the working day: work and workers only appear in contemporary economics under the guise of the "labor market."[28] In the never-never land of free market economics, we don't work; we sell our weekdays in order to buy our weekends. Economists don't get up in the morning to go to work; they go off to truck and barter their human capital. For most of us, however, capitalism remains what Marx described: "anarchy in the social division of labor, despotism in that of the workshop."[29] The labor market – getting a job – is an anarchic world we try to avoid as much as possible. The reality of capitalism is not the market, but the working day, day after day. Even Tocqueville recognized that "between workman and master there are frequent relations but no true association." The workplace remains the fundamental *unfree* association of civil society, without civil liberties or rights, without freedom of speech and with little freedom of association, assembly or opposition.[30]

And yet, the difficult, exhausting, and often demoralizing struggle by people to organize and mobilize at their place of work, has, as I have tried to suggest, been one of the fundamental driving forces of modern democracy. Unions, like other institutions, have their flaws, but they remain the most democratic institution of civil society, voluntary associations where leaders are elected in contested elections, where oppositions can organize, where ordinary people represent themselves. As a result, vital unions are central to a vital democracy; the decay and collapse of unions, as we have witnessed over the past decades, is a decay and collapse of democracy.

Much has made in recent years about the decline in civic participation among Americans over the last three decades; we're all bowling alone, as Robert Putnam put in. But though Putnam notes the decline in union membership as an aspect of this decline in civic participation, he pays little attention to it, not even noting that the decline was involuntary. There was no organized campaign against people forming bowling leagues; there has been an organized campaign against people forming unions. Across the country, we have seen repeated attacks – informal and formal – on the attempt to organize and associate. The market has efficiently allocated resources to a thriving industry of antiunion managerial consultants. If graduate teachers are not bowling alone, it is because they are striking together.[31]

Moreover, unions are one of the few forms of civic engagement that are *not* skewed toward wealthier citizens. Critics of the civic-engagement literature have often noted that since those with more time and more money are more likely to participate in politics, civic engagement can have antidemocratic consequences. The historic tendency of the labor movement has been to empower the least powerful, to protect the rights of its members by the practice of what Walt Whitman called the "great word" of democracy: "Solidarity."[32] It is true that unions have often been skewed to workers with more skills and more "market power," especially white workers and male workers. But the labor movement has struggled to reach across the divisions created by the labor market, divisions between "skilled" and "unskilled," "blue-collar" and "white-collar," the "employed" and the "unemployed," "men's work" and "women's work," "white work" and "colored work," to forge alliances where an injury to one is an injury to all. Anyone who reads the Human Rights Watch case studies of black, Latino, and women workers battling for their rights on the job can see why the right to organize is now a crucial civil rights issue.

The right to organize is the fundamental democratic issue of our time. One hundred million Americans working for a living do not have the democratic protections of a union. No democratization of civil society or revival of civic participation will be accomplished without their achieving the right to organize; no change in the inequality of wealth and income will come without that organization. The struggles for union recognition at Yale may seem like a local matter, hardly visible in the distant democratic vista, but the Democracy has always been about the struggles of ordinary people in the here and now.

But this is also a part of a wider struggle against the antidemocratic forces of globalization, of what is called around the world "neoliberalism." The extraordinary proletarianization of millions of the world's peoples on a global assembly line – the world working class has doubled in the last thirty years[33] – may well lead to a renewed Democracy. It has already generated a new social movement unionism, pioneered in the 1980s by Brazilian, South African, and South Korean workers, and now sparking new forms of organization and militancy by the young women in the world's *maquiladoras*, where toys, textiles, and electronics are processed for export. The 1999 protest against the WTO in Seattle by environmentalists and unionists, "turtles and Teamsters," was only the most visible part of the new century's Democracy. The first year of the new century witnessed general strikes against government austerity programs in South Korea, South Africa, Argentina, Uruguay, Nigeria, and India: in India, where twenty million workers went out May 11, 2000, a strike leader said that "the strike was aimed against the surrender of the country's economic sovereignty before the WTO and the IMF,"[34] the surrender of political and social democracy to economic despotism.

It is crucial to reclaim democracy from the antidemocrats, from those who would tell us that democracy is capitalist and American. When we think of democracy, we must remember "the Democracy," the social movements of working people that have been the driving force of the modern democracy around the world. It is working people who must, in the words of that old manifesto, "win the battle of democracy."

12

A CULTURAL FRONT IN THE AGE OF THREE WORLDS?

The late 1990s saw a new attention to labor and the labor movement in the world of culture and the arts. Slacker acquired a new meaning on college campuses as Student Labor Action Committees (SLACs) have generated a wave of antisweatshop campaigns, Union Summer organizers and "labor teach-ins." The *New York Times Magazine* even did a cover story on the "union kids." One of the "little magazines" of the 1990s, *The Baffler*, called on its writers to rediscover the "facts of working life," and published stories and essays on labor struggles. It is hard to recall the last time a major US novelist was someone who had also written a nonfiction account of a strike, as Barbara Kingsolver did in *Holding the Line*. Or a time when an English professor collaborated with a photographer to tell the story of workers in a North Carolina furniture factory, as did Cathy Davidson and Bill Bamberger in *Closing*.

In part, this ferment was an echo of the promise of change in the labor movement itself, symbolized by the election of the "New Voice" candidates to AFL-CIO leadership. But it also appeared to mark a larger change in American society. For many who were heartened by the glimmer of a culture that notices, honors, and even argues about working people and their organizations, it seemed to be a sign of reconciliation, the end of a generation of division between labor and intellectuals, unions and artists. Steven Fraser and Joshua Freeman argue in their introduction to *Audacious*

Democracy – the volume that grew out of the 1996 Columbia Labor Teach-in – that before 1948 "a world of writers and artists and intellectuals took up the labor question as its own and made common cause with the moral ambitions of the labor movement. . . . But then that alliance withered away and for nearly a half-century vanished from the public stage." People disagree on the causes of the divorce – some stress the reactionary response of the Meany AFL-CIO to black self-organization, feminism, and the invasion of Vietnam; others point to New Left disdain for labor and the rise of identity politics and a cultural or lifestyle left – but they tend to agree on the fact of the estrangement. For most of the age of three worlds – the late 1940s to the late 1980s – it seemed that labor and culture had no relation. There was no "cultural front," to use a phrase of the earlier age of the CIO.[1]

But is this accurate? Is the relationship between labor and culture during the Cold War simply a story of the cold war between labor and culture, between the Meany dinosaurs and the Sixties counterculture, between hard-hats and hippies, an endless retelling of *All in the Family*'s battle between Archie Bunker and his son-in-law, the Meathead? Was the new laborism of the 1990s an overdue reaction to the so-called identity politics of the New Left, a return to class and labor after a detour through race and gender, as many recent commentators have suggested? I think not, and we misunderstand the contemporary moment if we fall prey to a nostalgia for the 1930s, and fail to see the shape of labor and culture in the age of three worlds.

There was clearly a break around 1948, because the Cold War began with a powerful and successful drive to divide and purge both labor and culture. The anti-Communist crusade became a civil war in the union movement and in the powerful cultural institutions (publishing, schools and universities, broadcasting and film studios). The cultural front – the alliance between writers, artists and the labor movement that had been built on the wave of CIO organizing in the needle trades and metal-working industries – collapsed in the face of blacklists and Congressional inquisitions. The forward march of labor seemed to come to a halt; union density in manufacturing peaked in 1953 and then steadily declined. In the early years of the Cold War, the image of labor and working people in US popular culture was caught between films of union racketeers and images of a newly prosperous blue-collar "middle class," which novelist Harvey Swados attacked in 1957 as "the myth of the happy worker."[2]

Moreover, early New Left artists and intellectuals did heed sociologist C. Wright Mills's call to abandon the "labor metaphysic," the sense that "'the working class' of the advanced capitalist societies" was "*the* historic agency" of social change. There is no more striking example than Betty Friedan. As Daniel Horowitz's biography showed, after Friedan transformed herself from a dedicated labor intellectual of the 1940s into a leading voice of the feminist movement of the 1960s, she rarely referred to labor. Labor, pictured in its Depression-era cap and overalls, receded from public visibility, and the cultural front of the 1930s and 1940s never reappeared.[3]

In a way, Mills, Friedan, and the young activists of the New Left social movements were not wrong; they did witness the remaking of the working classes. Radicals of the old and new lefts saw what they perceived as – and called – the "embourgeoisment" of the working class: the moving of UE, ILG, and UAW families to the new suburbs, the rise of mass higher education and apparently non-working-class white-collar work for their children, and the infiltration of plebeian styles and accents into the "middle-class" mass media of television and colleges. Moreover, Popular Front and New Left radicals had a difficult time recognizing the masses of migrants from the South as a new working class: they were the poor people of Michael Harrington's *Other America*, the civil rights martyrs of Birmingham and Oxford, the margins of the affluent society.

This is because class images last longer than classes in capitalism. While a capitalist economy continually reshapes workplaces and the working population, destroying "old" industries and workforces while drawing new workers from around the globe and moving plants to new regions, we remain caught in the class maps we inherited from family, school, and movies. People thought the American working class was Irish long after that was no longer true: this is why Jack Conroy and James Farrell were the only writers immediately recognized in the 1930s as "proletarian writers." Similarly, the Depression image of "what workers look like" led a generation of postwar Americans to see the transformation and decline of the CIO working class, a specific historical class formation, as the disappearance of class itself and the passing of the "labor question."

Looking from the end of the century, however, what is striking about the Cold War decades is less the disappearance of labor in its Depression form than the appearance of a new working class in the midst of identity or, more accurately, liberation politics. First, the dramatic migration of black and white Southerners to the North and West during and after World War II – the largest internal migration in US history – transformed American class and racial formations. This change was first registered in popular music as the Southern musics once marketed as "race" and "hillbilly" records became nationally known under their new names of "rhythm and blues," "country and western," and "rock and roll," and displaced the tunes of Tin Pan Alley. The Cold War years were shaped by a vast cultural divide between the followers of Frank Sinatra, the son of working-class Hoboken and the laureate of the CIO working class, and those of Elvis Presley, the son of Mississippi sharecroppers. By the 1980s, the "Southernization" of American culture – and of American working-class culture – could be glimpsed when Jesse Jackson, in his rainbow coalition, was seen flanked by Stevie Wonder and Willie Nelson.

Second, the migration from Asia and Latin America – shaped by US Cold War interventions in Korea, Vietnam, the Caribbean, and Central America, and taking off after the Immigration Act of 1965 – changed the complexions, cultures, and languages of American workers. California's factories in the fields had a long history of recruiting Latin and Asian migrants, so the farmworkers' struggle for union recognition marked a turning point for American labor. The march from Delano to Sacramento and the solidarity campaigns – the grape and lettuce boycotts – brought a labor struggle to the forefront of the social movements. César Chávez became the foremost labor icon of the 1960s, much like California's Harry Bridges in the 1930s, and writers like John Gregory Dunne and Peter Matthiessen took up the legacy of Steinbeck, publishing eyewitness narratives of the strike. The United Farm Workers also sparked a Chicano cultural renaissance, as the satirical *actos* of Luis Valdez and *El Teatro Campesino* (the Clifford Odets and Group Theater of the 1960s) moved from picket line allegories to films like *Zoot Suit* and *La Bamba*.

Finally, one of the central, yet overlooked, legacies of the 1960s was the invisible labor movement – the tremendous wave of union organizing by white-collar, service, and public-sector employees, particularly women. If Franklin D. Roosevelt's National Industrial Recovery Act of 1933 kicked off two decades of industrial unionism, so John F. Kennedy's executive order of 1962 giving federal employees the right to bargain collectively kicked off two decades of a new unionism, closely connected to the struggles for black liberation and women's liberation. The strikes of Memphis sanitation workers in 1968 and of Charleston hospital workers in 1969 are as central to the history of the 1960s as the Flint sit-downs were to the 1930s; by the mid-1970s, 48 percent of public sanitation workers and 42 percent of public hospital employees were unionized.[4]

It is true that the labor struggles of the 1960s, 1970s, and 1980s were – like those of the 1930s and 1940s – usually ignored by the mainstream media and institutions. But they left a deeper imprint on American culture than is often thought. It is still too early to summarize confidently the cultural politics of that extraordinary burst of white-collar unionism that mixed laborism and feminism – the nine-to-five working class. And few have been able to figure out the cultural meanings of the most celebrated strikes of the period – those of baseball players. The life histories of those who took part in the sanitation workers' strikes, the hospital workers' strikes, the teachers' strikes, and the postal strikes are only beginning to be written. We still have little sense of the shape of its cultural front, the "proletarian culture" of the age of soul. However, the apparent divide between these labor struggles and the artists of the counterculture will, I think, eventually prove to be an illusion. Consider a figure like Barbara Garson, a veteran of the Berkeley Free Speech Movement and the author of the classic antiwar satire *Macbird*, who turned from working in avant-garde theater to collecting testimonies of contemporary work in books like *All the Livelong Day: The Meaning and Demeaning of Routine Work* and *The Electronic Sweatshop*. Similarly, Cynthia Young's forthcoming book on the cultural politics of the Third World left – ranging from the documentary films of Third World Newsreel to the cultural initiatives of 1199, the health and hospital workers' union, supported by the activist artists Ruby Dee and Ossie Davis – powerfully shows how labor battles, civil rights struggles, and anti-imperialist solidarity politics came together in a culture of soul and salsa.

From *Salt of the Earth*, the 1953 film about the strike of Mexican American miners made by blacklisted film workers, to *Finally Got the News*, the classic documentary made by Detroit's League of Revolutionary Black Workers in 1970, independent filmmaking was marked by the labor struggles of the Cold War decades. This legacy continues in the films of Barbara Kopple, John Sayles, Charles Burnett, Gregory Nava, and Michael Moore. Even Hollywood films have not been immune. It is hard to think of any Hollywood films of the studio's golden age of the 1930s that represented labor struggles with as much power as *Norma Rae* (1979), *9 to 5* (1980), and *Silkwood* (1983). Both *Norma Rae* and *Silkwood* were built around the stories of actual women organizers and union campaigns: *Norma Rae* on Crystal Lee and the Amalgamated Clothing and Textile Workers Union's struggle to organize the J. P. Stevens textile mills; and *Silkwood*, on the health and safety struggles that led to the death of Oil, Chemical and Atomic Workers (OCAW) activist Karen Silkwood.

Norma Rae, directed by Martin Ritt, a figure with roots in the cultural front of the 1930s, was the closest to the Popular Front's factory-centered vision of labor. *9 to 5*, on the other hand, was a slapstick comedy of the new office factory, where fantasies of revenge against the boss are mixed with utopias of a transfigured office: the secretaries run the office, instituting job sharing, flexible hours, and a day care center. The film was based on the experiences and stories of clerical workers – the film's producer later said it was made as a comedy because of the funny and bizarre fantasies of getting even with the boss that the clerical workers had described. And its unlikely cast was itself a sign of the changing face of class: Jane Fonda, not only the daughter of the great Depression icon Henry Fonda (who had played Tom Joad in *The Grapes of Wrath*) but also a leading antiwar activist in Hollywood's New Left; the comedian Lily Tomlin, the Detroit daughter of migrants from the Kentucky hill country (her father was a toolmaker in a brass factory) who got her start in the radical theater of the 1960s, Detroit's Unstabled Coffeehouse, before emerging on television comedies in the role of the telephone operator,

Ernestine; and Dolly Parton, the daughter of Tennessee sharecroppers who began as a child gospel singer and became the leading woman country singer in the late 1960s and early 1970s with a series of songs embodying a Nashville feminism.

These films appeared at the end of two decades of labor movement advance, halted by Reagan's second Cold War, and in many ways they seem as distant as *On the Waterfront* (1954), another contradictory film made at the end of a period of labor advance. The end of the Cold War – the end of the age of three worlds, the period when the world seemed divided into First, Second and Third Worlds – yielded a new world economy that we metaphorically call globalization, which continues to creatively destroy work and workers in new international divisions of labor. The "rediscovery" of labor in the 1990s was not a rediscovery of the CIO working class, a Rip Van Winkle-like awakening to 1930s notions of the primacy of class; it was rather the recognition of a new working class that was formed by the restructurings and migrations of the Cold War decades, a remaking that the artists and intellectuals of the liberation movements tried to fathom and represent. The post-Fordist world of deindustrialized, apartheid cities dominated by universities and hospitals is inhabited by a two-tier working class: on the one hand, unionized white-collar and professional workers, better educated than the general population and more likely to see their work as a career rather than a job; on the other hand, a predominantly black, Latino, and Asian American working class laboring in nonunion sweatshops that provide the basic care and feeding of the nation, from chicken processing plants to restaurant kitchens.

If a new cultural front is to be built, it depends not only on the self-organization of the downsized and subcontracted culture industry workers, but on the solidarity across tiers of writers and artists, teachers and professionals, joining with the part-timers, the casual workers, the immigrants in sweatshop restaurants and garment factories across the nation. That solidarity is not simply a matter of novelists walking picket lines and scholars and artists joining boycotts. For if a new cultural front is to be built, it cannot recycle the old images of labor, the stock figures of Archie Bunker, or even Homer Simpson. Writers, musicians, and artists have long been responsible for the stories and pictures by which we see the world; it is they who can redraw the maps of class and work and workers that we all carry around unconsciously, and allow us to see new forms of struggle and solidarity in places we never thought to look.

NOTES

1 Introduction

1. Francis Mulhern, *Culture/Metaculture* (London: Routledge, 2000); Terry Eagleton, *The Idea of Culture* (Malden: Blackwell, 2000).
2. Immanuel M. Wallerstein, *The Essential Wallerstein* (New York: New Press, 2000), 133.
3. This Wallersteinian account of cultural studies is, I will note, different from Wallerstein's own account of cultural studies, which sees it as simply a version of the thought of 1968: see Wallerstein, *The Essential Wallerstein*, 198–99.
4. Daniel Bell, *The End of Ideology: On the Exhaustion of Political Ideas in the Fifties* (New York: Free Press, 1962), 313. Bell's discussion originally appeared in 1959, in *Encounter*.
5. E.P. Thompson, "The Point of Production," *New Left Review*, no. 1 (January–February 1960), 68.
6. Beatriz Sarlo, "Cultural Studies Questionnaire," *Journal of Latin American Cultural Studies*, vol. 6, no. 1 (1997), 90.
7. Beatriz Sarlo, "The Modern City: Buenos Aires, The Peripheral Metropolis," in *Through the Kaleidoscope: The Experience of Modernity in Latin America*, edited by Vivian Schelling (London: Verso, 2000); Beatriz Sarlo, *Scenes from Postmodern Life* (Minneapolis: University of Minnesota Press, 2001), 72; Dipesh Chakrabarty, *Habitations of Modernity: Essays in the Wake of Subaltern Studies* (Chicago: University of Chicago Press, 2002), 138–40.

8. For the parallels between Candido and Williams, I am indebted to Maria Elisa Cevasco, "Raymond Williams and Cultural Studies: A Brazilian Perspective," *Pretexts: Studies in Writing and Culture*, vol. 7, no. 2 (1998), 235–48.
9. Eagleton, *The Idea of Culture*, 128.

2 Globalization and Culture: Process and Epoch

1. Karl Marx and Frederick Engels, *Collected Works*, vol. 6 (New York: International Publishers, 1976), 487–8.
2. Fredric Jameson, "Preface," to Fredric Jameson and Masao Miyoshi, eds., *The Cultures of Globalization* (Durham: Duke University Press, 1998), xi.
3. Anthony D. King, ed., *Culture, Globalization and the World-System: Contemporary Conditions for the Representation of Identity* (Minneapolis: University of Minnesota Press, 1997), viii.
4. Leslie Sklair, "Social Movements and Global Capitalism," in Jameson and Miyoshi, *The Cultures of Globalization*, 297; Manthia Diawara, "Toward a Regional Imaginary in Africa," in Jameson and Miyoshi, *The Cultures of Globalization*, 120–1; Geeta Kapur, "Globalization and Culture: Navigating the Void," in Jameson and Miyoshi, *The Cultures of Globalization*, 199, 201.
5. Lisa Lowe, "Work, Immigration, Gender: New Subjects of Cultural Politics," in Lisa Lowe and David Lloyd, eds., *The Politics of Culture in the Shadow of Capital* (Durham: Duke University Press, 1997), 360.
6. Arjun Appadurai, *Modernity at Large: Cultural Dimensions of Globalization* (Minneapolis : University of Minnesota Press, 1996), 4.
7. Thomas L. Friedman, *The Lexus and the Olive Tree* (New York: Farrar, Straus & Giroux, 1999).
8. Walter D. Mignolo, "Globalization, Civilization Processes, and the Relocation of Languages and Cultures," in Jameson and Miyoshi, *The Cultures of Globalization*, 47.
9. Enrique Dussel, "Beyond Eurocentrism: The World-System and the Limits of Modernity," in Jameson and Miyoshi, *The Cultures of Globalization*, 3–31.
10. Eric Hobsbawm, *The Age of Extremes: A History of the World, 1914–1991* (New York: Vintage 1996), 288. This was also, as D.A. Low argues in his fine survey of Asia and Africa, a social revolution that abolished large aristocratic landlord rule: see his *The Egalitarian Moment: Asia and Africa, 1950–1980* (Cambridge: Cambridge University Press, 1996). Immanuel Wallerstein, "Antisystemic Movements: History and Dilemmas," in *Transforming the Revolution: Social Movements and the World-System*, by Samir Amin, Giovanni Arrighi, Andre

Gunder Frank, and Immanuel Wallerstein (New York: Monthly Review Press, 1990), 34.

11. Theodore Levitt, "The Globalization of Markets," *Harvard Business Review* (May–June 1983), 92–102.
12. Robert W. McChesney, "Global Media, Neoliberalism, and Imperialism," *Monthly Review*, vol. 52, no. 10 (March 2001), 3.
13. Sherif Hetata, "Dollarization, Fragmentation, and God," in Jameson and Miyoshi, *The Cultures of Globalization*, 277.
14. Few of my students took up an early challenge to consider the globalization of sport – particularly soccer, cricket, baseball and basketball. And no "Rough Guide to World Sport" yet exists. However, C.L.R. James's once-forgotten and now-revived account of the place of cricket in the Caribbean is rightly seen as a founding text in the analysis of the culture of globalization; it has been followed by a lively debate over the indigenization of cricket in other parts of the world. Muhammad Ali is surely one of the canonic cultural figures of the age of three worlds, and he is understood not merely as an American, as the documentary *When We Were Kings* demonstrates.

3 A Global Left? Social Movements in the Age of Three Worlds

1. Naomi Klein, *No Logo: Taking Aim at the Brand Bullies* (New York: Picador, 1999), xix.
2. Ranajit Guha, *Elementary Aspects of Peasant Insurgency in Colonial India* (Durham: Duke University Press, 1999), 108, 12.
3. Alexander Cockburn, Jeffrey St. Clair, and Allan Sekula, *5 Days That Shook the World* (London: Verso, 2000), 58.
4. Doug McAdam, *Political Process and the Development of Black Insurgency, 1930–1970* (Chicago: University of Chicago Press, 1982), 21.
5. "The Non-Governmental Order," *The Economist* (December 11, 1999), 20.
6. Frances Fox Piven and Richard A. Cloward, *The Breaking of the American Social Compact* (New York: New Press, 1997), 268.
7. "Cronologia e Geografia dos Novos Movimentos," http://pages.hotbot.com/edu/stop.wto/cronologia_en.html
8. Andre Gunder Frank and Marta Fuentes, "Civil Democracy: Social Movements in Recent World History," in *Transforming the Revolution*, by Amin, Arrighi, Gunder Frank, and Wallerstein, 139–80.
9. E.P. Thompson, *The Making of the English Working Class* (New York: Random House, 1966), 197.

10. Ibid., 487, 491.
11. Ibid., 451.
12. Manuel Castells, *The Power of Identity* (Oxford: Blackwell, 1997), 69, 3.
13. Immanuel Wallerstein, "1968, Revolution in the World-system," from his *Geopolitics and Geoculture: Essays on the Changing World-system* (Cambridge: Cambridge University Press, 1991).
14. Nick Dyer-Witheford, *Cyber-Marx: Cycles and Circuits of Struggle in High-Technology Capitalism* (Urbana: University of Illinois Press, 1999).
15. George Katsiaficas, *The Imagination of the New Left: A Global Analysis of 1968* (Boston: South End Press, 1987); Adam Michnik, "Anti-Authoritarian Revolt: A Conversation with Daniel Cohn-Bendit," in his *Letters from Freedom: Post-Cold War Realities and Perspectives* (Berkeley: University of California Press, 1998).
16. There are three good short accounts of the coalition: from the corporate point of view, the leaked Burson-Marsteller memo, "Guide to the Seattle Meltdown: A Compendium of Activists at the WTO Ministerial," http://www.commondreams.org/headlines/031000–03.htm; from the mainstream point of view, William Finnegan, "After Seattle," *New Yorker* (April 17, 2000), 40ff.; and from the left, Dan La Botz, "Moving for Social Justice," *Against the Current*, no. 88 (September–October 2000), 33–38.
17. John Walton and David Seddon, *Free Markets and Food Riots: The Politics of Global Adjustment* (Oxford: Blackwell, 1994), 290, 173.
18. Monty Neill, with George Caffentzis and Johnny Machete, "Toward the New Commons: Working Class Strategies and the Zapatistas," http://www.geocities.com/CapitolHill/3843/mngcjm.html
19. Walton and Seddon, *Free Markets and Food Riots*, 106, 42.
20. Ibid., 201.
21. Susan L. Woodward, *The Balkan Tragedy: Chaos and Dissolution after the Cold War* (Washington, DC: The Brookings Institution, 1995), 46–81.
22. *New York Times*, June 20, 1994, quoted in Jeremy Brecher and Tim Costello, *Global Village or Global Pillage: Economic Reconstruction from the Bottom Up* (Boston: South End Press, 1998), 30.
23. Midnight Notes Collective, "The New Enclosures," in *Midnight Oil: Work, Energy, War, 1973–1992* (Brooklyn: Autonomedia, 1992).
24. Walton and Seddon, *Free Markets and Food Riots*, 126.
25. Kim Moody, "Global Labor Stands Up to Global Capital," *Labor Notes* (July 2000), 8–9.
26. Karl Marx, *Writings of the Young Marx on Philosophy and Society*, edited and

translated by Loyd D. Easton and Kurt H. Guddat (Garden City: Anchor Books, 1967), 214.

4 The Novelists' International

1. Gregory Rabassa's English translation (1970) had immense influence in breaking up the formalisms that dominated the official modernism of the US literary world; in the USSR, the 1970 Foreign Literature translation made it a model for writers trying to break with bureaucratic socialist realism. Katerina Clark, *The Soviet Novel: History as Ritual* (Chicago: University of Chicago Press, 1985), 267.
2. Richard Wright, *Later Works: Black Boy (American Hunger), The Outsider* (New York: Library of America, 1991), 302, 303, 328.
3. Gerald Martin, *Journeys through the Labyrinth: Latin American Fiction in the Twentieth Century* (London: Verso, 1989), 94.
4. Régine Robin, *Socialist Realism: An Impossible Aesthetic* (Stanford: Stanford University Press, 1992).
5. Jürgen Rühle, *Literature and Revolution: A Critical History of the Writer and Communism in the Twentieth Century* (New York: Frederick A. Praeger, 1969).
6. See H-J Schulz, *German Socialist Literature 1860–1914: Predicaments of Criticism* (Columbia, SC: Camden House, 1993).
7. The phrase comes from Perry Anderson's account of the coordinates of the modernist conjuncture in his "Modernity and Revolution," *New Left Review*, no. 144 (March–April 1984), 104.
8. "Second International Conference of Revolutionary Writers," *Literature of the World Revolution* (Special Number, 1931), 180, 176.
9. Maxim Gorky, *Mother*, trans. Margaret Wettlin (New York: Collier Books, 1962), 13.
10. Anisimov quoted in Rühle, *Literature and Revolution*, 464; Rühle, *Literature and Revolution*, 3.
11. Four distinct moments emerge from the historiography: the original Proletkult, formed in the midst of the revolution by left-wing Bolsheviks who had developed circles of worker writers in exile, and which became a state-funded haven for socialist intellectuals during the Civil War, before evaporating in the wake of the Kronstadt uprising; the post-Civil War Soviet cultural renaissance of 1921–1928, which saw the emergence of several rival proletarian literary groups in Moscow and Leningrad, publishing journals (*Na Postu [On Guard]*,

October, Kuznitza [Smithy]) and the first celebrated proletarian novels, particularly Gladkov's *Cement*; the Stalinist "cultural revolution" of 1928–1932, as Fitzpatrick calls it, a turbulent moment when the promotion of young workers into higher education and the arts created a new Soviet intelligentsia, and when one wing of the proletarian literature avant-garde, RAPP, was unleashed to conduct a literary class war against the older, established intelligentsia; and the end of the "cultural revolution" after 1932, when the advocates of proletarian literature were purged, traditional Russian culture was reasserted, and a middlebrow sense of "socialist realism" was officially sanctioned. See Lynn Mally, *Culture of the Future: The Proletkult Movement in Revolutionary Russia* (Berkeley: University of California Press, 1990); and Sheila Fitzpatrick, *The Cultural Front: Power and Culture in Revolutionary Russia* (Ithaca: Cornell University Press, 1992).

12. Clark, *The Soviet Novel*, 256.
13. Ibid., 192.
14. In China, the radical literary movement emerged out of two moments: the cultural renaissance associated with the student May Fourth Movement of 1919, and the turn to the Marxist left following the suppression of the Shanghai strikes of 1927. A number of left literary circles and journals appeared in the late 1920s, most notably the League of Left Writers, founded in Shanghai in 1930, and led by Lu Xun, a key figure of the New Culture movement of 1919. Its major figures, including Mao Dun and Ding Ling, became central literary figures in the early People's Republic after the victory of the Communists in 1949. See Tang Tao, ed., *History of Modern Chinese Literature* (Beijing: Foreign Languages Press, 1993); Liu Kang, *Aesthetics and Marxism: Chinese Aesthetic Marxists and their Western Contemporaries* (Durham: Duke University Press, 2000). The Korean proletarian literary movement began among Korean students studying in Japan in the early 1920s; the Korean Proletarian Art Federation (KAPF) was founded in 1925. See Brian Myers, *Han Sorya and North Korean Literature: The Failure of Socialist Realism in DPRK* (Ithaca: Cornell University East Asia Series, 1994); Kim Yoon-Shik, "Phases of Development Of Proletarian Literature in Korea," *Korea Journal*, vol. 27, no. 1 (January 1987), 31–36.
15. In Japan, the strike wave of 1917–19 led to the formation of the Japanese Socialist League in 1920, and an explosion of Marxist discussion and debate. The left-wing literary journal *Tanemaku hito [The Sower]* appeared in 1921, directly inspired by Barbusse's *Clarté*. Though it ceased publication during the crackdown on the left that followed the Tokyo earthquake in 1923, a successor journal, *Bungen sensen [Literary Arts Front]* appeared a year later, helping to

organize the Japanese Proletarian Literary Arts League in 1925. The movement was crushed in the early 1930s, as writers were arrested and forced to issue a *tenko*, a disavowal of their politics. After the war, however, members of the proletarian writers movement, like Nakano Shigeharu, organized left-wing writer's groups that became a major force in Japanese literature. See Cecil H.Uyehara, "Proletarian Cultural Movement," in his *Left-Wing Social Movements in Japan: An Annotated Bibliography* (Tokyo: Charles Tuttle Company, 1959); G.T. Shea, *Leftwing Literature in Japan: A Brief History of the Proletarian Literary Movement* (Tokyo: Hosei University Press, 1964); Miriam Silverberg, *Changing Song: The Marxist Manifestos of Nakano Shigeharu* (Princeton: Princeton University Press, 1990). In Germany, the League of Proletarian-Revolutionary Writers (BPRS) with its journal *Die Linkskurve* emerged in Weimar Germany as an alliance between former expressionist poets and playwrights and working-class writers in the orbit of the Communist Party; forced into exile by the Nazi regime, many of these writers became the core of an international antifascist cultural front. See Rühle, *Literature and Revolution.*

16. Margarida Lieblich Losa, *From Realist Novel to Working-Class Romance: An Introduction to the Study of the Brazilian, Italian, and Portuguese New Social Realist Novel, 1930–1955, In Light of New Critical Theory on Realism, Fiction and Reader-Response*, Ph.D. dissertation 1989.
17. In the United States, the John Reed Clubs and magazines like the *New Masses* brought together young modernists like Dos Passos, Josephine Herbst, and John Steinbeck (whose epic tale of southwestern migrant farmworkers, *The Grapes of Wrath*, 1939, became internationally known) with a generation of plebeian writers, children of a largely immigrant working class, including Pietro di Donato, Tillie Olsen, and Henry Roth. In the Andean republics, Ecuador's Guayaquil Group, including Enrique Gil Gilbert, Joaquin Gallegos Lara, and Demetrio Aguilera Malta, launched radical writing with the celebrated collection, *Los Que Se Van*, and the historic 1922 general strike and massacre became the subject of Gallegos Lara's *Cruces Sobre el Agua* [*Crosses on the Water*] (1946). In Brazil, proletarian writing became associated with the "novel of the Northeast," including the works of Rachel de Queiroz, Graciliano Ramos, and Jorge Amado. All three were imprisoned at various points in the 1930s. De Queiroz had been a member of the Communist Party in 1931 but was expelled for Trotskyist sympathies; both Amado and Graciliano Ramos joined the Communist Party during the war years. If Amado was to become Brazil's most widely-read novelist, Graciliano Ramos's brief and stark novel of refugees, *Vidas secas* [*Barren Lives*] (1938), stands as a landmark of Brazilian modernism. Like Brazil, Chile had a strong Communist and Marxist

tradition, based in the militant nitrate miners of the north and figured by the great poet Pablo Neruda; the election of Latin America's only Popular Front government in 1938 marked the emergence of a slightly younger "generation of 1938," which included the proletarian novelists Nicomedes Guzmán and Volodia Teitelboim, both of whom wrote novels of the nitrate mines. See Michael Denning, *The Cultural Front: The Laboring of American Culture in the Twentieth Century* (London: Verso, 1997); Martin, *Journeys through the Labyrinth*; Lon Pearson, *Nicomedes Guzmán: Proletarian Author in Chile's Literary Generation of 1938* (Columbia: University of Missouri Press, 1976).

18. Richard Wright, "Blueprint for Negro Writing," *New Challenge*, vol. 2, no. 2 (Fall 1937), 58.

19. On India, see Priyamvada Gopal, *Midnight's Labors: Gender, Nation and Narratives of Social Transformation in Transitional India, 1932–1954*, Cornell University Ph.D. dissertation, 2000; Sudhi Pradhan, ed., *Marxist Cultural Movement in India* (Volume 1, Calcutta: National Book Agency, 1979; Volume 2, Calcutta: Navana, 1982; Volume 3, Calcutta: Pustak Bipani, 1985); and Carlo Coppola, ed., *Marxist Influences and South Asian Literature*, two volumes (East Lansing: Michigan State University Asian Studies Center, 1974). For Indonesia, see Keith Foulcher, *Social Commitment in Literature and the Arts: The Indonesian Institute of People's Culture 1950–1965* (Clayton: Monash University Center for Southeast Asian Studies, 1986); Keith Foulcher, "Literature, Cultural Politics, and the Indonesian Revolution," in D.M. Roskies, ed., *Text/Politics in Island Southeast Asia* (Athens: Ohio University Center for International Studies: Southeast Asia Series Number 91, 1993). Proletarian literary movements emerged throughout Southeast Asia, including the Marxist Thakin movement in Burma, the Angkatan Sasterawan 50 founded in Singapore, and the Philippine Writers League, organized in 1939: see Anna J. Allott, "Continuity and Change in the Burmese Literary Canon," in David Smyth, ed., *The Canon in Southeast Asian Literatures* (Richmond, Surrey: Curzon, 2000); Robert H. Taylor, *Marxism and Resistance in Burma 1942–1945* (Athens: Ohio State University, 1984); Tham Seong Chee, ed., *Essays on Literature and Society in Southeast Asia* (Singapore: Singapore University Press, 1981); Manuel E. Arguilla and others, eds., *Literature under the Commonwealth* (Manila: Philippine Writers' League, 1940); Milagros Guerrero, "Proletarian Consciousness in Philippine Literature, 1930–1970," in Wang Gungwu, M. Guerrero & D. Marr, eds., *Society and the Writer: Essays on Literature in Modern Asia* (Canberra: Australian National University Press, 1981); E. San Juan, *Towards a People's Literature: Essays in the Dialectics of Praxis and Contradiction in Philippine Writing*

(Quezon City: University of the Philippines Press, 1984). In the British Caribbean, the impulse dates from the circle around C.L.R. James and *The Beacon* in the early 1930s, but reaches a flowering in the figures of the early 1950s: George Lamming, Roger Mais, and V.S. Reid, among others. In the French Caribbean, the major figures include the poet Aimé Césaire and the novelist Edouard Glissant. See Hazel V. Carby, "Proletarian or Revolutionary Literature? C.L.R. James and the Politics of the Trinidadian Renaissance," in her *Cultures in Babylon* (London: Verso, 1999); and Selwyn R. Cudjoe, *Resistance and Caribbean Literature* (Athens: Ohio University Press, 1980). In Africa, Peter Abrahams was the pioneering figure among writers in English, and Sembene Ousmane among writers in French. See Chidi Amuta, *The Theory of African Literature* (London: Zed Books, 1989); George M. Gugelberger, ed., *Marxism and African Literature* (Trenton: Africa World Press, 1985); and Neil Lazarus, *Resistance in Postcolonial African Fiction* (New Haven: Yale University Press, 1990). In West Asia and North Africa, there were major left-wing literary movements in Turkish literature, whose key figures include the poet Nazim Hikmet and the novelist Yashar Kemal, and in Arabic, where the socialist ideas of Salamah Musa had a powerful impact on a generation of young social realists in the 1940s, including Naguib Mahfouz. See Yashar Kemal, *On His Life and Art* (Syracuse: Syracuse University Press, 1999); M.M. Badawi, ed., *Modern Arabic Literature* (Cambridge: Cambridge University Press, 1992); Edward Said, "After Mahfouz," *Reflections on Exile and Other Essays* (Cambridge: Harvard University Press, 2000).

20. Ngugi wa Thiong'o, "The Links that Bind Us," was an address to the 1973 Afro-Asian Writers' conference, reprinted in his *Writers in Politics* (London: Heinemann, 1981). See also Akram Aminov, "Afro-Asian Writers' Movement in its 15th Year," *Freedomways*, vol. 12, no. 3 (1972).
21. Miguel Angel Asturias's *Viento fuerte* (1949), *El papa verde* (1954), *Los ojos de los enterrados* (1960); Naguib Mahfouz's *Bayn al-Qasrayn* (1956), *Qasr al-Shawq* (1957), *al-Sukkariyya* (1957); Pramoedya Ananta Toer's *Anak semua bangsa* (1980), *Bumi manusia* (1981), *Jejak langkah* (1985), *Rumah kaca* (1988). Similar multivolume novels that are written in this period by inheritors of the left-wing writers' movements include the Anatolian village trilogy of Turkish novelist Yashar Kemal – *Ortadirek* (1960), *Yer Demir Gök Bakir* (1963), *Ölmez otu* (1968) – and the Rosario saga of Filipino writer F. Sionel José – *The Pretenders* (1962), *Tree* (1978), *My Brother, My Executioner* (1979), *Mass* (1982), *Po-on* (1984).
22. It is striking that the two novels by Willi Bredel that were the subject of

Lukács's famous critique were a factory novel and a tenement novel. See Georg Lukács, "The Novels of Willi Bredel," in Lukács, *Essays on Realism* (Cambridge: MIT Press, 1981).

23. Takiji Kobayashi, *The Factory Ship, and The Absentee Landlord*, trans. Frank Motofuji (Seattle: University of Washington Press, 1973), xvii–xviii.
24. Michael Folsom, ed., *Mike Gold: A Literary Anthology* (New York: International Publishers), 64–5.
25. It is beyond the scope of this chapter but it is worth noting the profound impact this literary movement had on world film, from postwar Italian neorealism and the noir films of the Hollywood left to the various new cinema movements of the Third World. The new Indian cinema of Satyajit Ray, Ritwik Ghatak, and Mrinal Sen was closely connected to the Marxist cultural movement; the Brazilian *cinema novo* followed the radical novelists in filming the Northeast, with Nelson Pereira dos Santos filming Graciliano Ramos's novel, *Vidas secas*; and Sembene Ousmane moved from the novel to become one of Africa's leading directors.
26. Hobsbawm, *The Age of Extremes*, 289–291.
27. Martin, *Journeys through the Labyrinth*, 376, n.11. See also Joe Lockard, "'Sugar Realism' in Caribbean Fiction," *Journal of Commonwealth and Postcolonial Studies*, vol. 2, no. 1 (Fall 1994), 80–103.
28. Jorge Amado, *The Violent Land*, trans. Samuel Putnam (New York: Knopf, 1945), 333, 249–250.
29. Alejo Carpentier, "On the Marvelous Real in America," in Lois Parkinson Zamora and Wendy B. Faris, eds., *Magical Realism: Theory, History, Community* (Durham: Duke University Press, 1995), 88.
30. Contrast with this Louis Aragon's earlier shift from surrealist desire to the socialist realism of his aptly named cycle *Le Monde réel.*
31. Gabriel García Márquez, *One Hundred Years of Solitude*, trans. Gregory Rabassa (New York: HarperPerennial, 1992), 315. I am indebted to the discussions in Gene H. Bell-Villada, "Banana Strike and Military Massacre: One Hundred Years of Solitude and What Happened in 1928," in his *Gabriel García Márquez's One Hundred Years of Solitude: A Casebook* (New York: Oxford University Press, 2002); and Franco Moretti, "Epilogue: One Hundred Years of Solitude," in his *Modern Epic: The World-System from Goethe to García Márquez* (London: Verso, 1996).
32. García Márquez, *One Hundred Years of Solitude*, 333, 320.
33. Ibid., 324, 327.

5 The Socioanalysis of Culture: Rethinking the Cultural Turn

1. Warren Susman, *Culture as History: The Transformation of American Society in the Twentieth Century* (New York: Pantheon Books, 1984), 153, 164.
2. Three of the most interesting accounts that take this position are Eagleton, *The Idea of Culture*; Mulhern, *Culture/Metaculture*; and David Lloyd and Paul Thomas, *Culture and the State* (New York: Routledge, 1998).
3. T.S. Eliot, *Notes towards the Definition of Culture*, in his *Christianity and Culture* (San Diego: Harcourt Brace & Company, 1976), 85. A.L. Kroeber and Clyde Kluckhohn, *Culture: A Critical Review of Concepts and Definitions* (New York: Vintage Books, n.d.), 3. See also Denys Cuche, *La Notion de culture dans les sciences sociales* (Paris: Éditions La Découverte, 1996).
4. Kroeber and Kluckhohn, *Culture*, 291–293. Matthew Arnold, *Culture and Anarchy and Other Writings*, edited by Stefan Collini (Cambridge: Cambridge University Press, 1993), 81, 141. Edward B. Tylor, *Collected Works, Volume Three: Primitive Culture* (London: Routledge, 1994), 1. Karl Marx, "Introduction to the *Grundrisse*," in Marx, *Later Political Writings*, edited by Terrell Carver (Cambridge: Cambridge University Press, 1996), 154. See also Raymond Williams, "Marx on Culture," in his *What I Came to Say* (London: Hutchinson Radius, 1989).
5. "*Culture and Society*," Williams noted twenty years later, "served as a bridge . . . but a bridge is something that people pass over. Still today many American readers say, oh yes, we agree with your position, we read *Culture and Society* . . . And I say that is not my position . . . I read this book as I might read a book by somebody else. It is a work most distant from me . . . ironically . . . the very success of the book . . . has created the conditions for its critique." Raymond Williams, *Politics and Letters* (London: Verso, 1981), 110, 107, 100.
6. Marx, "Introduction to the *Grundrisse*," 149–150 (translator's brackets). Max Horkheimer and Theodor W. Adorno, *Dialectic of Enlightenment* (New York: Seabury Press, 1972), 131.
7. Eliot, *Notes*, 105.
8. One can see the shift in the difference in tone between Arnold and Eliot: if Arnold's culture of 1869 was still optimistic and expanding – "culture, or the study of perfection, leads us to conceive of no perfection as being real which is not a *general* perfection, embracing all our fellow-men" (with only a small caveat about the popular literature which condescended to the masses) – Eliot's culture of 1948 was a shrinking terrain caught between the market and the state. Arnold, *Culture and Anarchy*, 174.

9. Pierre Bourdieu, *Distinction: A Social Critique of the Judgement of Taste* (Cambridge: Harvard University Press, 1984); R. Laurence Moore, *Selling God: American Religion in the Marketplace of Culture* (New York: Oxford University Press, 1994).
10. Eliot, *Notes*, 83. Bell, *The End of Ideology*, 313.
11. The notion of socioanalysis, coined as an echo of psychoanalysis, seems to have originated with the American socialist Leon Samson, *The American Mind: A Study in Socio-analysis* (New York: J. Cape & H. Smith, 1932). Robert Heilbroner picked up Samson's neologism in his insightful discussion of Marxism: *Marxism: For and Against* (New York: Norton, 1980).
12. Kenneth Burke, "Curriculum Criticum," in his *Counter-Statement* (Chicago: University of Chicago Press, 1957), 215.
13. Stuart Hall, David Morley, and Kuan-Hsing Chen, *Stuart Hall: Critical Dialogues in Cultural Studies* (London: Routledge, 1996), 442.
14. Paul A. Baran and Paul M. Sweezy, *Monopoly Capital: An Essay on the American Economic and Social Order* (Harmondsworth: Penguin Books, 1968).
15. C. Wright Mills, "Letter to the New Left," *New Left Review*, no. 5 (September–October 1960), 18–23; C. Wright Mills, "On the New Left," *Studies on the Left*, vol. 2, no. 1 (1961), 63–72.
16. The critical theory of the German New Left also included several powerful elaborations of the Frankfurt School themes. See Hans Magnus Enzensberger, *The Consciousness Industry* (New York: Continuum Books, 1974); Wolfgang Fritz Haug, *Critique of Commodity Aesthetics* (Minneapolis: University of Minnesota Press, 1986); and Oskar Negt and Alexander Kluge, *Public Sphere and Experience: Toward an Analysis of the Bourgeois and Proletarian Public Sphere* (Minneapolis: University of Minnesota Press, 1993).
17. Fredric Jameson, "Reification and Utopia in Mass Culture," in his *Signatures of the Visible* (New York: Routledge, 1992).
18. Etienne Balibar argues that ideology and fetishism are not two halves of the same theory but two different theories: "the theory of ideology is fundamentally a *theory of the State* (by which we mean the mode of domination inherent in the State), whereas that of fetishism is fundamentally a *theory of the market* (the mode of subjection or constitution of the 'world' of subjects and objects inherent in the organization of society as market and its domination by market forces)." The first, he suggests, develops out of Marx's critique of Hegel on the state; the second out of Marx's critique of political economy. Etienne Balibar, *The Philosophy of Marx* (London: Verso, 1995), 77–78.
19. Michel Foucault, *Discipline and Punish* (New York: Pantheon Books, 1978), 217.

20. Walter Benjamin, *Charles Baudelaire: A Lyric Poet in the Era of High Capitalism* (London: NLB, 1973), 166.
21. Gramsci quoted in Stuart Hall, "Gramsci's Relevance for the Study of Race and Ethnicity," in Hall, Morley, and Chen, *Stuart Hall: Critical Dialogues in Cultural Studies*, 429. Stuart Hall, *The Hard Road to Renewal: Thatcherism and the Crisis of the Left* (London: Verso, 1988), 71.
22. Hall, *The Hard Road*, 170.
23. Wallerstein, *Geopolitics and Geoculture*, 158. Nancy Fraser, *Justice Interruptus: Critical Reflections on the "Postsocialist" Condition* (New York: Routledge, 1997).
24. Karl Marx, *Capital: A Critique of Political Economy, Volume One*, translated by Ben Fowkes (New York: Penguin Books, 1976), 284.
25. Harry Braverman, *Labor and Monopoly Capital* (New York: Monthly Review Press, 1975), 126, 174.
26. Karl Marx and Friedrich Engels, *The German Ideology*, edited by C. J. Arthur (New York: International Publishers, 1970), 53.
27. Eric Lott, "The Aesthetic Ante: Pleasure, Pop Culture, and the Middle Passage," *Callaloo*, vol. 17, no. 2 (1994), 545–55. Eric Lott, *Love and Theft: Blackface Minstrelsy and the American Working Class* (New York: Oxford University Press, 1993), 10–11.
28. Tillie Olsen, *Silences* (New York: Delta, 1978), ix.
29. David Harvey, *The Limits to Capital* (Chicago: University of Chicago Press, 1982), 163.
30. Karl Marx, *Wage-Labour and Capital* (New York: International Press, 1976), 33.

6 The End of Mass Culture

1. See in particular Stuart Hall, "Cultural Studies: Two Paradigms," *Media, Culture and Society* 2 (1980), 57–72; Richard Johnson, "Three Problematics: Elements of a Theory of Working-Class Culture," in *Working-Class Culture: Studies in History and Theory*, edited by John Clarke, Chas Critcher, and Richard Johnson (London: Hutchinson, 1979); and Tony Bennett, "The Politics of the 'Popular' and Popular Culture," in *Popular Culture and Social Relations*, edited by Janet Woollacott, Colin Mercer, and Tony Bennett (Milton Keynes: Open University Press, 1986).
2. Donald Lazere, ed., *American Media and Mass Culture: Left Perspectives* (Berkeley: University of California Press, 1987). Despite its date, more than two-thirds of its essays were written in the 1970s.

3. Fredric Jameson, "Reification and Utopia in Mass Culture," *Social Text*, no. 1 (Winter 1979), 130–48; Stuart Hall, "Notes on Deconstructing 'The Popular'," in *People's History and Socialist Theory*, edited by Raphael Samuel (London: Routledge & Kegan Paul, 1981). I would also note the somewhat earlier essay by Gareth Stedman Jones, "Class Expression Versus Social Control?" *History Workshop*, no. 4 (1977), 163–70.
4. For example, Jackson Lears noted that "left cultural historians have discovered traces of collective memory in Hollywood films, early network television programs, and other supposed citadels of social amnesia," and went on to say that he thought "such arguments may exaggerate the significance of the dissent embodied in mass cultural forms. There is too strong a tendency to elevate what is often a univocal, closed system of imagery into an elegant Bakhtinian conversation, where every neofascist utterance by Clint Eastwood implies a counterfascist critique of 'late capitalism.'" Jackson Lears, "Power, Culture, and Memory," *Journal of American History*, vol. 75 (1988), 139. Similarly, Judith Williamson (like Lears an analyst of advertising) complained of "left-wing academics . . . picking out strands of 'subversion' in every piece of pop culture from Street Style to Soap Opera" (quoted in Meaghan Morris, "Banality in Cultural Studies," *Discourse*, vol. 10, no. 2 [1988], 3).
5. Jameson, "Reification and Utopia in Mass Culture,"139; Hall, "Notes on Deconstructing 'The Popular'," 234, 239.
6. Hall, "Notes on Deconstructing 'The Popular'," 233; Jameson, "Reification and Utopia in Mass Culture," 144.
7. Hall, "Notes on Deconstructing 'The Popular'," 229; Jameson, "Reification and Utopia in Mass Culture,"134, 139–40.
8. Hall, "Notes on Deconstructing 'The Popular'," 233.
9. Theodor Adorno, "Letters to Walter Benjamin," in Ernst Bloch and others, *Aesthetics and Politics* (London: NLB, 1977), 123.
10. Garry Wills, *Reagan's America: Innocents at Home* (Garden City, NY: Doubleday, 1987); Michael Rogin, *Ronald Reagan, the Movie and Other Episodes in Political Demonology* (Berkeley: University of California Press, 1987); Stuart Hall, "The Great Moving Right Show," *Marxism Today*, January 1979, is collected in his *The Hard Road to Renewal.*
11. On the romance, see Janice A. Radway, *Reading the Romance: Women, Patriarchy, and Popular Literature* (Chapel Hill: University of North Carolina Press, 1984); and Tania Modleski, *Loving with a Vengeance: Mass-Produced Fantasies for Women* (Hamden, Conn.: Archon Books, 1982). On Hollywood melodrama, see Christine Gledhill, ed., *Home is Where the Heart is: Studies in Melodrama and the Woman's Film* (London: British Film Institute, 1987). One

of the first appropriations of Jameson's "reification and utopia" framework came in one of Radway's early essays on romance fiction.

12. Jameson, "Reification and Utopia in Mass Culture," 133.
13. Paul Buhle, ed., *Popular Culture in America* (Minneapolis: University of Minnesota Press, 1987), xxiv.
14. Jean Paul Sartre, *Search for a Method* (New York: Vintage Books, 1968), 56.
15. Jameson, "Reification and Utopia in Mass Culture,"140.
16. Fredric Jameson, "Postmodernism, Or the Cultural Logic of Late Capitalism," *New Left Review*, no. 146 (1984), 53–92; Fred Pfeil, "Makin' Flippy-Floppy: Postmodernism and the Baby Boom PMC," *The Year Left*, no. 1 (1985).
17. Bourdieu, *Distinction*, 569, 81, 87.
18. The key intervention was Jackson Lears, "The Concept of Cultural Hegemony," *American Historical Review*, vol. 90 (1985), 567–93. The term also emerged in the controversy between Thomas Haskell and David Brion Davis over the relation between capitalism and abolitionism: Thomas Haskell, "Convention and Hegemonic Interest in the Debate Over Antislavery," *American Historical Review*, vol. 92 (1987), 829–78, and has recently been the subject of an illuminating symposium on labor history and the concept of hegemony in the *Journal of American History*, vol. 75 (June 1988), 115–161.
19. Eric Foner, "Why is There no Socialism in the United States?" *History Workshop*, no. 17 (1984), 64; Haskell, "Convention and Hegemonic Interest in the Debate Over Antislavery," 834.
20. Lears, "The Concept of Cultural Hegemony," 568; George Lipsitz, "The Struggle for Hegemony," *Journal of American History*, vol. 75 (1988), 146.
21. Bourdieu, *Distinction*, 88.
22. Raymond Williams, *Culture* (London: Fontana, 1981), 93.
23. Bourdieu, *Distinction*, 32.
24. "The End of Mass Culture" was originally written for a 1988 international colloquium in Paris, sponsored by the journals *International Labor and Working-Class History* and *Le Mouvement Social*. It was subsequently published in *International Labor and Working-Class History*, no. 37 (Spring 1990) and was followed by several critiques. This response first appeared in *International Labor and Working-Class History*, no. 38 (Fall 1990).
25. Luisa Passerini, "The Limits of Academic Abstraction," *International Labor and Working-Class History*, no. 37 (Spring 1990), 27–8.
26. Adelheid von Saldern, "The Hidden History of Mass Culture," *International Labor and Working-Class History*, no. 37 (Spring 1990), 32–40.
27. William R. Taylor, "On the Dangers of Theory Without History," *International Labor and Working-Class History*, no. 37 (Spring 1990), 29–31; von

Saldern, "The Hidden History of Mass Culture." Leo Lowenthal's *Literature, Popular Culture and Society* (Englewood Cliffs: Prentice-Hall, 1961) was an important exception. For a fine account of the debates over mass culture in the US since World War II, see Andrew Ross, *No Respect: Intellectuals and Popular Culture* (London: Verso, 1989). See also Michael Denning, *Mechanic Accents: Dime Novels and Working-Class Culture in America* (London: Verso, 1987); and Michael Denning, *Cover Stories: Narrative and Ideology in the British Spy Thriller* (London: Routledge & Kegan Paul, 1987).

28. Janice Radway, "Maps and the Construction of Boundaries," *International Labor and Working-Class History*, no. 37 (Spring 1990), 23.
29. Radway, "Maps and the Construction of Boundaries," 25, 23, 25.
30. Raymond Williams, *Problems in Materialism and Culture* (London: Verso, 1980).
31. Radway, "Maps and the Construction of Boundaries," 26.
32. Quoted in Arnold Krupat, *The Voice in the Margin* (Berkeley: University of California Press, 1989), xi.
33. Radway, "Maps and the Construction of Boundaries," 26.

7 The Academic Left and the Rise of Cultural Studies

1. *New York Times*, 5 May 1991, 32. The key news stories about political correctness include Richard Bernstein's "The Rising Hegemony of the Politically Correct," *New York Times*, 28 October 1990, E1. The *Newsweek* "Thought Police" cover story appeared 24 December 1990; *New York* magazine jumped on the bandwagon with the "Are You Politically Correct?" cover story on 21 January 1991. *Time* headlined "U.S. Campuses: The New Intolerance," on 1 April 1991. The right-wing critique had been simmering for years: see Edward E. Ericson, Jr., *Radicals in the University* (Stanford: Hoover Institution Press, 1975), and Stephen Balch and Herbert London, "The Tenured Left," *Commentary*, vol. 82, no. 4 (October 1986). Balch and London went on to found the National Association of Scholars (NAS), whose quarterly journal *Academic Questions* began during the 1987–88 academic year. For a brief history of NAS, see Sara Diamond, "Readin', Writin' and Repressin'," *Z*, February 1991. The book-length attacks include Roger Kimball's *Tenured Radicals* (New York: Harper & Row, 1990) and Dinesh D'Souza's *Illiberal Education* (New York: Free Press, 1991), latter-day versions of William Buckley's *God and Man at Yale*. The Wisconsin populism of Charles Sykes's *Profscam* (Washington: Regnery Gateway, 1988) is more amusing,

mixing taxpayer outrage at university boondoggles with McCarthyite red-baiting.

2. Irving Howe, "The Value of the Canon," *New Republic*, 18 February 1991, 42. Barbara Epstein, "'Political Correctness' and Collective Powerlessness," *Socialist Review*, vol. 91, no. 3–4 (July–Dec 1991), 26, 32. Louis Menand, "Lost Faculties," *New Republic*, 9 and 16 July 1990, 39.
3. Balch and London, "The Tenured Left," 51.
4. Brian Morton, "How Not to Write for *Dissent*," *Dissent*, vol. 37, no.3 (Summer 1990).
5. There are three basic lineages for the phrase: it may be a descendent of the old Communist left's notion of a "correct line"; it has antecendents in the Maoist-influenced part of the New Left, which picked up "correct" from the translations of Mao; and its first verifiable uses are in the women's movement. A good history is Ruth Perry, "Historically Correct," *Women's Review of Books* (February 1992), 15.
6. One of the best articles on the controversy over university speech codes was written by Miss Manners. Judith Martin and Gunther Stent, "Attack Ideas, Not People," *New York Times*, 20 March 1991, A29.
7. Jerry Adler and others, "Taking Offense," *Newsweek*, 24 December 1990, 54.
8. Epstein, "'Political Correctness' and Collective Powerlessness"; Barbara Ehrenreich, "The Challenge for the Left," *Democratic Left* (July/August 1991); Richard Flacks, *Making History: The American Left and the American Mind* (New York: Columbia University Press, 1988), 168.
9. Henry Louis Gates, Jr., "Good-bye Columbus? Notes on the Culture of Criticism," *American Literary History*, vol. 3, no. 4 (Winter 1991), 716.
10. Balch and London, "The Tenured Left," 43. *The Condition of the Professoriate* (Princeton: Carnegie Foundation for the Advancement of Teaching, 1989).
11. Martin Finkelstein, *The American Academic Profession: A Synthesis of Social Scientific Inquiry Since World War 2* (Columbus: Ohio State University Press, 1984), 169–73.
12. Harold Bloom, ed., *Ralph Waldo Emerson* (New York: Chelsea House, 1985), 8.
13. David Bromwich, "The Future of Tradition," *Dissent*, vol. 36, no. 4 (Fall 1989), 541–57.
14. Finkelstein, *The American Academic Profession*, 173.
15. Lewis Coser, *Men of Ideas* (New York: Free Press, 1965).
16. See Clyde Barrow, *Universities and the Capitalist State: Corporate Liberalism and the Reconstruction of American Higher Education 1894–1928* (Madison: University of Wisconsin Press, 1990); Ellen Schrecker, *No Ivory Tower: McCarthyism and*

the Universities (New York: Oxford University Press, 1986); and Christopher Phelps, "The Second Time as Farce: The Right's 'New McCarthyism'," *Monthly Review*, vol. 43, no. 5 (October 1991).

17. Like Louis Menand, Epstein dissociates the academic left from radical social movements, arguing that the tenured radicals are *not* the former student activists of the New Left. See Epstein, "'Political Correctness' and Collective Powerlessness," 31 and Louis Menand, "Illiberalisms," *New Yorker*, 20 May 1991, 103.
18. Kimball, *Tenured Radicals*, 39.
19. For a British formulation, see Stuart Hall, "The Emergence of Cultural Studies and the Crisis of the Humanities," *October* no. 53 (Summer 1990), 11–23. See also Dennis L. Dworkin, *Cultural Marxism in Postwar Britain: History, the New Left, and the Origins of Cultural Studies* (Durham: Duke University Press, 1997). The best accounts of the translation are Joel Pfister, "The Americanization of Cultural Studies," *Yale Journal of Criticism*, vol. 4, no. 2 (1991), 199–229, and Alan O'Connor, "The Problem of American Cultural Studies," *Critical Studies in Mass Communication*, vol. 6 (1989), 404–413.
20. Coser, *Men of Ideas*, 267.
21. I deal with the work of these figures in *The Cultural Front*.
22. Paul Berman, ed., *Debating P.C.* (New York: Laurel, 1992), 14.
23. Wallerstein, "Culture as the Ideological Battleground of the Modern World-system," from his *Geopolitics and Geoculture*, 158–9.
24. Donna Haraway, "'Gender' for a Marxist Dictionary: The Sexual Politics of a Word," from her *Simians, Cyborgs, and Women* (New York: Routledge, 1991), 130.
25. Edward Said, *Orientalism* (New York: Vintage, 1979), 45.
26. Thus the finest immanent critique of cultural studies remains Walter Benjamin's critique of the cultural history of German social democracy embodied in the exemplary figure of Eduard Fuchs: see "Eduard Fuchs, Collector and Historian," in *One-Way Street and Other Writings* (London: Verso, 1979).
27. The introduction to Lennard Davis and Bella Mirabella's collection, *Left Politics and the Literary Profession* (New York: Columbia University Press, 1990), is a particularly striking example of the attempt to overcome the polarization of the literary left.
28. Not only did this academic craft unionism create a set of left counter-disciplinary journals, but it structures Bertell Ollman and Edward Vernoff's useful surveys of the left academy. See Ollman and Vernoff, *The Left Academy: Marxist Scholarship on American Campuses*, Vol. 1 (New York: McGraw-Hill, 1982), Vol. 2 (New York: Praeger, 1984), Vol. 3 (New York: Praeger, 1986).

29. John Searle, "The Storm over the University," in Berman, *Debating P.C.* 121. Watkins's corrosive critique of the work of universities is a powerful if implicit reply to works like *Profscam* where ideologues of the market find themselves horrified by the workings of the academic labor market, with its star systems and its neglect of teaching. Evan Watkins, *Work Time* (Stanford: Stanford University Press, 1989).
30. Daniel Bell, *The Reforming of General Education* (New York: Columbia University Press, 1966), 20.
31. William Cain, "An Interview with Irving Howe," *American Literary History*, vol. 1, no. 3 (Fall 1989).
32. Epstein, "'Political Correctness' and Collective Powerlessness," 33–4; Menand, "Lost Faculties," 40; Berman, *Debating P.C.*, 24.

8 What's Wrong with Cultural Studies?

1. Sue Kim and Cheryl Higashida, "Questions for Roundtable on Cultural Studies and Historical Materialism," *After Postcolonialism, Beyond Minority Discourse: Postcolonial, Ethnic and American Studies* conference, Cornell University, November 14, 19–21, 1999.
2. Wallerstein, *The Essential Wallerstein*, 265
3. Steve Fraser and Gary Gerstle, eds., *The Rise and Fall of the New Deal Order, 1930–1980* (Princeton: Princeton University Press, 1989), xix.
4. Wai Chee Dimock and Michael T. Gilmore, eds., *Rethinking Class: Literary Studies and Social Formations* (New York: Columbia University Press, 1994), 1.
5. C.L.R. James, *Amercan Civilization* (Cambridge: Blackwell, 1993), 36.
6. Stuart Hall, "Gramsci and Us," in Hall, *The Hard Road to Renewal*; Stuart Hall, "Gramsci's Relevance for the Study of Race and Ethnicity," in Hall, Morley, and Chen, *Stuart Hall: Critical Dialogues*; David Forgacs, ed., *An Antonio Gramsci Reader: Selected Writings, 1918–1935* (New York: Schocken Books, 1988).
7. Antonio Gramsci, *Selection from the Prison Notebooks* (New York: International Publishers, 1971), 127, 324, 52.
8. Ibid., 52; Ranajit Guha, "Preface," in Ranajit Guha and Gayatri Chakravorty Spivak, eds., *Selected Subaltern Studies* (New York: Oxford University Press, 1988), 35.
9. Antonio Gramsci, *Letters from Prison* (New York: Harper and Row, 1973), 79–80. Antonio Gramsci, *Selections from Cultural Writings* (Cambridge: Harvard University Press, 1985), 376, 349, 207–8, 101–2.

10. Gramsci, *Selections from the Prison Notebooks*, 177.
11. Ibid., 133, 130, 132, 340.
12. Eagleton, *The Idea of Culture*, 128.
13. The phrase "merely cultural" is used by Judith Butler in her reply to Nancy Fraser in a debate which deals with similar issues: see Nancy Fraser, "From Redistribution to Recognition? Dilemmas of Justice in a 'Post-Socialist' Age," *New Left Review*, no. 212 (July–August 1995); and Judith Butler, "Merely Cultural," *New Left Review*, no. 227 (January–February 1998).
14. Priyamvada Gopal, in the abstract of her contribution to the conference's roundtable on "Political and Intellectual Visions and Models." Preliminary Documents, *After Postcolonialism, Beyond Minority Discourse* conference, Cornell University, November 14, 19–21, 1999.
15. James C. Scott, *Domination and the Arts of Resistance: Hidden Transcripts* (New Haven: Yale University Press, 1990), 45, 86.
16. Andrew Ross, *Real Love: In Pursuit of Cultural Justice* (New York: New York University Press, 1998).

9 "The Special American Conditions": Marxism and American Studies

1. Karl Marx and Friedrich Engels, *Letters to Americans, 1848–1895* (New York: International Publishers, 1953), 26. Robert Sklar, "The Problem of an American Studies 'Philosophy': A Bibliography of New Directions," *American Quarterly*, vol. 27 (August 1975), 260. Frank Lentricchia, *Criticism and Social Change* (Chicago: University of Chicago Press, 1983), 6. Perry Anderson, *In the Tracks of Historical Materialism* (London: Verso, 1983), 24. One can get a good overview in the three volumes of Bertell Ollman and Edward Vernoff, eds., *The Left Academy*. It is striking that they do not include an essay on Marxism and American studies.
2. Leon Samson, "Americanism as Surrogate Socialism," in John Laslett and Seymour Martin Lipset, eds., *Failure of a Dream?: Essays in the History of American Socialism* (New York: Anchor, 1974), 426. For introductions, see Perry Anderson, *Considerations on Western Marxism* (London: Verso/NLB, 1976), and Martin Jay, *Marxism and Totality: The Adventures of a Concept from Lukács to Habermas* (Berkeley: University of California Press, 1984). Fredric Jameson, *Marxism and Form* (Princeton: University of Princeton Press, 1971). See also the special issue "Engagements: Postmodernism, Marxism, Politics," *boundary 2*, no. 11 (Fall-Winter 1982–1983). On the British Marxist historians

in the US, see *Radical History Review*, no. 19 (Winter 1978–1979). A right-wing critique also noticed the European-centered nature of US Marxists: "So far, the Marxist humanistic program in the universities has concentrated on criticism, social history, and the history of Marxist thought itself. It has nevertheless failed to develop a distinctive, persuasive critique of American culture comparable to the work of Adorno and Benjamin in the 1930s in the European context." Norman Cantor, "The Real Crisis in the Humanities Today," *New Criterion*, no. 3 (June 1985), 32.

3. Susman, *Culture as History*. Gene Wise, "'Paradigm Dramas' in American Studies: A Cultural and Institutional History of the Movement," *American Quarterly*, vol. 31 (Bibliography 1979), 293–337. For Boorstin's testimony, see Eric Bentley, ed., *Thirty Years of Treason: Excerpts from Hearings before the House Committee on Un-American Activities, 1938–1968* (New York: Viking, 1971), 601–12. Daniel Boorstin: *The Americans: The Colonial Experience* (New York: Random House, 1958); *The Americans: The National Experience* (New York: Random House, 1965); *The Americans: The Democratic Experience* (New York: Vintage, 1974). For a representative Cold War text, see Clinton Rossiter's influential *Marxism: A View from America* (New York: Harcourt, Brace & World, 1960).
4. Alan Trachtenberg, "Myth and Symbol," *Massachusetts Review*, vol. 25 (Winter 1984), 670–71. Kenneth Lynn, *New York Times Book Review*, 10 January 1982, 29.
5. In the original published version of this chapter, I added, parenthetically: "(There are moments when one wishes it were so, as when Frank Lentricchia attempts to claim Kenneth Burke as a 'Western Marxist'; but there are also moments when one must decline: consider the confusion of Marxism with economic determinism as a result of the influence of Beard's 'economic interpretation' of history.)" Though I would continue to insist on the difference between Marx and Beard – see the discussion in Eugene Genovese, *In Red and Black: Marxian Explorations in Southern and Afro-American History* (New York: Pantheon, 1971), 318–20, 337–39 – I now accept Lentricchia's account of Burke as a Western Marxist. See Lentricchia, *Criticism and Social Change*, 23; and my subsequent *The Cultural Front*, 434–45.
6. For the "Americanist" perspective, see "What is Americanism? A Symposium on Marxism and the American Tradition," *Partisan Review & Anvil*, vol. 3 (April 1936), 3–16, with statements by Burke, Arvin, and Frank among others. For the modernist position calling for the "Europeanization of American literature," see William Phillips and Philip Rahv, "Literature in a Political Decade," in Horace Gregory, ed., *New Letters in America* (New York: W.W.

Norton, 1937). For a fine account of this conflict which emphasizes its effect in the historiography of American politics, see Christopher Lasch, "Foreword," to Richard Hofstadter, *The American Political Tradition* (New York: Vintage, 1974).

7. F.O. Matthiessen, *The Responsibilities of the Critic* (New York: Oxford University Press, 1952), 184–99. See also the Matthiessen memorial issue of *Monthly Review*, vol. 2 (October 1950), and, for an extended discussion of the cultural criticism of the Popular Front, see my "American Culture and Socialist Theory," in *The Cultural Front.*
8. For an example of the union of the New Left and this critical American studies, see Charles Newman and George Abbott White, eds., *Literature in Revolution* (New York: Holt, Rinehart and Winston, 1972), which included essays by New Left activists (Carl Oglesby on Melville, Todd Gitlin on TV, and Paul Buhle on comics), an essay on Matthiessen, and essays by Leo Marx and Raymond Williams.
9. Leo Marx, "Double Consciousness and the Cultural Politics of F.O. Matthiessen," *Monthly Review*, vol. 34 (February 1983), 48. T.J. Jackson Lears, "The Concept of Cultural Hegemony," *American Historical Review*, vol. 90 (June 1985), 567–93.
10. F.O. Matthiessen, *American Renaissance: Art and Expression in the Age of Emerson and Whitman* (New York: Oxford University Press, 1941); Leo Marx, *The Machine in the Garden: Technology and the Pastoral Idea in America* (New York: Oxford University Press, 1964); Richard Hoggart, *The Uses of Literacy: Changing Patterns in English Mass Culture* (Boston: Beacon Press, 1961); Raymond Williams, *Culture and Society* (New York: Columbia University Press, 1958).
11. See Stuart Hall et al., *Culture, Language, Media* (London: Hutchinson, 1980) for a history of British cultural studies and a selection of work from the journal *Working Papers in Cultural Studies*, and Stuart Hall et al., *Policing the Crisis* (London: Macmillan, 1978).
12. Sean Wilentz, "Against Exceptionalism: Class Consciousness and the American Labor Movement," *International Labor and Working-Class History*, no. 26 (Fall 1984), 1–24; Eric Foner, "Why is there no Socialism in the United States?" *History Workshop*, no. 17 (Spring 1984), 57–80; Seymour Martin Lipset, "Why No Socialism in the United States?" in S. Bialer, ed., *Sources of Contemporary Radicalism* (Boulder: Westview Press, 1977); Jerome Karabel, "The Failure of American Socialism Reconsidered," *The Socialist Register* (1979), 204–27.
13. One might, crudely, distinguish four Marxisms of the last half-century: the state ideologies of the postcapitalist societies; the "Eastern Marxisms" which critically interrogate the historical experience of those societies, from Kollantai,

Trotsky, and the circle of Bakhtin, to Bahro and Medvedev; the Third World Marxisms which have theorized imperialism, colonialism, and the relations between national liberation and socialist transformation, from the early Mao Zedong and José Carlos Mariátegui to C.L.R. James and Amilcar Cabral; and the Western Marxisms I draw on in this essay, which have since Gramsci and Lukács addressed the resilience of the advanced capitalist nations, particularly in culture and ideology.

14. Louis Hartz, *The Founding of New Societies* (New York: Harcourt, Brace & World, 1964), 6; see also Hartz, *The Liberal Tradition in America* (New York: Harcourt, Brace & World, 1955), 254n. On European Marxist views of the US, see Lipset, "Why no Socialism?"; R. Laurence Moore, *European Socialists and the American Promised Land* (New York: Oxford University Press, 1970); and *Marx and Engels on the United States* (Moscow: Progress Publishers, 1979).
15. Hartz, *The Liberal Tradition*, 252.
16. This chapter is based on an essay orginally commissioned and published by the institutional journal in American studies, *American Quarterly*. I have not tried to update its account of American studies scholarship; thus the following section must now be read less as a review of contemporary work than as a portrait of the work of the New Left American studies scholars who transformed the field in the 1970s and early 1980s. In this survey of the Marxist scholarship, two qualifications are necessary. First, for a variety of reasons, including the recurrent "red scares" in the American academy and the disarray of the American left, there is no sure litmus test for Marxist scholarship. I have based this survey neither on party affiliation nor on political activity; rather I have cited work which either calls itself Marxist, is predominately influenced by leading Marxist theorists, or uses Marxist categories and a materialist conception of history. I am more interested in sending the reader to this work than in precise labels. Second, my focus on the the New Left years was a result of a sense that, as Ronald Aronson has noted, though "the two earlier heydays of American Left activity – centered on the pre-World War I Socialist Party and the Communist Party of the 1930s – were virtually barren of Marxist culture, . . . the New Left has led to the first significant intellectual advances for an American Marxism." Ronald Aronson, "Historical Materialism," *New Left Review*, no. 152 (July/August 1985), 79. For the history of earlier American Marxisms, see David Herreshoff, *The Origins of American Marxism* (New York: Monad Press, 1973); Oakley Johnson, *Marxism in United States History Before the Russian Revolution* (New York: Humanities Press, 1974); the still indispensable Donald Drew Egbert and Stow Persons, eds., *Socialism and American Life*, 2 vols (Princeton: Princeton University Press, 1952); Cedric Robinson, *Black*

Marxism: The Making of the Black Radical Tradition (London: Zed Press, 1983); and Stanley Aronowitz, "Culture and Politics," in his *The Crisis of Historical Materialism* (New York: Praeger, 1991). For bibliographies, see the second volume of Egbert and Persons; Lee Baxandall, *Marxism and Aesthetics: A Selected Annotated Bibliography* (New York: Humanities Press, 1968); and Chris Bullock and David Peck, *Guide to Marxist Literary Criticism* (Bloomington: Indiana University Press, 1980).

17. Harry Henderson, *Versions of the Past: The Historical Imagination in American Fiction* (New York: Oxford University Press, 1974); Myra Jehlen, "New World Epics," *Salmagundi*, no. 36 (Winter 1977), 49–68; see also her *Class and Character in Faulkner's South* (New York: Columbia University Press, 1976); Michael T. Gilmore, *American Romanticism and the Marketplace* (Chicago: University of Chicago Press, 1985); Carolyn Porter, *Seeing and Being: The Plight of the Participant Observer in Emerson, James, Adams, and Faulkner* (Middletown, Conn.: Wesleyan University Press, 1981), xvii.

18. June Howard, *Form and History in American Literary Naturalism* (Chapel Hill: University of North Carolina Press, 1985); Rachel Bowlby, *Just Looking: Consumer Culture in Dreiser, Gissing and Zola* (New York: Methuen, 1985); Alan Wald, *James T. Farrell: The Revolutionary Socialist Years* (New York: New York University Press, 1978); Alan Wald, *The Revolutionary Imagination: The Poetry and Politics of John Wheelwright and Sherry Mangan* (Chapel Hill: University of North Carolina Press, 1983); Robert Rosen, *John Dos Passos: Politics and the Writer* (Lincoln: University of Nebraska Press, 1983); H. Bruce Franklin, *The Victim as Criminal and Artist: Literature from the American Prison* (New York: Oxford University Press, 1978).

19. For accounts of Marxist-feminist work, see Nancy Hartsock, *Money, Sex, and Power: Toward a Feminist Historical Materialism* (New York: Longman, 1983), and Lise Vogel, *Marxism and the Oppression of Women* (New Brunswick, NJ: Rutgers University Press, 1983). Elizabeth Fox-Genovese offers a Marxist account of women's history in "Placing Women's History in History," *New Left Review*, no. 133 (May–June 1982), 5–29. Lillian Robinson, *Sex, Class, and Culture* (Bloomington: Indiana University Press, 1978); Rachel Blau DuPlessis, *Writing Beyond the Ending: Narrative Strategies of Twentieth-Century Women Writers* (Bloomington: Indiana University Press, 1985). Ann Snitow, "Mass Market Romance: Pornography for Women is Different," in A. Snitow, C. Stansell, and S. Thompson, *Powers of Desire: The Politics of Sexuality* (New York: Monthly Review Press, 1983). Tania Modleski, *Loving With a Vengeance: Mass-produced Fantasies For Women* (Hamden, Conn.: Archon, 1982); Radway, *Reading the Romance*.

20. See the journal *Science Fiction Studies*; H. Bruce Franklin's *Future Perfect: American Science Fiction of the Nineteenth Century*, rev. ed. (New York: Oxford University Press, 1978); and his *Robert A. Heinlein: America as Science Fiction* (New York: Oxford University Press, 1980); Fredric Jameson's essays on science fiction: "World Reduction in Le Guin," *Science Fiction Studies*, vol. 2 (1975), 221–30; "After Armageddon," *Science Fiction Studies*, vol. 2 (1975), 31–42; "Progress versus Utopia: or, Can We Imagine the Future?" *Science Fiction Studies*, no. 27 (1982), 147–58; and Darko Suvin's *Metamorphoses of Science Fiction: On the Poetics and History of a Literary Genre* (New Haven: Yale University Press, 1979).
21. Henry Nash Smith, *Virgin Land: The American West as Myth and Symbol* (Cambridge: Harvard University Press, 1950); Richard Slotkin, *Regeneration Through Violence: The Mythology of the American Frontier, 1600–1860* (Middletown, Conn.: Wesleyan University Press, 1973); Annette Kolodny, *The Land Before Her: Fantasy and Experience of the American Frontiers, 1630–1860* (Chapel Hill: University of North Carolina Press, 1984); Richard Slotkin, *The Fatal Environment: The Myth of the Frontier in the Age of Industrialization, 1800–1890* (New York: Atheneum, 1985), 47; Michael P. Rogin, *Fathers and Children: Andrew Jackson and the Subjugation of the Indians* (New York: Knopf, 1975); Michael P. Rogin, *Subversive Genealogies: The Politics and Art of Herman Melville* (New York: Knopf, 1983); Ronald Takaki, *Iron Cages: Race and Culture in 19th-Century America* (Seattle: University of Washington Press, 1979). See also Susan Willis' readings of American writers through the lens of dependency theory: "Aesthetics of the Rural Slum," *Social Text*, no. 2 (Spring 1979), 82–103; "A Literary Lesson in Historical Thinking," *Social Text*, no. 3 (Fall 1980), 136–43; and "Eruptions of Funk," in H. L. Gates, Jr., ed., *Black Literature and Literary Theory* (New York: Methuen, 1984).
22. Saul Padover, ed., *The Letters of Karl Marx* (Englewood Cliffs, NJ: Prentice-Hall, 1979), 335–36. This work was begun, in a non-Marxist way, by the classic exponent of American exceptionalism, Louis Hartz, who focused on ideological issues in his *The Founding of New Societies*, and it has been practiced particularly in the fields of comparative frontiers and comparative slavery and race relations. See Stanley Greenberg, *Race and State in Capitalist Development* (New Haven: Yale University Press, 1980) for a Marxist example of such work; and William Cronon, *Changes in the Land: Indians, Colonists, and the Ecology of New England* (New York: Hill & Wang, 1983) for a discussion of the ecological consequences of the transformation in the mode of production after the European invasion of North America.
23. Karl Marx, *Capital*, Vol. I (Harmondsworth: Penguin, 1976), 414. For treat-

ments of the Communist Party and black Americans, see Harold Cruse, *The Crisis of the Negro Intellectual* (New York: William Morrow & Co., 1967) and Mark Naison, *Communists in Harlem during the Depression* (Urbana: University of Illinois Press, 1983). Robinson, *Black Marxism*, is a key treatment of black Marxist thinkers. For the place of Marxism in the rise of Afro-American studies in the 1960s and 1970s, see Genovese, *In Red and Black*; Manning Marable, *Blackwater: Historical Studies in Race, Class Consciousness and Revolution* (Dayton, OH: Black Praxis Press, 1981); Manning Marable, *How Capitalism Underdeveloped Black America* (Boston: South End Press, 1983). See also Alexander Saxton's review essay, "Historical Explanations of Racial Inequality," *Marxist Perspectives*, no. 6 (Summer 1979), 146–68, and the critique and reconstruction of Marxist theories of racial formation in Michael Omi and Howard Winant, "By the Rivers of Babylon: Race in the United States," *Socialist Review*, no. 71 (September–October 1983), 31–65, and no. 72 (November–December 1983), 35–68.

24. Cornel West, "The Dilemma of the Black Intellectual," *Cultural Critique*, no. 1 (Fall 1985), 114. Eugene Genovese, *Roll, Jordan, Roll: The World the Slaves Made* (New York: Pantheon, 1974); Cornel West, *Prophecy Deliverance!: An Afro-American Revolutionary Christianity* (Philadelphia: Westminster Press, 1982); V. P. Franklin, *Black Self-Determination: A Cultural History of the Faith of the Fathers* (Westport, CT: Lawrence Hill & Co., 1984). On black music, see Sidney Finkelstein, *Jazz: A People's Music* (New York: Citadel Press, 1948); Theodor Adorno, "Perennial Fashion – Jazz," (1953), in his *Prisms* (London: Neville Spearman, 1967); Francis Newton [Eric Hobsbawm], *The Jazz Scene* (London: MacGibbon and Kee, 1959); Frank Kofsky, *Black Nationalism and the Revolution in Music* (New York: Pathfinder Press, 1970); Ben Sidran, *Black Talk* (New York: Holt, Rinehart & Winston, 1971); and Paul Garon, *Blues and the Poetic Spirit* (London: Edison Press, 1975).

25. Amiri Baraka, *Daggers and Javelins* (New York: William Morrow and Co., 1984); Houston Baker, *Blues, Ideology, and Afro-American Literature: A Vernacular Theory* (Chicago: University of Chicago Press, 1984); John Brown Childs, "Concepts of Culture in Afro-American Political Thought, 1890–1920," *Social Text*, no. 3 (Fall 1981), 28–43; John Brown Childs, "Afro-American Intellectuals and the People's Culture," *Theory and Society*, vol. 13 (1984), 69–90; Hazel V. Carby, *Reconstructing Womanhood: The Emergence of the Afro-American Woman Novelist* (New York: Oxford University Press, 1987).

26. Susman, *Culture as History*, 41. For the mode of production debate, see *Radical History Review* (Winter 1977), no. 18 (Fall 1978), no. 22 (Winter 1979–1980).

27. Sacvan Bercovitch, *The American Jeremiad* (Madison: University of Wisconsin

Press, 1978), 176, 141, 13. But he did not title his chapter, "The Ritual of Consensus," "The Ritual of Hegemony." Samson, "Americanism as Surrogate Socialism," 426. The major treatments of Samson's "Americanism" thesis are Lipset, "Why no Socialism?"; Susman, "Socialism and Americanism," in his *Culture as History*; Michael Harrington, *Socialism* (New York: Saturday Review Press, 1972); Daniel Bell, "The End of American Exceptionalism," in his *The Winding Passage* (Cambridge: Abt Books, 1980); and Irving Howe, *Socialism and America* (New York: Harcourt Brace Jovanovich, 1985). Howe explicitly invokes Bercovitch's work on the Puritan covenant.

28. Though I am focusing on culture in this essay, it is important to note that for Marxists, "Americanism" signifies not only mass consumer culture, but also the reconstruction of the labor process on "Taylorist" and "Fordist" principles. So the studies of the capitalist reshaping of technology and the labor process by Harry Braverman, *Labor and Monopoly Capital* (New York: Monthly Review Press, 1974); David Noble, *America by Design: Science, Technology, and the Rise of Corporate Capitalism* (New York: Oxford University Press, 1977); David Montgomery, *Workers' Control in America* (Cambridge: Cambridge University Press, 1979); and Michael Buroway, *The Politics of Production* (London: Verso, 1985), among others, are essential for American cultural studies.
29. Gramsci, *Selections from the Prison Notebooks*. For a selection and bibliography of the work of the Frankfurt School, see Andrew Arato and Eike Gebhardt, eds., *The Essential Frankfurt School Reader* (New York: Urizen Books, 1978). Bernard Rosenberg and David M. White, eds., *Mass Culture* (Glencoe, IL: Free Press, 1957).
30. For an account of the Frankfurt critique of mass culture, see Martin Jay, *The Dialectical Imagination* (Boston: Little, Brown and Co., 1973), 173–218; Patrick Brantlinger, *Bread and Circuses: Theories of Mass Culture as Social Decay* (Ithaca: Cornell University Press, 1984), represents the recent critique. For the differences between Adorno and Benjamin, see their correspondence in Bloch and others, *Aesthetics and Politics*. For a brilliant reading of Adorno against the grain, see Andreas Huyssen, "Adorno in Reverse: From Hollywood to Richard Wagner," *New German Critique*, no. 29 (Spring/Summer 1983), 8–38.
31. Jameson, "Reification and Utopia in Mass Culture," 133–34, 144.
32. Stuart Ewen, *Captains of Consciousness: Advertising and the Social Roots of Consumer Culture* (New York: McGraw-Hill, 1976); see the important review essay by Susan Porter Benson, "Advertising America," *Socialist Review*, no. 43 (January–February 1979), 143–55; Elizabeth Ewen and Stuart Ewen, *Channels of Desire: Mass Images and the Shaping of American Consciousness* (New York:

McGraw-Hill, 1982). The works of Herbert Schiller include: *Mass Communications and American Empire* (Boston: Beacon, 1971); *The Mind Managers* (Boston: Beacon, 1973); *Communication and Cultural Domination* (White Plains, NY: International Arts and Sciences Press, 1976); *Who Knows: Information in the Age of the Fortune 500* (Norwood, NJ: Ablex Pub. Corp., 1981); and *Information and the Crisis Economy* (Norwood, NJ: Ablex Pub. Corp., 1984). Ariel Dorfman and Armand Mattelart, *How to Read Donald Duck: Imperialist Ideology in the Disney Comic* (London: International General, 1975); Ariel Dorfman, *The Empire's Old Clothes: What the Lone Ranger, Babar, and Other Innocent Heroes Do To Our Minds* (New York: Pantheon, 1983); Todd Gitlin, *The Whole World is Watching: Mass Media in the Making and the Unmaking of the New Left* (Berkeley: University of California Press, 1980); Todd Gitlin, *Inside Prime Time* (New York: Pantheon, 1983).

33. Editors of *Cahiers du Cinéma*, "John Ford's *Young Mr. Lincoln*," in *Screen Reader 1: Cinema/IdeologyPolitics* (London: Society for Education in Film and Television, 1977); Laura Mulvey, "Visual Pleasure and Narrative Cinema," *Screen*, vol. 16 (1975), 6–18. Bill Nichols, *Ideology and the Image: Social Representation in the Cinema and Other Media* (Bloomington: Indiana University Press, 1981); E. Ann Kaplan, *Women and Film: Both Sides of the Camera* (New York: Methuen, 1983); Peter Biskind, *Seeing is Believing: How Hollywood Taught Us to Stop Worrying and Love the Fifties* (New York: Pantheon, 1983); Robert B. Ray, *A Certain Tendency of the Hollywood Cinema, 1930–1980* (Princeton: Princeton University Press, 1985). See also Flo Leibowitz's review essay, "Marxist Film Theory," *Socialist Review*, no. 80 (March–April 1985), 127–39.

34. Martin Sklar, "On the Proletarian Revolution and the End of Political-Economic Society," *Radical America*, vol. 3 (May-June 1969), 1–39; Barbara Ehrenreich and John Ehrenreich, "The Professional-Managerial Class," in Pat Walker, ed., *Between Labor and Capital* (Boston: South End Press, 1979). Jean-Christophe Agnew's "A Touch of Class," *democracy*, vol. 3 (Summer 1983), 59–72, is a fine survey of the "new class" controversy. The major works in the "culture of abundance" vein include Susman, *Culture as History*; and T.J. Jackson Lears, *No Place of Grace: Antimodernism and the Transformation of American Culture, 1880–1920* (New York: Pantheon, 1981); and, somewhat earlier, Christopher Lasch, *The New Radicalism in America, 1889–1963: The Intellectual as a Social Type* (New York: Knopf, 1965). Feminist discussions include Barbara Ehrenreich and Deidre English, *For Her Own Good: 150 Years of the Experts' Advice to Women* (Garden City, NY: Anchor, 1978); and Dolores Hayden, *The Grand Domestic Revolution: A History of Feminist Designs for American Homes,*

Neighborhoods, and Cities (Cambridge: MIT Press, 1981). An Italian Marxist treatment of this cultural transformation is Giorgio Ciucci *et al.*, *The American City from the Civil War to the New Deal* (Cambridge: MIT Press, 1979). See also Richard Ohmann, *Selling Culture: Magazines, Markets, and Class at the Turn of the Century* (London: Verso, 1996).

35. Stanley Aronowitz, *False Promises: The Shaping of American Working Class Consciousness* (New York: McGraw-Hill, 1973). Herbert Gutman's *Work, Culture and Society in Industrializing America* (New York: Knopf, 1976) was an ambitious synthesis of a Thompsonian conception of class and the Marxist anthropology of Sidney Mintz and Eric Wolf; nevertheless, as David Montgomery noted, its force was blunted by the language of modernization theory. Montgomery, "Gutman's Nineteenth-Century America," *Labor History*, vol. 19 (Summer 1978), 416–29.
36. Susman, *Culture as History*, 192; Dan Schiller, *Objectivity and the News: The Public and the Rise of Commercial Journalism* (Philadelphia: University of Pennsylvania Press, 1981); Denning, *Mechanic Accents*; Roy Rosenzweig, *Eight Hours For What We Will: Workers and Leisure in an Industrial City, 1870–1920* (Cambridge: Cambridge University Press, 1983); Sarah Eisenstein, *Give Us Bread But Give Us Roses: Working Women's Consciousness in the United States, 1890 to the First World War* (London: Routledge and Kegan Paul, 1983); Elizabeth Ewen, *Immigrant Women in the Land of Dollars: Life and Culture on the Lower East Side, 1890–1925* (New York: Monthly Review Press, 1985); Kathy Peiss, *Cheap Amusements: Working Women and Leisure in Turn-of-the-Century New York* (Philadelphia: Temple University Press, 1986); George Lipsitz, *Class and Culture in Cold War America* (South Hadley, Mass.: J.F. Bergin, 1982); Alan Trachtenberg, *The Incorporation of America: Culture and Society in the Gilded Age* (New York: Hill and Wang, 1982).
37. Fredric Jameson, *The Political Unconscious: Narrative as a Socially Symbolic Act* (Ithaca: Cornell University Press, 1981). See the special issue on *The Political Unconscious*, *Diacritics*, vol. 12 (Fall 1982).
38. Aronowitz, *The Crisis in Historical Materialism*; Bertell Ollman, *Alienation: Marx's Conception of Man in Capitalist Society* (Cambridge: Cambridge University Press, 1976); Richard Ohmann, *English in America: A Radical View of the Profession* (New York: Oxford University Press, 1976); Michael Ryan, *Marxism and Deconstruction: A Critical Articulation* (Baltimore: Johns Hopkins University Press, 1982); John Fekete, *The Critical Twilight: Explorations in the Ideology of Anglo-American Literary Theory from Eliot to McLuhan* (Boston: Routledge & Kegan Paul, 1977); Lentricchia, *Criticism and Social Change*; West, *Prophecy*

Deliverance!; Cornel West, *The American Evasion of Philosophy: A Genealogy of Pragmatism* (Madison: University of Wisconsin Press, 1989); Edward Said, *The World, the Text, and the Critic* (Cambridge: Harvard University Press, 1983).

39. Said, *The World, the Text, and the Critic*, 29.
40. Ibid., 174.
41. Marvin Harris, *Cultural Materialism: The Struggle for a Science of Culture* (New York: Random House, 1979). Harris's "cultural materialism" ought not be confused with Raymond Williams's use of that phrase. For a Marxist critique of demographic determinism, see Wally Seccombe, "Marxism and Demography," *New Left Review*, no. 137 (January–February 1983), 22–47.
42. For Marxist discussions of the original metaphor, see Raymond Williams, "Base and Superstructure in Marxist Cultural Theory," in his *Problems in Materialism and Culture* (London: NLB, 1980), and Stuart Hall, "Rethinking the Base/Superstructure Metaphor," in Jon Bloomfield, ed., *Class, Hegemony, and Party* (London: Lawrence and Wishart, 1976).
43. Louis Althusser, *Lenin and Philosophy and Other Essays* (New York: Monthly Review Press, 1971); Jameson, *The Political Unconscious*; Fredric Jameson, "Ideology, Narrative Analysis, and Popular Culture," *Theory and Society*, no. 4 (1977), 543–59; Terry Eagleton, *Criticism and Ideology* (London: NLB, 1976); Terry Eagleton, "Ideology, Fiction, Narrative," *Social Text*, no. 2 (Summer 1979), 62–81. Perhaps the best review and synthesis is Göran Therborn, *The Power of Ideology and the Ideology of Power* (London: NLB, 1980).
44. Lears, "The Concept of Cultural Hegemony," discusses the relation between "consensus" and "hegemony," without, to my mind, escaping the consensus model.
45. Raymond Williams, *Marxism and Literature* (New York: Oxford University Press, 1977), 5. See also his *The Sociology of Culture* (New York: Schocken, 1982).
46. Said, *The World, the Text, and the Critic*, 166.

10 The Peculiarities of the Americans: Reconsidering *Democracy in America*

1. Aileen S. Kraditor, *The Radical Persuasion 1890–1917* (Baton Rouge: Louisiana State University Press, 1981), 39; Lentricchia, *Criticism and Social Change*, 6.
2. John Diggins, "Comrades and Citizens: New Mythologies in American Historiography," *American Historical Review*, vol. 90 (June 1985), 615.
3. Rossiter quoted in Lynn L. Marshall and Seymour Drescher, "American

Historians and Tocqueville's *Democracy*," *Journal of American History*, vol. 55 (December 1968), 515–6; Robert Nisbet, "Many Tocquevilles," *American Scholar*, vol. 46 (Winter 1976–77), 60: Marshall and Drescher, "American Historians and Tocqueville's *Democracy*," 514; George Wilson Pierson, *Tocqueville and Beaumont in America* (New York: Oxford University Press, 1938); Susman, *Culture as History*, 59.

4. Louis Hartz, *The Liberal Tradition in America* (New York: Harcourt, Brace & World, 1955), 11, 135, 277, 236–7.
5. Alexis de Tocqueville, *Democracy in America*, translated by George Lawrence (Garden City: Anchor, 1969), 18; Lewis Feuer, "The Alienated Americans and Their Influence on Marx and Engels," in his *Marx and the Intellectuals* (Garden City, NY: Anchor, 1969).
6. Tocqueville quoted in Pierson, *Tocqueville and Beaumont in America*, 102.
7. Tocqueville, *Democracy in America*, 267, 266, 269, 270.
8. Ibid., 454; Tocqueville quoted in Pierson, *Tocqueville and Beaumont in America*, 32; Tocqueville quoted in Marshall and Drescher, "American Historians and Tocqueville's *Democracy*," 523–4.
9. Tocqueville, *Democracy in America*, 9, 417.
10. Ibid., 50, 543.
11. Edward Pessen, "The Egalitarian Myth and the American Social Reality: Wealth, Mobility, and Equality in the 'Era of the Common Man'," *American Historical Review*, vol. 76 (October 1971), 989–1034.
12. Tocqueville, *Democracy in America*, 504.
13. Ibid., 518, 520, 513.
14. Ibid., 522, 517, 63, 278n
15. Ibid., 517, 521, 558.
16. Matthiessen, *American Renaissance*, 533.
17. Tocqueville, *Democracy in America*, 478, 204.
18. Ibid., 468.
19. Ibid., 403.
20. Ibid., 176.
21. Feuer, "The Alienated Americans," 200.
22. Tocqueville, *Democracy in America*, 316.
23. Ibid., 324, 318.
24. Ibid., 409, 635, 638–9, 639.
25. Hartz, *The Founding of New Societies*, 95; Rogin, *Fathers and Children*.
26. Donald Denoon, *Settler Capitalism* (New York: Oxford University Press, 1983), 2, 209, 225.

11 Neither Capitalist nor American: The Democracy as Social Movement

1. Richard McKeon, ed., *Democracy in a World of Tensions: A Symposium Prepared by UNESCO* (Chicago: University of Chicago Press, 1951), 522. Gordon Wood, "Democracy and the American Revolution," in John Dunn, ed., *Democracy: The Unfinished Journey* (Oxford: Oxford University Press, 1992), 91. Tocqueville, *Democracy in America*, 454, 456, 238, 580, 620n.
2. Perronet Thompson from the *Oxford English Dictionary*; Tocqueville is quoted in French in Jens Christophersen, *The Meaning of "Democracy" As Used in European Ideologies from the French to the Russian Revolution* (Oslo: Universitets-forlaget, 1966), 80; I quote Tocqueville's nineteenth-century translator, Henry Reeve, in this case because he preserves Tocqueville's use of this meaning of the democracy; Mill is quoted in Christopherson, 160; the *Times* of London is quoted in Francis Wheen, *Karl Marx* (New York: W.W. Norton, 2000), 325.
3. Russell L. Hanson, *The Democratic Imagination in America* (Princeton: Princeton University Press, 1985), 56. Gordon Wood, "Democracy and the American Revolution," in Dunn, *Democracy*, 98.
4. Peter Linebaugh and Marcus Rediker, *The Many-Headed Hydra: Sailors, Slaves, Commoners, and the Hidden History of the Revolutionary Atlantic* (Boston: Beacon Press, 2000), 211–47.
5. Christophersen, *The Meaning of "Democracy"*, 322, 323. Hal Draper, *Karl Marx's Theory of Revolution: Volume Two* (New York: Monthly Review Press, 1978), 76.
6. Quoted in Draper, *Karl Marx's Theory of Revolution*, vol. 2, 212n
7. Carlyle and Guizot quoted in Christophersen, *The Meaning of "Democracy"*, 63, 77. The point about emancipation is made by Bonnie Anderson, *Joyous Greetings: The First International Women's Movement, 1830–1860* (New York: Oxford University Press, 2000), 114. Marx and Engels, *Collected Works*, vol. 20, 14.
8. Walsh quoted in Sean Wilentz, *Chants Democratic: New York City and the Rise of the American Working Class, 1788–1850* (New York: Oxford University Press, 1984), 331. Marx and Engels, *Collected Works*, vol. 11, 374.
9. Robert Dahl, *On Democracy* (New Haven: Yale University Press, 1998), 3.
10. Barrington Moore, *The Social Origins of Dictatorship and Democracy* (Boston: Beacon Press, 1966), 418.
11. Göran Therborn, "The Rule of Capital and the Rise of Democracy," *New Left Review*, no. 103 (January–April 1977). Dietrich Rueschemeyer, John D.

Stephens, and Evelyne Huber Stephens, *Capitalist Development and Democracy* (Chicago: University of Chicago Press, 1992), 98; see also 270.

12. Rueschemeyer, Stephens, and Stephens, *Capitalist Development and Democracy*, 271.
13. Perry Anderson, "The Affinities of Norberto Bobbio," in his *A Zone of Engagement* (London: Verso, 1992), 124.
14. See, in particular, Ruth Berins Collier, *Paths Toward Democracy: The Working Class and Elites in Western Europe and South America* (Cambridge: Cambridge University Press, 1999).
15. Alexander Keyssar, *The Right to Vote: The Contested History of Democracy in the United States* (New York: Basic Books, 2000), 70.
16. See David Montgomery, *Citizen Worker: The Experience of Workers in the United States with Democracy and the Free Market During the Nineteenth Century* (Cambridge: Cambridge University Press, 1993).
17. Keyssar, *The Right to Vote*, 169.
18. Alexander Hicks, *Social Democracy and Welfare Capitalism: A Century of Income Security Politics* (Ithaca: Cornell University Press, 1999), 20. Patrick Heller, *The Labor of Development: Workers and the Transformation of Capitalism in Kerala, India* (Ithaca: Cornell University Press, 1999), 6–7.
19. Ellen Meiksins Wood, *Democracy Against Capitalism: Renewing Historical Materialism* (Cambridge: Cambridge University Press, 1995), 214. Montgomery, *Citizen Worker*, 2, 12.
20. Midnight Notes, *Midnight Oil: Work, Energy, War, 1973–1992* (New York: Autonomedia, 1992).
21. Tocqueville, *Democracy in America*, 513, 517, 521.
22. Bobbio quoted in Anderson, "The Affinities of Norberto Bobbio," 116. Norberto Bobbio, *Democracy and Dictatorship* (Minneapolis: University of Minnesota Press, 1989), 157.
23. *Unfair Advantage: Workers' Freedom of Association in the United States under International Human Rights Standards* (New York: Human Rights Watch, 2000), 8, 10.
24. Jonathan D. Rosenblum, *Copper Crucible: How the Arizona Miners' Strike of 1983 Recast Labor-Management Relations in America* (Ithaca, NY: ILR Press, 1995), 123, 224.
25. *Unfair Advantage*, 196.
26. Rebecca Ruquist, statement made in conjunction with my DeVane Tercentennial Lecture, Yale University, February 13 2001.
27. Peg Tamulevich, statement made in conjunction with my DeVane Tercentennial Lecture, Yale University, February 13 2001.

28. When I was first approached about delivering the lecture this chapter was based on – a lecture in a series on democracy – I was asked to address democracy and the labor market.
29. Karl Marx, *Capital: Volume One*, in Marx and Engels, *Collected Works*, vol. 35, 362.
30. Tocqueville, *Democracy in America*, 558.
31. Robert Putnam, *Bowling Alone: The Collapse and Revival of American Community* (New York: Simon & Schuster, 2000).
32. Walt Whitman, "Democratic Vistas," in *Leaves of Grass and Selected Prose* (New York: Modern Library, 1950), 477.
33. World Bank, *World Development Report 1995: Workers in an Integrating World* (Oxford: Oxford University Press, 1995), 9.
34. Quoted in Kim Moody, "Global Labor Stands Up to Global Capital," *Labor Notes*, no. 256 (July 2000), 9.

12 A Cultural Front in the Age of Three Worlds?

1. Steven Fraser and Joshua B. Freeman, eds., *Audacious Democracy: Labor, Intellectuals, and the Social Reconstruction of America* (Boston: Houghton Mifflin, 1997), 3.
2. Harvey Swados, "The Myth of the Happy Worker," *The Nation*, 17 August 1957.
3. C. Wright Mills, *Power, Politics and People: The Collected Essays of C. Wright Mills* (New York: Ballantine, 1963), 256; Daniel Horowitz, *Betty Friedan and the Making of the Feminine Mystique: The American Left, the Cold War, and Modern Feminism* (Amherst, Mass.: University of Massachusetts Press, 1998).
4. Kim Moody, *An Injury to All: The Decline of American Unionism* (London: Verso, 1988), 212.

ACKNOWLEDGMENTS

A number of these essays were written for particular occasions, and several were published in earlier forms. My thanks to the colleagues and editors who invited me and responded to the work, as well as to the audience members who raised challenges and offered suggestions and criticisms. My particular thanks to Jane Hindle at Verso, who has been a wonderful editor. Thanks as well to my colleagues in the Marxism and Cultural Theory group, in the American Studies program, and in the program in Ethnicity, Race and Migration; thanks also to all those involved in Scholars, Artists and Writers for Social Justice (SAWSJ). A particular thanks to Brenda Choresi Carter, Michael Cohen, Tucker Foehl, Megan Glick, Sumanth Gopinath, John Mackay, Bethany Moreton, Steve Pitti, Alicia Schmidt Camacho, Zach Schwartz-Weinstein, Vicki Shepard and Ivy Wilson for their help and suggestions. And thanks to Hazel Carby and Nicholas Carby-Denning, without whom this book would not have been possible.

An earlier version of chapter 2 appeared in *European Journal of Cultural Studies*, vol. 4, no. 3 (2002). It was originally written for a conference at Cornell University, *Writing Across the Curriculum*, as a reflection on teaching two seminars on culture in the age of three worlds. I am grateful to the students in the seminars, and particularly to Josh Jelly-Schapiro, Cindy Kang, Ben Landy, Terra Lawson-Remer, Simon Rodberg, and Quinnie Tan.

Chapter 3 was originally developed during a seminar on social movements and subaltern insurrections. My thanks to the students in the seminar. A version appeared in Portuguese in Isabel Loureiro, José Corrêa Leite, and Maria Elisa Cevasco, eds., *O Espírito de Porto Alegre* (São Paulo: Paz e Terra, 2002).

Chapter 4 was inspired by Franco Moretti's invitation to contribute to his world history of the novel. An Italian translation appeared in Franco Moretti, ed., *Il romanzo. Volume terzo: Storia e geografia* (Torino: Einaudi, 2002).

Chapter 5 grew out of a number of seminars on cultural theory in Yale's American Studies graduate program. An earlier version was published in Donald Pease and Robyn Wiegand, eds., *The Futures of American Studies* (Durham: Duke University Press, 2002).

Chapter 6 was originally written for an international conference on mass culture and working-class culture held in Paris. Earlier versions of chapter 6 were published in *International Labor and Working-Class History*, no. 37 (Spring 1990) and in James Naremore and Patrick Brantlinger, eds., *Modernity and Mass Culture* (Bloomington: Indiana University Press, 1991). The version in *International Labor and Working-Class History* was accompanied by responses from Janice Radway, Luisa Passerini, William Taylor, and Adelheid von Saldern. The final section of chapter 6 is based on my reply to those critics; it first appeared in a slightly different version in *International Labor and Working-Class History*, no. 38 (Fall 1990).

Chapter 7 grew out of discussions in the Southern New England Left Triangle. Earlier versions were published in *Radical History Review*, no. 54 (Fall 1992) and in Isabel Caldeira, ed., *O Cânone Nos Estudos Anglo-Americanos* (Coimbra: Livraria Minerva, 1994). My thanks as well to Laura Wexler, Rachel Bowlby, Kathy Newman, Jon Wiener, and Michael Rosenthal.

Chapter 8 is based on several conference talks, each of which was a reply to questions about cultural studies and cultural politics posed by conference organizers. My thanks to the organizers, fellow panelists, and audiences at the *After Postcolonialism, Beyond Minority Discourse* conference at Cornell; the *Seeds of Liberation* conference at the Stony Brook Humanities Institute (a conference in memory of Michael Sprinker, a friend and editor of two earlier books of mine); the "Does Cultural Studies Neglect Class?" panel at the American Studies Association convention in Pittsburgh; the "Dead Dog or New Research Agenda?: Gramsci in Cultural Studies" panel at the International Crossroads in Cultural Studies conference in Birmingham; and the "Culture and Political Practice" panel at the 2003 World Social Forum in Porto Alegre. One section of chapter 8 was published in an earlier form in the online journal *Politics and Culture* (2001: Issue 1). Particular thanks to Sue Kim, Cheryl Higashida, Priya Gopal, Steve Shapiro, and Maria Elisa Cevasco.

An earlier version of chapter 9 appeared in *American Quarterly* 38.3 (1986). My thanks to Jean-Christophe Agnew, Joseph De Plasco, Robert Fogarty, Richard Slotkin, Werner Sollors, and Alan Trachtenberg.

Chapter 10 was originally delivered at Wesleyan University's Center for the Humanities as part of series of talks reconsidering the canon in social theory.

Chapter 11 was originally written and delivered as part of Yale University's De Vane Tercentennial series of lectures on democracy, "Democratic Vistas." My particular thanks to Rebecca Ruquist and Peg Tamulevich for their statements.

An earlier version of chapter 12 appeared in *New Labor Forum*, no. 4 (Spring/Summer 1999). My thanks to Steve Fraser and Paula Finn.

INDEX

1968 social movements 8, 41–4, 43

Abrahams, Peter 67
Achebe, Chinua
  Things Fall Apart 30
Adorno, Theodor 100
  culture industries 87
  Mass Culture 184
advertising 185
African National Congress 42
Afrika Bambaataa
  "Planet Rock" 30
Agnew, Spiro T. 153
Althusser, Louis 43, 82, 190
  ideological state apparatuses 87
  Reading Capital 156
Amado, Jorge 63
  The Violent Land 69
American studies 13
  interdisciplinary method 189–91
  labor and culture 227–34
  Marxism and 169, 170–8
  New Left revisionism 178–87
  Puritanism 182–3
  race and slavery 181–2
Americanization 31, 115–16
Amin, Samir 82
Anand, Mulk Raj 63–4
Anderson, Benedict
  Imagined Communities 89
Anderson, Perry 11, 82, 170, 216
Anisimov, Ivan 60
anti-globalization movement
  see Seattle protest
Apocalypse Now (film) 30
Appadurai, Arjun 23
Argentina 46–7, 48
Aristotle 92
Arnold, Matthew
  Culture and Anarchy 77–80
Aronowitz, Stanley 82, 187
  False Promises 155, 186
Asturias, Miguel Angel 64, 69–70
Aum Shinrikyo 42

Baker, Houston 182
Balch, Stephen 123, 129
Balibar, Etienne 82, 89
Bandung Conference 64
Baraka, Amiri 182
Barbusse, Henri 57
Baroja, Pio
  La Lucha Por La Vida 56
Barthes, Roland 7, 82
  Mythologies 84
Baudrillard, Jean 82, 91
The Beatles 30
Bell, Daniel 5, 81, 83
Beloved (Morrison) 30
Benedict, Ruth
  Patterns of Culture 76
Benjamin, Walter 85, 184

Bercovitch, Sacvan 109, 183
Berger, John 82
Berman, Paul 140, 146
Black Skins, White Masks (Fanon) 20
Bloom, Allan 144
Bloom, Harold 130
Bobbio, Norberto 220
Boorstin, Daniel
  The Americans 172
Bourdieu, Pierre 80, 82
  on class 153–4
  class and aesthetics 113
  cultural capital 86, 106, 107–8, 112
Bowlby, Rachel 179
Braverman, Harry 82
  Labor and Monopoly Capital 91–3, 94, 155, 156
Brazil 46–7
Brazilian Centro Popular de Cultura (CPC) 7
Brecher, Johannes 61
Brenner, Robert
  The Economics of Global Turbulence 27
Britain
  Chartists and democracy 211, 213, 214, 217
  cultural studies 136–7, 175–6
Bromwich, David 122, 130–1, 133, 134
Buhle, Paul 103
Bulosan, Carlos 68
Burke, Kenneth 83, 111, 139–40, 146, 148
Burke, Peter
  Popular Culture in Early Modern Europe 97
Bush Sr, George 121

Cabral, Amilcar 82
Calvertson, V. F. 174
Canclini, Néstor García 9
Candido, Antonio
  Formation of Brazilian Literature 7
capitalism
  Appadurai's global flows of 23
  bourgeois democracy and 214–19
  culture and 21, 103–4
  relation to labor 91
Carby, Hazel 9, 182
Carlyle, Thomas 213
Carpentier, Alejo 69–70
Carter, Jimmy 101
Castells, Manuel
  The Powers of Identity 42
Chakrabarty, Dipesh 7, 10
Chand, Prem 63–4
Chase, Richard 178
Chávez, Hugo 48, 49
Childs, John Brown 182
Chomsky, Noam 43, 82
civil society 13
  associations and 199–202, 220
  democracy and 219–26
  public sphere 11
Clark, Katerina 61
class
  and cultural commodities 104–11
  in cultural studies 140–1, 151–5
  drawing boundaries 116–20
  social crisis of 152–3
  social realism 56
Cliff, Jimmy 30
Cloward, Richard 41, 43
  Poor People's Movements (with Pliven) 38–9
Coca-Cola Corporation 31–2
Cockburn, Alexander
  Seattle, Five Days that Shook the World (with St Clair) 36, 37
Cohn-Bendit, Daniel 43
Colletti, Lucio 82
Columbia University 143–4
communication 4, 83–4
communism 7
  literature and 52–4, 60–2
Coppola, Francis Ford
  Apocalypse Now 30
  The Godfather 30
Cornell University 148
Coronil, Fernando
  The Magical State 27
Coser, Lewis 131–2
cultural materialism
  forms of culture and 112–13
  Marxism and 190–1
  social class and 104–11
cultural studies
  British origins 175–6
  class and 151–5
  commodity theories 84–6
  concept of culture 76–81
  defending 147–8
  definition and scope of 148–51
  "discovery" of 75–6
  drawing boundaries 116–20
  emergence in US 135–7
  Gramsci's influence 155–61
  hegemony theories of 87–90

cultural studies (*cont.*)
  labor theory and 90–6
  magazines and journals of 137–9
  means of communication 83–4
  New Left generation 81–3
  products and social class 104–6
  race/class/gender-ism 140–1, 152
  rise of 1–3
  social science and politics 3–4
  see also American studies
culture
  body of global texts 29–34
  concept of 2
  defining 90
  in groups 140
  "high and low" 107
  homogenization 20
  labor struggle and 227–34
  politics of 161–6
  postmodern concept of 160–1
culture industries 4
  forms and social class 104–11
  global market in 30–1

Dahl, Robert 214
Davis, Angela 21, 82
Davis, Mike 47
Davis, Miles 30
Debord, Guy 85
decolonization
  see liberation/decolonization
democracy
  bourgeois revolution of 214–19
  in civil society 219–26
  defining 210
  narrowed meaning of 14
  social movement of 211–14
  US perspective on 209–11
  workers and 221–4
Democracy in America (de Tocqueville) 13–14
Denning, Michael
  Mechanic Accents 186
Denoon, Donald 206–7
Derrida, Jacques 82
Diawara, Manthia 20
Diggins, John 193
Dimock, Wai Chee
  Rethinking Class (with Gilmore) 153
Direct Action Network 44–5
Dominican Republic 46
Dorfman, Ariel 82, 185
Douglass, Frederick 213
DuPlessis, Rachael Blau 179
Dussel, Enrique 25
Dyer-Witheford, Nick 43
Dylan, Bob 33, 86

Eagleton, Terry 3, 10, 118–19, 161
economics 20
  see also capitalism; socialism
education
  for adults 2
  anti-communism 134–5
  canon and theory 124–5
  conservative attacks 121–2
  emergence of universities 28
  further 165
  general 142–5
  interdisciplinary Marxism 189–91
  perception of radicals in 128–35
  reforming 145–6
Ehrenreich, Barbara 128, 134, 139, 155, 185–6
Ehrenreich, John 185–6
Eisenstein, Sarah 186
Eliot, T. S.
  Notes Towards a Definition of Culture 76, 77
Ellison, Ralph
  Invisible Man 30
Engels, Friedrich 169
  The Communist Manifesto (with Marx) 18
  democracy and 211, 213
Enzensberger, Hans Magnus 82
Epstein, Barbara 122, 128, 136, 145
Erskine, John 144
ethnic studies 21–2
Ewen, Elizabeth 185, 186
Ewen, Stuart 185

Fanon, Frantz 82
  Black Skins, White Masks 20
  "Racism and Culture" 7
fascism 61–2
Fela 31
feminism
  1968 movements 43
  American studies and 179–80
  democracy and 219
  political correctness and 125–6
  popular culture and 101–2
Fernández Retamar, Roberto 82
Feuer, Lewis 203

Fiedler, Leslie 178
film
  labor struggle 232–3
  world 20, 32–3
Flacks, Richard
  Making History 128
Fonda, Jane 232
Foner, Eric 109–10
food riots 45–6
Foucault, Michel 82, 154
  Discipline and Punish 43, 86–7, 91
Frank, Andre Gunder 38, 82
Frankfurt School 184–5
Franklin, H. Bruce 179
Fraser, Steven 227–8
  The Rise and Fall of the New Deal Order (with Gerstle) 152
Frears, Stephen 20
free-market fundamentalism 8
Freeman, Joshua 227–8
Friedan, Betty 82, 229
  The Feminine Mystique 29
Friedman, Thomas 24
Fukuyama, Francis 23

Galvao, Patrícia 66
Gates, Henry Louis 129, 130
gender
  boundaries and 117
  in cultural studies 140–1
Gerstle, Gary
  The Rise and Fall of the New Deal Order (with Fraser) 152
Gil, Gilberto 33
Gilmore, Michael T. 179
  Rethinking Class (with Dimock) 153
Gilroy, Paul
  Between Camps 9–10
  The Empire Strikes Back 9–10
Gitlin, Todd 185
Gladkov, Feodor 61
globalization 11
  body of texts 29–34
  defining 17
  transdisciplinary debate 22–4
  varying narratives of 17–24
Gold, Michael 66, 67
Gopal, Priya 162
Gorky, Maxim
  Mother 55, 59, 65
Gorz, André 82
Gramsci, Antonio 8–9, 190
  cultural commodities 109–11
  culture and 79, 87–8
  influence on cultural studies 148, 155–61
  mental labor 93
  Prison Notebooks 155–61
Grieder, William
  One World, Ready or Not 27
Guha, Ranajit 41, 157, 163
  The Elementary Aspects of Peasant Insurgency in Colonial India 37
Guizot, Francois 213
Gutiérrez, Gustavo 82

Habermas, Jürgen 82
habitus 106
  see also Bourdieu, Pierre
Hall, Stuart 9, 82, 151, 155
  on hegemony 88–9, 110
  influence of 156
  "Notes on deconstruction of 'the popular'" 97–104
  relations of representation 84
Hamilton, Thomas 195–6
Haraway, Donna 141
Harrington, Michael 229
Hartz, Louis 177–8, 194–5, 205–6
Harvey, David 96
Haug, Frigga 82
Haug, Wolfgang 82
Heller, Patrick 218
Henderson, Harry 178
Hetata, Sherif 32
Hicks, Alexander 218
Hicks, Granville 174
history
  Age of Three Worlds 26–7
  Gramsci on 158–9
  new historicism 10, 118
  periodization 24–7
Hitchcock, Alfred 30
Hobsbawm, Eric 32
  character of Three Worlds 27–8
  on death of peasantry 67–8
  narrative of globalization 17–18
Hoggart, Richard
  The Uses of Literacy 175
Honda, Inoshiro
  Godzilla 30
Horkheimer, Max 87
Howard, June 179

Howe, Irving 122, 133, 144–5
Human Rights Watch
  workers' rights 221–4
Hungary 46–7
Huntingdon, Samuel 210, 216–17

identity politics 42, 123
ideology, end of 5
India 48
Indonesia 64
intellectuals
  market 131–2
  socialist 133–4
  see also education and academe
International Monetary Fund (IMF) 45–6

Jackson, Andrew 206, 213
Jackson, Michael 30
Jacoby, Russell 130, 133, 139
Jamaica 46
James, C. L. R. 21
  American Civilization 154, 155
  The Black Jacobins 26
  cultural politics 81
  Minty Alley 67
  on sport 114
Jameson, Fredric 82, 105, 151
  The Cultures of Globalization (with Miyoshi) 20
  globalization as new 19
  labor theory of culture 95
  Marxism and Form 171, 186–7
  The Political Unconscious 187
  on postmodernism 106
  "Reification and Utopia in Mass Culture" 97–104, 184–5
  symbolic acts 146
Jehlen, Myra 178–9
Jordan, Michael 30
Jubilee 2000 38

Kapur, Geeta 21
Katsiaficas, George 43
Kazin, Michael
  The Populist Persuasion 41
Kennedy, John F. 153
Keyssar, Alexander 217
Kimball, Roger 136, 141, 145
King, Anthony
  Culture, Globalization and the World-System 19
Kingsolver, Barbara
  Holding the Line 227
Klein, Naomi 35–6
Kluckhohn, Clyde 76–80
Kluge, Alexander 82
Kolodny, Annette
  The Land Before Her 180
Kraditor, Aileen 192
Kroeber, A. L. 76–80
Kureishi, Hanif
  My Beautiful Laundrette 20

labor
  assembly lines 49
  cultural theory and 90–6
  culture of 227–34
  international division of 20
  on living by culture 118–19
  right to strike 221–4
  social change and 152–3
  strike narratives 65–6
Laclau, Ernesto 41
Ladysmith Black Mambazo 31
Las Casas, Bartolomé de 25
Latin America 62–3
Lears, Jackson 174–5
  "The Concept of Cultural Hegemony" 109–10
Lentricchia, Frank 169
Lessing, Doris 82
Levitt, Theodore 30
Lewis, R. W. B. 178
liberalism 130
liberation/decolonization
  1968 movements 42–4, 49–50
  literature of 57–8
  proletarian literature 62–5
  revolutionary experience of 7
Linebaugh, Peter 212
Lipsitz, George 110
literature
  the canon 143–4
  comparative 20
  forms of novels 65–72
  globalization of the novel 11–12
  Gramsci and 157–8
  intellectuals and 132
  "international" or "ethnic" 145
  little magazines and 139
  magical realism 32, 51
  modernity 25

radical forms 54
rise of world novels 51–3
Lloyd, David
The Politics of Culture Under the Shadow of Capital (with Lowe) 21–2
Lodge, David
Nice Work 131
London, Herbert 123, 129
Los Angeles riots 47
Lott, Eric 95
Louis Napoleon 88
Lowe, Lisa
The Politics of Culture Under the Shadow of Capital (with Lloyd) 21–2
Lowenthal, Leo
Mass Culture 184
Lu Xun 55
Lucas, George
Star Wars 30
Luce, Henry 13
Lukács, György 61, 84–5
American studies and 178–9
culture and 79
Luther, Seth 217, 218
Luxemburg, Rosa 38

McChesney, Robert 31
MacIntyre, Alasdair 6
McLuhan, Marshall
The Mechanical Bride 83
Understanding Media 83
magical realism 32, 51
Mahfouz, Naguib 64, 70
Mandel, Ernest 152
Manley, Michael 46
Mao Dun 61
Midnight 66
Mapfumo, Thomas 31
Marcuse, Herbert 184
Marley, Bob 20, 31, 32, 33
Márquez, Gabriel García
One Hundred Years of Solitude 29, 51, 70–2
Martin, Gerald 54
Marx, Karl 8
abstraction of culture 78
black liberation and 181
The Communist Manifesto (with Engels) 18
democracy and 211, 213–14
The Eighteenth Brumaire of Louis Napoleon 27, 88
on labor 92, 93, 96
pleasures of the laborer 6
Marx, Leo 81, 82, 174
The Machine in the Garden 175
Marxism
American studies and 169, 170–8
commodity theories 85–6
culture and 79
fetishism and ideology 90–1
as interdisciplinary method 189–91
international discourse of 187–9
new historicism 118
New Left reflections 149–51
Tocquville and 207–8
mass media 4
Mattelart, Armand 1955
Mapping World Communication 83
Matthiessen, F. O. 172–3, 174
American Renaissance 175–6
on Tocqueville 202
Melville, Herman 173
Menand, Louis 123, 135, 145–6
Merry Christmas, Mr Lawrence (Oshima) 20
Michnick, Adam 43
Middleton, Faith 127
Mignolo, Walter 25
Mill, John Stuart 211
Mills, C. Wright 82, 84, 229
Mintz, Sidney 31
Mitchell, Juliet 82
Miyamoto, Shigeru 32
Miyoshi, Masao
The Cultures of Globalization (with Jameson) 20
modernism 3
modernity 25
Montgomery, David 219
Moore, Barrington 215
Morocco 47
Morrison, Toni 30
Mulhern, Francis 3
multiculturalism/pluralism 152
cultural studies and 89–90
Multilateral Agreement on Investment (MAI) 38
music
global culture and soundtracks 33

nationalism
anticolonial 21
proletarian literature 62–3

Native Americans
  de Tocqueville and 204–8
  dispossession of 13
Negri, Antonio 82
Neruda, Pablo
  Canto General 30
New Left
  in age of three world 4–8
  defeat and repression 8
  revision of American studies 178–87
  three moments of 8
Nexo, Martin Anderson
  Pelle Erobreren 56
Ngugi wa Thiong'o 64, 82
  Petals of Blood 68
Nigeria 47, 48
Nike Corporation 29, 31–2
Nixon, Richard M. 101, 153
Nizan, Paul 158
non-governmental organizations (NGOs)
  Seattle protest and 38, 44–5
North American Free Trade Agreement
    (NAFTA) 48

Ohmann, Richard 82
Olsen, Tillie
  Silences 95
One Hundred Years of Solitude (Márquez) 29
Ong, Aihwa 10, 21
Open University 2
Oshima, Nagisa
  Merry Christmas, Mr Lawrence 20
Ousmane, Sembene 32
  God's Bits of Wood 66

Parton, Dolly 233
Passerini, Luisa 115–16
Peiss, Kathy 186
Pérez, Carlos 47
Pessen, Edward 199
Pfiel, Fred 106–7
philosophy 25
Pierson, George 196
Piven, Frances Fox 41, 43
  Poor People's Movements (with Cloward)
    38–9
"political correctness"
  conservative attack on 121–8
  meaning and manners of 125–8
politics
  academic leanings 128–35
  cultural 3–4, 161–6
  see also uprisings and resistance
Poovey, Mary 153
popular culture
  aesthetics of 113–14
  boundaries and value 100–1
  confused with Americanization 115–16
  forms and value of 112–114
  Jameson and Hall's interpretations 97–104
  political importance of 99
  in the Reagan year 12
  victory of 103–4
Porter, Carolyn
  Seeing and Being 179
post-structuralism 98
postmodernism
  concept of culture 6, 80–1
  cultural studies 3
  Jameson and 102
Poulantzas, Nicos 190
power
  Foucault on 86
  hegemony theories of 87–90
Pramoedya Ananta Toer 64
proletarian culture 32
  communism and fascism 60–2
  forms of novels 65–72
  nationalist and anticolonial 62–5
  rise of literature 58–60
  see also social realism
Public Enemy 30
Putnam, Robert 225
Pynchon, Thomas
  Gravity's Rainbow 30

race and ethnicity
  black American studies 181–2
  boundaries and 117
  civil rights and democracy 217–18
  Columbia University 143–4
  in cultural studies 140–1
  de Tocqueville and 204–8
  political correctness and 125–6
"Racism and Culture" (Fanon) 7
Radway, Janice 116–20
Reagan, Ronald 12, 97, 101, 121
Rediker, Marcus 212
Rio de Janeiro Earth Summit 38
Robin, Régine 55
Robinson, Lillian 179
Rodney, Walter 82

Rogin, Michael 180, 181, 206
Ronald Reagan, The Movie 101
Roosevelt, Franklin D. 153
Rosen, Robert 179
Rosenzweig, Roy 186
Rossiter, Clinton 193
Roth, Henry 67
Ruckus Society 44–5
Rühle, Jürgen 60
Ruquist, Rebecca 223
Rushdie, Salman
The Satanic Verses 20, 30
Russell, Lord John 214

Said, Edward 1955
Culture and Imperialism 87
dividing human reality 141
Gramsci and 156
Marxism and 187–8, 190
Orientalism 87, 162
St Clair, Jeffrey
Seattle, Five Days that Shook the World (with Cockburn) 36
Samson, Leon 171, 183
San Juan, E. 82
Sarlo, Beatriz 6–7
Sartre, Jean-Paul 104
Schiller, Dan
Objectivity and the News 186
Schumpter, Joseph 210
Scott, James 163
Searle, John 142, 145
Seattle protests
coalition of forces 44–5
development of movement 35–41
Seddon, David
Free Markets and Food Riots (with Walton) 45
Segher, Ann
The Seventh Cross 62
Shumpter, Joseph 215
Simon, Paul
Graceland 33
Sinclair, Upton
The Jungle 56
Sklair, Leslie 20
Sklar, Martin 185
Sklar, Robert 169
slavery 13, 25
de Tocqueville and 204–8
Slotkin, Richard 180, 181, 189
Smith, Adam 78
social movements
1968 and 8, 41–4
cultural resistance 163–6
democracy as 14
development of Seattle protest 36–41
global culture and 11
Hobsbawm on 28
as long processes 40–1
social realism
effect of Russian revolution 57–60
social sciences 3–4
socialism
American exceptionalism 175–8
de Tocqueville and 198–9
intellectuals and 133–4
socialist realism 32
nineteenth-century beginnings 55–7
transnationalism and politics 52–4
Sombart, Werner 176, 192
Sontag, Susan 82
Sony Corporation 31–2
Sorya, Han 61
South Africa 46, 48
South Asia
proletarian literature 63–4
Soviet Union
revolution and literature 57–61
socialist realism 55
Spivak, Gayatri 82, 90
sport 114
Sprinker, Michael 147
Stalinism 5
Star Wars series (films) 30
state
1968 movements 43
Steinbeck, John
Grapes of Wrath 68
subaltern studies 9, 21
cultural studies and 87–90
Gramsci and 157
reshaped lives 5
Sudan 46
Sunao, Tokunanga
The Street without Sun 61–2
Susman, Warren 75, 172, 182, 186, 194

Takaki, Ronald 180, 181
Takiji, Kobayashi 66
Tamulevich, Peg 223
Thatcher, Margaret 97, 101

Thein Pe Myint
  The Student Boycotter 63
Therborn, Göran 215, 217
Thompson, E. P. 6, 82, 98–9, 192
  The Making of the English Working Class 40–1
Thompson, Thomas Perronet 211
Tocqueville, Alexis de 13–14
  democracy and 209–10
  freedom of association 199–202, 220
  Marxism and 207–8
  master concepts of 197–202
  race and slavery 204–8
  rhetorical strategy 202–4
  status of *Democracy in America* 193–5
  viewpoint and context of 195–6
Tomlin, Lily 232
Trachtenberg, Alan 172, 186
transnational corporations 28
Trilling, Diana 126, 127
Trilling, Lionel 127
Tylor, E. B.
  Primitive Culture 76, 77–81

United States
  class and democracy 214–19
  peculiarities 192–3
  perspective on democracy 209–11
  populism 152
  radical literature 63
  see also American studies; Tocqueville, Alexis de
universities
  see education
uprisings and resistance 28
  cultural politics 163–6
  Marxist revolution 165–6
  struggle for democracy 211–14
urban life 28, 67–9
Uruguay 48

Valéry, Paul 104
Vallejo, César 63
value 112
Veblen, Thorstein 107, 196
Veloso, Caetano 33
Venezuela 47

Wald, Alan 179
Wallerstein, Immanuel 82
  defines culture 90
  on groups 140, 151
  indigenization of state apparatus 28
  on social sciences 4
  world-system 19–20, 43
Walton, John
  Free Markets and Food Riots (with Seddon) 45
Watkins, Evan 142
Wenders, Wim
  Paris, Texas 20
West, Cornel 181
Williams, Raymond 82, 89
  classifying cultures 162–3
  Communications 83
  cultural materialism 112–13
  on "culture" 75
  Culture and Society 5, 7, 77, 79–81, 175–6
  labor and further education 165
  The Long Revolution 80, 81
  Marxism and Literature 118
  production and consumption of culture 190
  rise of cultural studies 137
Willis, Paul 155
  Learning to Labour 9
Wills, Garry
  Reagan's America 101
Wolfensohn, James 38
Wood, Ellen Meiksins 219
Wood, Gordon 209, 211
Workers Educational Association 2
World Trade Organization (WTO) 35–6
World-systems theory 19–20
Wright, Richard
  "Blueprint for Negro Writers" 63
  Native Son 68
  on world novels 51

Yugoslavia 46–7

Zaheer, Sajjad 63
Zapatistas 42, 48
Zola, Emile 56